LEADING A CULTURE OF REASONING
READING

How to Ignite & Sustain a Love of Literacy in Your School Community

LORRAINE M. RADICE

Solution Tree | Press

Copyright © 2024 by Solution Tree Press

Materials appearing here are copyrighted. With one exception, all rights are reserved. Readers may reproduce only those pages marked "Reproducible." Otherwise, no part of this book may be reproduced or transmitted in any form or by any means (electronic, photocopying, recording, or otherwise) without prior written permission of the publisher.

555 North Morton Street
Bloomington, IN 47404
800.733.6786 (toll free) / 812.336.7700
FAX: 812.336.7790

email: info@SolutionTree.com
SolutionTree.com

Visit **go.SolutionTree.com/literacy** to download the free reproducibles in this book.

Printed in the United States of America

Library of Congress Cataloging-in-Publication Data

Names: Radice, Lorraine M., author.
Title: Leading a culture of reading : how to ignite and sustain a love of
   literacy in your school / Lorraine M. Radice.
Description: Bloomington, IN : Solution Tree Press, [2023] | Includes
   bibliographical references and index.
Identifiers: LCCN 2023024246 (print) | LCCN 2023024247 (ebook) | ISBN
   9781958590195 (paperback) | ISBN 9781958590201 (ebook)
Subjects: LCSH: Literacy programs--United States.
Classification: LCC LC151 .R34 2023 (print) | LCC LC151 (ebook) | DDC
   379.2/40973--dc23/eng/20230814
LC record available at https://lccn.loc.gov/2023024246
LC ebook record available at https://lccn.loc.gov/2023024247

Solution Tree
Jeffrey C. Jones, CEO
Edmund M. Ackerman, President

Solution Tree Press
President and Publisher: Douglas M. Rife
Associate Publishers: Todd Brakke and Kendra Slayton
Editorial Director: Laurel Hecker
Art Director: Rian Anderson
Copy Chief: Jessi Finn
Production Editor: Alissa Voss
Copy Editor: Evie Madsen
Proofreader: Madonna Evans
Text and Cover Designer: Abigail Bowen
Acquisitions Editor: Hilary Goff
Assistant Acquisitions Editor: Elijah Oates
Content Development Specialist: Amy Rubenstein
Associate Editor: Sarah Ludwig
Editorial Assistant: Anne Marie Watkins

ACKNOWLEDGMENTS

The words on these pages are reflective of students, teachers, administrators, colleagues, parents, caregivers, family members, community members, authors, editors, and publishers. Many people have supported and executed the work this book describes, solidifying the collaborative and participatory nature of how school culture and literacy practices grow.

Jennifer Gallagher, superintendent of Long Beach Public Schools: thank you for your vision to elevate the importance of reading and create a culture within the school district that prioritizes all aspects of literacy. Establishing the importance of reading was one of your first priorities as superintendent. As a teacher and leader, I can't express enough the appreciation I feel for your recognition of reading and a culture that celebrates reading matters. Thank you for believing in me and the importance of literacy work, and for encouraging creative thinking in leadership.

The central office team in Long Beach Public Schools: thank you to Michele Natali for seeing me as a teacher and school district leader, and how those two responsibilities are symbiotic. Thank you to Michael DeVito for prioritizing books and rich literacy curriculum experiences in a complex and vast budgeting process each year. Your support and encouragement are invaluable to the process of providing book access to students. Thank you to Paul Romanelli for allowing my literacy leadership to be a canvas with many colors. You welcome new thinking and partner with me to engage school community members in doing what is best for the reading lives of students. Thank you for always welcoming me. *So, I have this idea . . . .*

The teachers and librarians in Long Beach Public Schools: your energy and enthusiasm for promoting reading in classrooms and libraries fuels this work. You have the greatest influence on students, and how you cultivate young readers matters. Thank you for sharing new and diverse books with students. Thank you for creating environments that value reading. Thank you for promoting reading initiatives and contributing to their success. Thank you for creating spaces where all students are invited to see themselves and discover the perspectives of others in text. And thank you for your kindness and encouragement as together we build a school experience where students are at the center of literacy experiences.

My school leadership colleagues and partners: the principal, assistant principal, director, and coordinator roles are keys to the success of school culture and initiatives. I share deep appreciation for your partnership, your support, and your efforts to promote reading and *book love* in your schools.

The contributors to this book: thank you for sharing your personal stories about literacy leadership and building reading culture in your schools and classrooms, and your own reading identities. Your stories exemplify the power of community in literacy work.

My former students in Long Beach Public Schools: being a student gives you one of the greatest gifts of all . . . to be a teacher. I learned invaluable lessons that enable me to do the work of a school district leader who represents all learners and supports all readers.

My teachers and colleagues at Hofstra University: it is the strong foundation in teaching, learning, literacy, and leadership you provided that granted me the tools and framework to lead with and from.

Hilary Goff at Solution Tree: thank you for your positive energy, insightful suggestions and revisions, and presence in many conversations throughout this writing process. Your responsiveness and kindness are invaluable.

My core: thank you to my parents for giving me the tools and love to believe in myself. Thank you to my husband, Josh, for being a thinking partner, a cheerleader, and a friend.

—Lorraine M. Radice

Solution Tree Press would like to thank the following reviewers:

Courtney Burdick
Apprenticeship Mentor Teacher
Spradling Elementary—
    Fort Smith Public Schools
Fort Smith, Arkansas

Doug Crowley
Assistant Principal
DeForest Area High School
DeForest, Wisconsin

John D. Ewald
Educator, Consultant, Presenter, Coach
Retired Superintendent, Principal, & Teacher
Frederick, Maryland

Alex Fangman
Principal
Summit View Academy
Independence, Kentucky

Colleen Fleming
Literacy Specialist
Calgary, Alberta, Canada

Kelli Fuller
Instructional Facilitator
Howard Perrin Elementary School
Benton, Arkansas

Eric Lindblad
Achievement Coach
Andover High School
Andover, Minnesota

Shanna Martin
Middle School Teacher & Instructional Coach
School District of Lomira
Lomira, Wisconsin

Paula Mathews
STEM Instructional Coach
Dripping Springs ISD
Dripping Springs, Texas

Lauren Smith
Assistant Director of Elementary Learning
Noblesville Schools
Noblesville, Indiana

Kory Taylor
Reading Interventionist
Arkansas Virtual Academy
Little Rock, Arkansas

Ringnolda Jofee' Tremain
K–8 Principal
Trinity Leadership Arlington
Arlington, Texas

Dianne Yee
Assistant Professor
Western University
London, Ontario, Canada

Allison Zamarripa
Reading & Language Arts Curriculum &
    Instructional Specialist
Pasadena Independent School District
Pasadena, Texas

TABLE OF CONTENTS

Reproducible pages are in italics.

About the Author ix

Introduction 1
    Features of This Book 4
    My Advice to You 6
    It's Time to Get Started 7

CHAPTER 1
#BrandReading
How to Leverage a Campaign in Your School Community and Attract Followers 9
    The Roots of This Work 11
    How to Make It Happen 13
    Sustain the Momentum of Your Reading Campaign 17
    Engage in Community Outreach Through Your New Campaign 20
    Summary 24
    Reflection Questions 24

CHAPTER 2
Developing Reading Role Models
How to Rally Adults to Explore Their Reading Lives 27
    The Roots of This Work 27
    How to Make It Happen 31
    A Goal to Personalize Culture 62
    Summary 62
    Reflection Questions 63
    Lift a Line Conversation Cards for an Adult Book Swap 64
    Book Discussion Questions List 65
    Reading Schedule for a Bookmark 66
    Book Club Launch Presentation Slides 67
    Books as Mirrors, Windows, and Sliding Glass Doors Thinking Chart 71
    Norms and Agreements 72

Book Tasting Presentation Slides 73

Book Tasting Recording Sheet, Primary 78

Book Tasting Recording Sheet, Upper Elementary and Secondary 79

CHAPTER 3
Sustaining the Culture
How to Make the Culture Visible, Participatory, and Celebratory 81

The Roots of This Work 81

How to Make It Happen 83

The Importance of Shared Planning 100

Summary 100

Reflection Questions 101

CHAPTER 4
Helping Students Become Literacy Leaders
How to Rally Students to Plan Reading Events 103

The Roots of This Work 104

How to Make It Happen 105

Summary 116

Reflection Questions 116

School Resources Tool Kit 118

Advertise Your Reading Event! 120

Thinking Routine for Selecting a Schoolwide Book Talk Book 121

Selecting a Book for a Schoolwide Book Talk Chart 122

CHAPTER 5
Positioning Authors as A-List Celebrities
How to Make Author Visits Part of the Reading Culture Experience 123

The Roots of This Work 124

How to Make It Happen 124

Summary 138

Reflection Questions 139

Author Visit Planning Page 140

Generating Questions for an Author Visit 141

Author Visit Welcome Address Planning Page 142

CHAPTER 6
Partnering With Home and School
How to Engage Families and Caregivers in Building Reading Culture 143

The Roots of This Work 143

How to Make It Happen 145

The Importance of Access and the Need for Ongoing Reflection.........................161
Summary..163
Reflection Questions 163
Tips for Caregivers *164*

CHAPTER 7
Elevating Reading When Other Endeavors Come Into Focus
How to Continue to Prioritize Reading and Reading Culture 165
The Roots of This Work..165
How to Make It Happen 167
Summary..176
Reflection Questions 176

EPILOGUE
Embracing *Some*..177

APPENDIX A
Recommended Book Lists 181

APPENDIX B
High-Interest Book Lists to Share With Caregivers 187

References & Resources 191

Index..197

ABOUT THE AUTHOR

 **Lorraine M. Radice, PhD,** is the preK–12 director of literacy in a public school district in New York. There, she leads curricular improvement and facilitates professional learning experiences for teachers. Radice leads teams to develop literacy curricula, monitor student engagement and progress, bridge literacy experiences between the school and community, and consistently build a culture that promotes and celebrates reading and literacy. Radice also teaches professional development courses for teachers that align with district goals. Prior to becoming a school leader, Radice was an English teacher and literacy specialist. She also taught in programs to support language acquisition for elementary, middle, and high school students learning English. Radice teaches undergraduate and graduate courses in childhood education and literacy at Hofstra University in New York.

Radice is a member of the National Council of Teachers of English and presents at its national conferences. Her writing has been featured on the NCTE blog. Radice is also a member of the International Literacy Association and has published in ILA's *Literacy Today*. Radice is committed to sharing in professional learning communities at the local, state, and national levels where she presents her research and field work. Radice's research on digital literacies in middle level classrooms was published in *Curriculum, Instruction, and Assessment: Intersecting New Needs and New Approaches*, a volume in *The Handbook of Research in Middle Level Education*. Student work from Radice's teams has been featured in ASCD's *Educational Leadership* magazine.

Radice earned a bachelor's degree in childhood education and psychology and a master's degree in literacy studies at Hofstra University. She earned an advanced certificate in Teaching English to Speakers of Other Languages (TESOL) from St. John's University. Radice also earned an advanced certificate in educational leadership and a doctorate in philosophy in literacy studies at Hofstra University.

To learn more about Lorraine M. Radice's work, visit www.lorrainemradice.com/blog.

INTRODUCTION

The year I became a school district leader I cried most days; I was a classroom teacher in mourning.

I transitioned from being a teacher in a classroom, where I was the primary decision maker for how to cultivate my students' reading lives and directly monitor their engagement, interests, motivations, and achievement. I was responsible for making my students accountable for their actions, feelings, and thinking in our learning space. If you are or have ever been a teacher, you know what I'm talking about.

Reading culture was important to me and my students. We regularly spoke about books. My students chose their own books to read, and there was time for reading in school. We also discussed individual plans for reading at home. Library visits were part of our routine. Reading, for both pleasure and academic purposes, was a priority. When I transitioned to school district leadership, I was asked to do what I had previously done within the four walls of my classroom on a district level: build a districtwide culture where everyone celebrated and emphasized reading to cultivate engagement.

I found myself working in multiple schools among many people, and was unsure as to how reading culture work would ever be relevant to so many at one time. I had moments of pause. There were moments when I stood still. My life as a literacy educator changed; I was no longer thinking of one learning space, I was thinking of several. But when I parked my insecurities and reconnected with my *teacher-self*, I embraced the simple ideas that guided my work with students in the classroom. While my role changed, my focus did not. It's always about students in literacy leadership.

Those simple ideas became the foundation for the work I started with teams as a school district leader. They are the five ideas that frame this book (see figure I.1).

1. *Reading* is important: Whether one is perusing the next great American novel or directions on how fill out an application, reading is how people make meaning and function in society.

2. *Engagement* is important: Personal investment will elevate any experience, including the work in a school.

3. *Joy* is important: School should be a place where adults and children want to be.

4. *Community* and the people in it are important: Educators are in the "people business"; they are their greatest assets.

5. *Everyone* is important: All stakeholders in a school community have the ability to impact a student's reading life.

FIGURE I.1: Principles of reading culture-building.

Visit  *for a free reproducible version of this figure.*

While I use the word *simple* to describe these ideas, simple does not mean easy. Simple does not mean these ideas are implied in literacy work. They are ideas educators and educational leaders should make explicit and constantly reflect on. They are simple ideas that become complex when working within a system with many people and moving parts to its operation. A challenge of leadership is to rally others—students, colleagues, staff, caregivers, community members—behind those ideas. What starts out as simple becomes complicated when the goal is to channel a shared vision throughout the building culture and action plans. That is where this book comes in. This book provides the action plans to rally people around the fundamental ideas of reading culture and community.

My first year of work in creating a culture that celebrates reading began at the elementary level and then expanded to the secondary level in the second year. You will read about this journey as you move through the chapters of this book. You will read about the research I shared with teams about the positive influence reading volume has on achievement for young people and the theoretical literacy framework as a sociocultural practice, providing the foundation for how to design the culture. In response to the research and theory, I created a reading campaign that spread across the district to promote the value the district places on reading and literacy work. I worked with teachers, librarians, and administrators to reflect on their adult reading identities and understand how their own perceptions and reading habits may influence their work with students.

My staff and I also spent our professional learning time immersed in activities related to books for classroom libraries and read-alouds. Teachers had opportunities to read samples of new books to share with students and make decisions about books they wanted to add to their libraries. We prioritized time for reading in school, and many teachers created new routines for independent reading and sharing about reading during class time. Teachers ensured all students had a book to read at all times and encouraged and prioritized reading at home. Teachers and leaders shared messages about the importance of reading with caregivers and held special events about the importance of reading to partner with caregivers in this work and culture building. Author visits also became a part of our literacy program so students could experience engagement with text and the art of writing in new ways.

These intentional acts of reading culture–building with the five "simple" ideas initially led to higher student achievement on multiple assessments in reading in grades K–5 than in previous years. One assessment measured the progress students made on meeting individual growth targets. Another assessment measured a combination of comprehension, decoding, and fluency. I also evaluated results from a state assessment for grades 3–5 when comparing achievement across the years. The messaging about the importance of reading influenced the time students spent reading in school and the ways in which parents and caregivers encouraged students to read at home. Students received more time to talk about their reading with peers and track their reading progress in personal and community spaces (see chapter 3, page 81). Teachers prioritized reading volume and choice.

While standardized measures reading achievement was not as high during the pandemic years (2019–2022) as the first year of beginning our culture work (2018–2019), the achievement remained higher than the years prior to reading culture–building. This is likely because schools sustained their commitment to encouraging reading during the challenging time of the COVID-19 pandemic. Trends in reading growth continued at the middle school level where, after two years of reading culture–work (that began during the first year of the COVID-19 pandemic,

2019–2020), there was significant growth in reading achievement on the schoolwide computer-based benchmark assessment.

The creation of a reading culture continues to be a positive influence on the development of classroom and school libraries, as well as curriculum plans. Teachers and librarians actively request new and diverse titles for libraries and make current titles available to students via book talks, book recommendation routines, book shopping, and visits to the library. The district leadership also made revisions to literacy curricula, including the following.

- Daily or weekly routines for sustained independent reading
- Units of study designed to include student choice for reading (for example, thematic book clubs)
- Learning engagements rooted in student identities

Reading and the threads of the culture work also developed into a theme that filters into several other areas of work in the school district. Stakeholder groups have independently initiated their own ways of engaging through the reading theme in their respective projects. The following list highlights some of the new events that emerged over several years since the reading culture–building work began. A mark of a rich and inclusive culture is when multiple people or groups of people with their own goals sustain related work. The established culture influences work happening in the learning community.

- Districtwide committees elected to evaluate the diversity in school libraries to discover if recommendations are necessary to provide more contemporary and inclusive texts to students.
- District and school committees facilitate book talks connected to districtwide goals (like exploring innovative classroom practices and providing equitable opportunities for students).
- The new-teacher mentor program added a book study component to the program. All new teachers and their mentors receive a copy of a professional book aligned with district goals. Monthly meetings incorporate reading and discussion.
- Schools host book drives and book swaps.
- Parent Teacher Association (PTA) groups host schoolwide events (like Bedtime and Books and PTA-sponsored author visits).
- The district developed an annual tradition of a summer book fair. Parents and caregivers host a summer book fair in one of our schools each summer, inviting families to attend. Students also attend camps and summer extended learning programs our schools host.
- Schools have grand celebrations of days (like World Read-Aloud Day and Read Across America Day) to boost engagement in reading in the school communities.

You will see references to studies on the positive relationship between reading volume and reading achievement in this book (Allington & McGill-Franzen, 2021; Lewis & Samuels, 2005; Mol & Bus, 2011; Torppa, Niemi, Vasalampi, Lerkkanen, Tolvanen, & Poikkeus, 2020; van Bergen, Vasalampi, & Torppa, 2021). The ideas in this book serve to capture student engagement in reading to work toward building reading volume. While achievement data are important, building reading culture undoubtedly has positive impacts on book access for students, relationships with the school community, and curricula beyond standardized assessments.

Features of This Book

This book aims to be a tool for any educator who is working to promote the importance of reading and develop students' engagement in reading and literacy work. This is not a book about teaching students *how* to read. If you are an educator who is doing the important work of teaching students how to read, I encourage you to consider how teacher and student motivation and a positive literacy environment can support students while learning to read. This book can be a tool to inspire motivation and a positive reading culture that helps teachers do curricular and instructional work.

While reading engagement is a primary focus, many of the strategies and events serve to support students in how they think about text, converse about text, and make meaning in response to navigating a text and discussion. As a result of participating in the events about reading or while working with a specific text or in a book club, students are developing their comprehension and analysis skills, offering opportunities for them to make connections between the text and themselves, others, and the world. You will find that in many of the activities I share, students are also writing in response to text or are learning specific techniques through author visits or author study. Reading hardly exists in a vacuum; a book or reading experience is often the catalyst to develop other areas of student literacy and learning. You will build those explicit connections as you work within your context in response to your school or class community's goals.

Roles and responsibilities differ among adults in a school or organization, but all adults are leaders for students. There are ideas, activities, and strategies in this book that educators can use in a classroom or library program or across one school or multiple schools simultaneously. I address how the content may apply in a classroom, in a school, or across schools. Educators are busy and have a lot of daily responsibilities; any resource that makes this important work just a little bit easier can be a lifeline. Consider this book your *phone a friend* option!

I wrote this book as a how-to guide for building a celebratory school reading culture and engaging school community members in reading literacy events. You may read it cover to cover, or you may visit a chapter that supports the goals of your current work. Many of the ideas in chapters 1 and 2 serve as ways to launch a reading culture campaign and to build a foundation for adults in the school community to initially embrace. The chapters can function independently, but chapters do cross-reference one another because of the interconnectedness of the work.

Chapter 1 explains how to launch a reading campaign as a way to initiate culture building and promote the importance of reading among school community members (Allington & McGill-Franzen, 2021). This chapter connects to the research about the growing use of social media among young people and adults, and describes how social media can help to enhance your reading campaign, not hinder it. Chapter 1 provides strategies for sharing the reading campaign (along with artifacts of real promotion) with stakeholders. I also narrate parts of my process in creating a reading campaign in my school district.

Chapter 2 addresses the importance of adults exploring their own reading lives as a way to prepare to support the reading lives of students. It provides activities and reflection protocols adults can use to consider their own reading lives and also share with students in the classroom. It also shares examples of how adult reading experiences can impact students in the classroom.

Chapter 3 establishes ways to make reading culture visible and participatory. This chapter highlights ways to transform your classroom, library, or school environment into a space that celebrates reading, as well as strategies for using technology to inspire community reading events.

Chapter 4 focuses on how to position students as literacy leaders in a classroom or school. It addresses different ways to integrate student literacy leadership into existing structures or position students as new literacy leaders. This chapter also provides a tool kit to support student leadership and thinking.

Chapter 5 provides guidance on how to make author visits part of students' reading experiences in school. It describes how to plan for an author visit (along with various planning tools) and encourage authentic student involvement.

Chapter 6 embraces the role of parents and caregivers in a student's reading life. This chapter explains various contexts in which caregivers can participate in and out of school. It provides resources to support caregivers and addresses considerations for equitable opportunities for caregiver participation.

Chapter 7 addresses the changing landscape of education and how to elevate reading culture through the work of other initiatives. It highlights creative ways that reading culture can support content-area work and shares opportunities for collaboration with content- and performance-based departments in school.

You will find the following features in the chapters.

- **The Roots of This Work:** The culture-building ideas shared in each chapter reflect the theoretical framework of literacy as a sociocultural practice. Literacies can form through social engagements and cultural experiences. The Roots of This Work sections explain and contextualize this research. These sections also provide references to research on teacher efficacy, technology use, branding, and leadership.

- **How to Make It Happen:** For each idea, you will find a step-by-step guide on how to execute a plan individually or with a team. You may choose to follow the steps or modify them to fit your context.

- **Reflections From Those Who Are Making It Happen:** You will meet other educators who have implemented the culture-building strategies and participated in similar work. These perspectives of various stakeholders in schools bring this work to life.

- **Visuals From the Reading Culture–Building in My Schools:** You will see images of social media posts, advertisements, reading events, planning tools, emails I sent to staff, and more throughout the book. These images serve as concrete representations of reading culture and will help you generate ideas for your work. You will find printable resources in the appendixes.

- **Representation and Resources for Grades PreK–12:** Each chapter is inclusive of students and educators in elementary, middle, and high school. I will explain how you can carry out some reading events similarly across the preK–12 continuum and customize other events to suit the students' age.

- **Book Lists . . . and More Book Lists:** Choosing books for reading events and to add to the curriculum and libraries is joyful work. It is also time-consuming and can be overwhelming due to the number of books available. I provide several book lists for you to use as tools to support the good literacy work you're doing.

My Advice to You

Building reading culture is a commitment, not a trend. The work requires educators to exercise their valuable skills—innovative thinking, problem solving, creativity, originality, technology use, flexibility, anticipatory planning, perseverance—to create meaningful experiences for school community members.

Building culture also requires risk taking. Growth and progress don't stem from hesitation and fear. American professor, author, and podcast host Brené Brown (2018) explains when people are afraid of being put down or ridiculed for trying something and failing, or even for putting forward a radical new idea, the best you can expect is the status quo. You may be aware of this, but it doesn't mean that fear or uncertainty don't challenge you. If thought bubbles were to appear over my head as I brainstorm reading-culture ideas or write emails to colleagues, you might read the following.

- Is this too much? Is this another thing for people to do?
- Will the students not be interested in this?
- Is this a burden?
- Will people not care?
- Is my passion irritating to others?
- Do others agree with this message?
- What if this isn't successful?

There may just be people who are uninterested or who do not want to participate in culture-building work. But, as a literacy leader, it's important to keep thinking, planning, and going because there *are* people who will lead and follow in this work with you. Throughout this book, I share times when I was unsure about the direction to go or worried about the perception and participation of stakeholders. There is always the fear (and the reality) that people won't join in, will just criticize, or don't believe in the work you are rallying the community to do for students. It is when you find yourself having those thoughts that you need bravery and courage most to push through the apprehension. Here is some advice to help manage and not give into the apprehension or uncertainty.

1. **Take the risk and be courageous:** You owe it to yourself, your students, and your colleagues. Brown (2018) writes, "Courage is contagious. To scale daring leadership and build courage in teams and organizations, we have to cultivate a culture in which brave work, tough conversations, and whole hearts are the expectation, and armor is not necessary or rewarded" (p. 12). Act in ways that you want others to contribute to your school community.

2. **Lead with passion for the work:** Part of effective leadership is making others believe in a vision bigger than their own area of influence. That is what *culture* is . . . an encompassing feeling and message that influences daily practices and decisions. Your passion will bring definition to the culture. And while there may or may not be others who share your passion for literacy, it is your responsibility to share passion with others.

3. **Develop a team to help build the reading culture:** Each chapter ends with discussion questions to explore the relationship between the ideas in the book and your school or class community. Use these questions to generate conversation. Get people talking about reading, books, and the community.

4. **Value the connections the work will create:** This work is about bringing people together through reading experiences. Courageous leaders must connect to the people they lead. Celebrate your early adopters (who connect to the culture-building initially); they will help propel the messaging. I write about this later in the book because it's something educators need to often remind themselves.

5. **Be fearless in your messaging:** As the leader of the literacy work in a school or classroom, be consistent with your message about the importance of reading. Be flexible in how the culture evolves, but never lose sight of *why* investing in reading culture is one of the best things you can do for your school or classroom.

6. **Share a firm belief that students need to belong to a community of readers:** Young people spend a lot of their time at home and school. One of Australian researcher Brian Cambourne's (1988) conditions of learning is *immersion*; young people need to be surrounded by interesting, high-quality texts and engaging reading-related experiences. This is not only true for young people but also for adults in a school community. School is a space where students can see adults with books in their hands and talk with peers about reading. A thriving reading culture normalizes reading for everyone and offers equitable opportunities for participation. Reading-culture events provide access and membership to a larger community.

7. **Building reading culture is a marathon, not a sprint:** The ideas, strategies, and resources I share in this book were developed over several years and are still in progress today. Decide what is relevant to your community and manageable for you and your team when developing your action plan. As your culture evolves and shapes, you may add more reading-culture events. This book is written to help in flexible approaches to planning.

It's Time to Get Started

In chapter 1, I share information about how to create a reading campaign as an anchor to the reading-culture work in your school or class community. However, you may be wondering about how to introduce the idea of promoting reading as a cornerstone to your culture, an entry point into the reading campaign chapter 1 describes. As the first of many book recommendations, I suggest *Just Read* by Lori Degman (2019) to inspire you toward the messages in this book.

CHAPTER 1

#BrandReading

How to Leverage a Campaign in Your School Community and Attract Followers

This Chapter Features...

Steps to Launching a Reading Campaign in Your School or Class Community

- Develop a vision for the work (page 13).
- Create a slogan or hashtag (page 13).
- Design a logo (page 14).
- Plan and launch your campaign (page 15).
- Engage in community outreach through your new campaign (page 20).

During my last year as a grade 6 teacher, I spent a lot of time thinking about new ways to authenticate my students' reading practices. I wanted my students to build a meaningful connection between their reading lives in the classroom and at home. Through surveys and conversations with my students, it became more and more apparent how dominant technology and media were becoming in their lives, both in and out of school. The one-to-one device initiative in our school granted all students access to a device at home and in the classroom and, with each passing year, there were more students who had access to a personal device and various types of media. My observations were congruent with research—95 percent of teens reported they had a smartphone or access to one, and 45 percent of teens reported they were online on a near-constant basis (Anderson & Jiang, 2018). Use of technology and media among tweens and teens has only increased, especially due to the COVID-19 pandemic. According to *The Common Sense Census: Media Use by Tweens and Teens* report, media use in tweens and teens has grown faster since the start of the pandemic than it did over the four years prior (Rideout, Peebles, Mann, & Robb, 2022).

Knowing technology use and media engagement were on the rise among young people, I started to pay more attention to how other readers in my social media feeds engaged in online reading communities and expressed their reading identities via social platforms. I noticed how readers posted pictures of the covers of books they were enjoying, how they engaged in chats about reading in the comment threads, and how they posted links to reviews on their Goodreads pages (https://goodreads.com).

I also noticed there was often a hashtag included with the postings: #IndependentBookstoreDay, #booknerd, #bookstoread, #BooksWorthReading, and others. Posting on social media is a welcome practice in my school, so I decided I was going to invite my next class of students to share pictures with me throughout the school year related to their reading lives (their favorite books, pictures of them reading in and out of school, book recommendations, and so on). We could then post them on a class social media page that would be identified with the slogan and hashtag #ReadersInRoom230. I planned to post on social media sites to document and share the reading lives of my students to inspire sharing about books, seeking new reads, documenting reading lives, and expressing reading identities. However, I never had the opportunity to carry out this plan because I didn't teach grade 6 the following school year; instead, my role had changed to the director of literacy.

I share this reflection with you because it is part of how I created the slogan and hashtag for my district reading campaign, *#LBReads*, and to encourage all educators to be innovative leaders of literacy. Whether working directly in a classroom, a library, or across a building or district, ideas take various shapes and forms depending on your context. What originated as an idea for my own classroom transformed into an idea carried out in many schools.

During my interview for the director of literacy position, the superintendent explained how she wanted to dedicate the following school year toward building a positive reading culture. She asked, "Do you have any ways that you might build our reading culture?" I decided to share what I had planned for #ReadersinRoom230. I wanted to work with school community members to implement a social media plan I originally designed for a classroom experience across the district and pointed out that media use is on the rise for young people and adults (Anderson & Jiang, 2018; Common Sense Media, 2020; Rideout et al., 2022). The superintendent welcomed the idea and it was soon brought to life.

Reading Culture in Action
Reflections From Those Who Are Making It Happen

In 2008–2009, I was principal of a middle school in the South Bronx, New York. Most of our students were several grade levels behind in reading when they joined us in the sixth grade, and my teachers were trying to balance teaching literacy and literature. In providing professional development for them, I discovered the inspiring book *Igniting a Passion for Reading* by Steven L. Layne (2009). While many books and speakers touched on strategies to build better readers, this was the first time an author tapped into something that all good readers already know: to be a good reader, it helps to *love* reading.

At that point, my staff and I shifted our focus a bit and tried to match readers to books of interest, even if the books weren't what one would consider great literary works. We tried every strategy we could think of to incentivize our students to read *anything*. We created book clubs, invited authors to speak to students, held reading parties—anything we could think of to get reluctant middle school readers to start to see the magic of getting lost in a story. It was no surprise to me that our reading scores jumped exponentially that year. More important, I started to see students "sneaking" to read under their desks when they were supposed to be doing other work (which secretly delighted me), and their schoolyard banter started to include discussions about what happened in the latest chapter of the book several students were reading *on their own*!

From that year, I learned the importance of creating a culture of literacy. When I became superintendent in Long Beach (New York), one of my first goals was to prioritize reading and literacy in our elementary schools. The district changed its elementary homework policy to make reading the focus, and I asked our literacy director to put together a plan to build a culture of reading there. I wanted to hear that schoolyard buzz about books again, and I wanted to see students and adults walking around with books and talking about the great things they read last night. When reading becomes something students chat about with friends, it stops being an assignment and starts becoming fun!

One of our first efforts was a bit of branding. We developed a hashtag, #LBReads, had students compete to design a logo for our reading campaign, and asked staff to include what they were currently reading in their email signatures. Classroom doors displayed what teachers were reading for pleasure. From the #LBReads hashtag and logo to book clubs, author talks, and many other initiatives led by our director of literacy, Lorraine Radice, I have seen our district literacy culture transformed over the past few years. And when I pop into classrooms and see students "sneaking" to read their favorite book under their desks, I am still delighted! A passion for reading is a lifelong gift and a key component of being a great learner. (J. Gallagher, superintendent, personal communication, December 20, 2022)

The Roots of This Work

The impact of leisure reading on reading achievement has been in question for years. Literacy experts and coauthors Richard L. Allington and Anne M. McGill-Franzen (2021) pose the question: Does extensive reading activity improve reading achievement, or does a high level of reading achievement result in more extensive reading activity? Several studies show in addition to school-related reading activities, reading for pleasure promotes reading development (Lewis & Samuels, 2005; Mol & Bus, 2011; Torppa et al., 2020; van Bergen et al., 2021).

It seems intuitive—the more students read, the better they get as readers. However, it's concerning that in the United States, the number of American nine-, thirteen-, and seventeen-year-olds who say they read for fun almost daily has dropped to the lowest levels since the mid-1980s (Schaeffer, 2021; see figure 1.1). Preteens (eight to twelve years old), tweens (ten to thirteen years old), and teens (thirteen to eighteen years old) are less interested in what is needed for them to grow in their academic and personal reading identities: an interest in and commitment to reading (Schaeffer, 2021).

Percent of U.S. students of each age who say they read for fun, by year

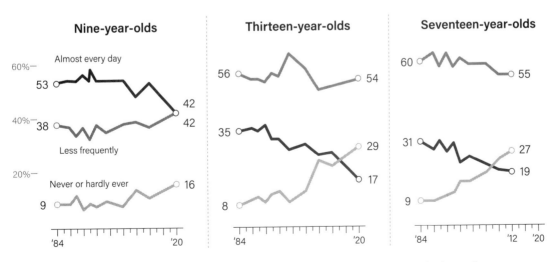

Note: 2020 assessment was not fielded to seventeen-year-olds. Totals may not sum to 100 percent due to rounding. "Less frequently combines responses of "once or twice a week," "once or twice a month," and "a few times a year."

Source: Pew Research Center, 2021. Used with permission.

FIGURE 1.1: U.S. nine- and thirteen-year-olds read for fun less often than they used to.

When I talk with teachers and librarians about these statistics, technology undoubtedly becomes part of the conversation. Elementary, middle school, and high school teachers and librarians agree that the use of technology is a distraction from other activities, like reading. While these are anecdotal observations from the classroom and maybe their own family lives, there is research showing the growing use of media and social media among various age groups, adults included. The following are statistics that capture the growing use of social media.

- Social media use among eight- to twelve-year-olds is growing as 38 percent of tweens have used social media, up from 31 percent in 2019 (Rideout et al., 2022).
- Teens, ages thirteen to eighteen years old, spend nearly an hour and a half using social media every day (Rideout et al., 2022).
- Young adults were among the early adopters of social media and continue to use sites at high levels, but usage by older adults has increased. In 2021, the following percentage of U.S. adults say they use at least one social media site: 84 percent of eighteen- to twenty-nine-year-olds, 81 percent of thirty- to forty-nine-year-olds, 73 percent of fifty- to sixty-four-year-olds, 45 percent of sixty-five-year-olds and older (Schaeffer, 2021).
- The top five social media sites teens have ever used are Instagram (53 percent), Snapchat (49 percent), Facebook (30 percent), Discord (17 percent), and Twitter (16 percent) (Rideout et al., 2022).
- For many adults, visiting social media sites is part of a daily routine. Here are the sites U.S. adults visit daily: Facebook (70 percent), Snapchat (59 percent), Instagram (59 percent), Twitter (46 percent), and YouTube (54 percent) (Schaeffer, 2021).

Knowing the number of young people who read for fun is steadily declining (Schaeffer, 2021), educators must find ways to use what students *do* find interesting as a way to bring reading back into their scope of interests, passions, or academic commitments. Building higher levels of engagement in reading is now priority work. There can be many reasons as to why young people recommit to reading. Connecting reading to social media is one way to illuminate the importance of reading via a platform that is second nature to young people and on the rise for adults. Publicizing reading and making it social elevates its relevance. Being social through technology is a normed and well-exercised practice in society.

There is a lot to learn from media branding when planning to build a school reading culture. Logos, slogans, and now hashtags have become vehicles to symbolize a particular meaning, brand, or cause. Logos and slogans are historically established symbols. A *hashtag* connects categorized content for people with similar interests and has become part of how people brand and spread ideas. The hashtag has emerged as a way to make content discoverable and build followings around that content. This concept of promotion can help in building a community reading campaign: attach a hashtag to a slogan and logo to memorialize your commitment to reading. #LBReads is the reading campaign in my school community.

Branding strategies help when developing a reading campaign, and eventually become a mechanism to make reading content discoverable when posting in physical space and on social media. My school community developed the #LBReads campaign so that the reading brand would encourage educators to generate content about students' reading lives and share that content through a digital platform or print displays in the school district. A branded campaign encourages school and class community members to join the movement and popularize the commitment to developing the reading lives of students. Whether teachers post reading-related content on bulletin boards in school hallways or on their social media pages, the campaign is an indicator to viewers that the content is in support of the reading lives of students. What you share in physical or digital space is an indicator of what you value. Borrow and repurpose ideas from the media industry to create a strong visual representation that contributes to perpetuating a positive reading culture.

Sharing the message about the importance of reading with all stakeholders and inviting them to embrace the campaign can build the capacity of the campaign itself. #LBReads became the brand of our district in Long Beach—a place that promotes a love of reading based on personal choice and interest, and is committed to developing the capacities of all members of a school community to support the reading identities of students. Shortly after creating the hashtag, a logo was designed to support the branding of the message. Figure 1.2 shows the logo that became the new face of our literacy work in Long Beach. The hashtag and logo became (and still are) widely used in the district and act as catalysts for a new age of literacy work. Publicity and visual cues are part of the world, and these are ways classrooms, libraries, and schools can move into 21st century culture.

How to Make It Happen

The following steps will help you create and implement a branded reading campaign in your school or district.

1. Develop a vision for the work.
2. Create a slogan or hashtag.
3. Design your logo.
4. Plan and launch your campaign.

Source: © 2018 Long Beach School District.
FIGURE 1.2: The final logo for the #LBReads campaign.

Develop a Vision for the Work

The purpose of branding reading is to build a positive reading culture to support students' engagement in reading. A thriving reading culture can inspire students to develop their reading identities and read often and diversely. The message is quite simple: *reading is important*. Sharing the vision and defining the message helps school or class community members know what you value and that becomes the heart of the culture work you're about to do. Every context is different. Think about what it is you want your school or class community to rally behind. Some reading-related themes a community may want to promote include prioritizing reading time at home and school, diversifying student book choices, embracing reading as a vehicle for learning, reading to explore, or integrating more reading into content-area disciplines. By defining your chosen theme, you create a vision for people to be part of and a unified message to share.

Create a Slogan or Hashtag

Once your vision is clear, create a slogan or hashtag to capture the message of the vision. Generate ideas for words and phrases that connect the school or class community and the message of the campaign. Figure 1.3 (page 14) shows samples of reading campaign ideas using *LB* as sample initials for my school district. Think about how your school's name would fit.

Vision or Message	Slogan or Hashtag
Reading is important.	#LBReads
Prioritize reading time at home and school.	#TimeToReadinLB
Students have access to a diverse collection of books representative of the community population.	#ReadingForWeInLB
Reading is a vehicle for new learning.	#LBReadstoLearn
Reading is a pathway to explore and make new discoveries.	#LBReadstoExplore
Reading can elevate learning in content-area disciplines.	#ReadEverywhere

FIGURE 1.3: Sample visions or messages with associated slogans or hashtags.

The articulation of letters is important. I still laugh when I think of an email from my superintendent that said to make sure the *R* in #LBReads is capitalized; otherwise it looks like we are promoting a bakery (#LBreads).

Design Your Logo

In advertising, there are two types of logos: (1) a descriptive logo and (2) a nondescriptive logo. A *descriptive* logo includes textual or visual design elements (or a combination of the two) and clearly communicates the type of brand or service. Burger King is an example of a company that has a descriptive logo; the logo includes a visual of two hamburger buns and the word *burger*. A *nondescriptive* logo contains design elements not indicative of the type of product or service the brand is selling. An example of a nondescriptive logo is McDonalds', which contains only two golden arches. Assistant marketing professors Jonathan Luffarelli, Antonios Stamatogiannakis, and Haiyang Yang (2019) find descriptive logos more favorably impact consumers' brand perceptions and are more likely to improve brand performance than nondescriptive logos. As a result of their study, Luffarelli and colleagues (2019) suggest including at least one textual or visual design element (or both) indicative of the type of product or service offered, or in the case of a reading campaign, the message being promoted. My district chose to add a descriptive logo to the #LBReads campaign.

Similar to the thought process when creating a hashtag, think of images that capture the messaging of the reading campaign and mesh with a theme or identity of the learning community. You may consider including an image that encompasses several areas of literacy—like reading, writing, creating, or thinking—to broaden your community's message about the importance of literacy and how integral reading is to literacy development overall. You may consider including school colors, a school mascot, or a symbol (or a combination) already represented in your school. You may also include a theme that resonates with your school community based on the identities of the broader community. For example, I work in a beach community where school buildings are just a ten-minute walk from the ocean. A beach theme is representative of an aspect that is already part of the community's identity.

There are several ways to go about creating your logo. In each of these scenarios, it is helpful to explain the purpose of your campaign, what specific text you wish to incorporate into the logo, and any other additional information about what makes your community unique (for example, colors, a school mascot, and so on).

- **Collaborate with the art or technology department:** Present the opportunity to design a reading campaign logo to colleagues who specialize in design. They may invite students with a special interest or talent in design to work on this project.
- **Host an open submission opportunity:** Invite all students in your school or class community to submit ideas for a logo design. You may select one of the submissions or use ideas from multiple submissions to create one logo that represents reading and your community. You may also select several submissions to reveal to the school or class community so they can vote on one new logo. This approach is student centered and invites students into the process of branding and messaging.
- **Partner with an artist who specializes in design:** If you aren't artistically inclined, it may be a good idea to hire a professional artist. You might like to partner with an artist from your community or search online for independent artists' websites. Alternatively, you could use a freelance services site such as Fiverr (www.fiverr.com), an online platform that offers digital services in several categories. After posting an inquiry to their message board, you can connect with a graphic design artist whose services can attend to your vision.

The #LBReads logo was designed by a professional graphic design artist. In my reflection, I developed an understanding of the importance of inclusivity and active participation in culture. After several years, the district leadership invited students in my school community to submit original designs for a new #LBReads logo so the reading campaign could have a new representation for students to share. Offering students the opportunity to design the logo is a way to build investment in developing the reading culture and make it an authentic representation of the school community. Having students at the center of all reading experiences is a priority. The more students are centered in the work, the better.

Plan and Launch Your Campaign

Depending on the context of the work, you may notice your role as a literacy leader takes different responsibilities and personalities. Get ready to dabble in the fields of public relations and advertising. You established your vision, defined your message, and now have a brand to capture that message. Now, on to the campaign!

If you are an administrator, work with teachers and other administrators to promote the campaign. If you are a teacher, communicate with building leaders, students, and caregivers to promote this work in your classroom. You cannot develop a reading culture alone (read more on that in chapter 2, page 27). In my case, district leadership shared the vision for #LBReads with the adults in the school community so they could begin supporting the campaign in the classroom.

Providing information about the research that confirms your initiative, as well as the standards it addresses, helps to provide context for the work. For example, I explained the research that supports the relationship between reading volume and student achievement (see The Roots of This Work, page 11), as well as how the state standards (in our case, the *New York State Next Generation English Language Arts Standards*) share expectations for readers in the "Lifelong Practices of Readers and Writers": "read often and widely from a range of global and diverse texts; read for multiple purposes, including for learning and for pleasure; and self-select texts based on interest" (New York State Education Department, 2017a, p. 8). Consider revisiting the standards in your state to see if there are specific standards that support your campaign work.

> ### What Does a Reading Campaign Help Promote?
>
> **A community embrace of a love of reading:** Students will develop a personal interest in reading with the support of school community members.
>
> **Reading books of choice:** Students will choose from a range of diverse texts in classroom and school libraries so they have a personal investment in their reading lives.
>
> **Reading often:** Students will have time to read every day in school, as well as encouragement to read at home.
>
> **Conversations about reading:** Students will be given time in school each day to talk about their reading with peers and adults, and to respond to reading in authentic ways.
>
> **A reading identity:** Students will develop a reading identity so they can talk about themselves as readers. (Educators expect students' reading identities will change over time.)

Use social media platforms to elevate awareness about a reading campaign among older students, educators, and caregivers a school community. After launching the #LBReads campaign, teachers and administrators post it on their individual and school social media accounts. We began to post #LBReads content to start the trend for followers to come (see figure 1.4). People now tag #LBReads when they post reading-related content.

We created an Instagram account to share the #LBReads work: @lbreadsbooks. All adults in the school community were invited to follow the account via email (see figure 1.5). People tag @lbreadsbooks when they post reading-related content on Instagram.

You can use multiple forms of communication to spread the word about your campaign to families and students.

FIGURE 1.4: A social media post to introduce the #LBReads reading campaign to school community members active on social media.

- Teachers can post information on their learning management system pages.
- Administrators can post branded campaign messages and images on the school district website.
- Inform families about the use of social media pages via paper mailings, email, and the school or district website.
- PTA representatives can share information about the campaign and related events on their social media pages and messaging platforms.
- Secondary teachers can invite students to follow a social media account directly. Confirm age requirements before sharing social media information with students. See figure 1.6 for the message I shared with secondary teachers to encourage students to follow the @lbreadsbooks Instagram account.

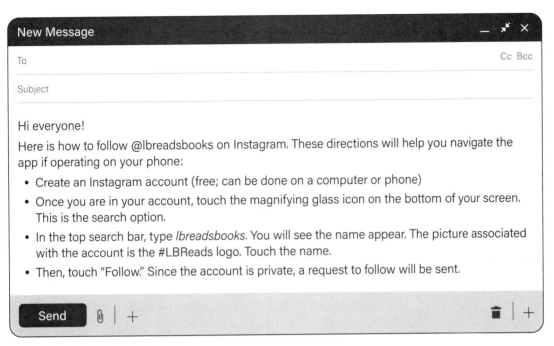

FIGURE 1.5: An email to invite adults in the school community to follow @lbreadsbooks on Instagram.

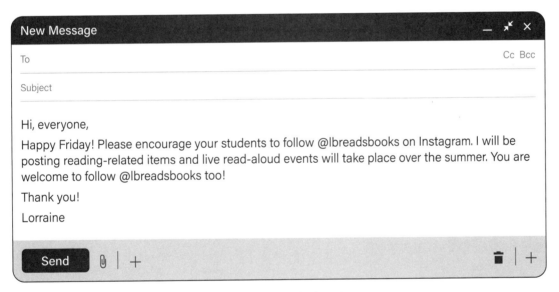

FIGURE 1.6: An email to invite secondary students to follow @lbreadsbooks on Instagram.

Please visit www.lorrainemradice.com/blog for more images showing how the #LBReads campaign spreads via social media networks.

Sustain the Momentum of Your Reading Campaign

The four steps I previously outlined are initial steps to take in creating a reading campaign: (1) develop a vision for the work, (2) create your hashtag, (3) design your logo, and (4) plan and launch your campaign. However, these steps are only the beginning. The way the reading campaign perpetuates a reading culture is through the leadership committing to branding the reading initiatives and communication with your hashtag and logo. A well-designed logo can offer substantial benefits to a brand, including piquing the interest of consumers, facilitating brand recognition, and conveying what a brand is all about (Luffarelli et al., 2019). Over time, your logo will attract followers to your reading campaign. Aim for school community members to recognize the reading campaign, become interested in the purpose of the campaign, and know why there is a commitment to the campaign.

You will see the #LBReads logo on images in the figures throughout this book to serve as examples of how to incorporate your reading campaign into reading events. It's one of the ways the campaign *lives*. The following list contains examples of how to build the brand of your reading campaign and maintain its presence.

- **Attach the campaign logo to initiatives related to reading:** Think about initiatives in your class or school related to reading and begin to brand those initiatives with your campaign logo. Include the logo on a website or in promotional material you share with students and caregivers. For example, *WRaP* (Wonder, Read, and Play) is my school district's approach to at-home learning. It utilizes the #LBReads logo on the school website to promote at-home learning. Another example shows an informational slide for caregivers from a kindergarten orientation presentation (see figure 1.7). As their children enter kindergarten, my district welcomes new families by explaining the strong commitment it has to reading culture and building the reading identities of students. The #LBReads campaign logo is one of the first images new caregivers see as they enter the district.

At-Home Learning

WRaP—Wonder, Read, and Play!

- An emphasis on reading and language development
- A commitment to personal inquiry
- The importance of purposeful play
- Caregivers as learning partners

FIGURE 1.7: An informational slide shared during a presentation for caregivers of students entering kindergarten.

- **Use the campaign logo on communication with staff, students, and caregivers:** Figure 1.8 is an invitation to caregivers to attend an author visit (see chapter 5, page 123, for more on author visits, and chapter 6, page 143, for more on including caregivers). Notice the #LBReads logo on this advertisement. #LBReads acts as a sponsor for the events happening in the school.

- **Design a T-shirt to incorporate into school spirit days or to wear at school events:** One part of building reading culture is to plan events. Consider designing a T-shirt that features your reading campaign logo. At school reading events, presenters and facilitators wear the T-shirt to support the campaign and show they value reading.

- **Share about your reading campaign with new educators:** There will be an initial launch of the reading campaign when you begin this work. Anticipate the need to keep launching (or sharing information about) the campaign and the vision for reading with new educators as they enter your school year after year. To relaunch the campaign as new staff join the district, host meetings to share about the reading campaign and your district's work to build reading culture. In addition to formal meetings, send an email to summarize the campaign message and provide resources to support the work ahead. Figure 1.9 is an example of an email I share with new staff at the start of a new school year.

FIGURE 1.8: Promotional material for a reading event features the #LBReads campaign logo.

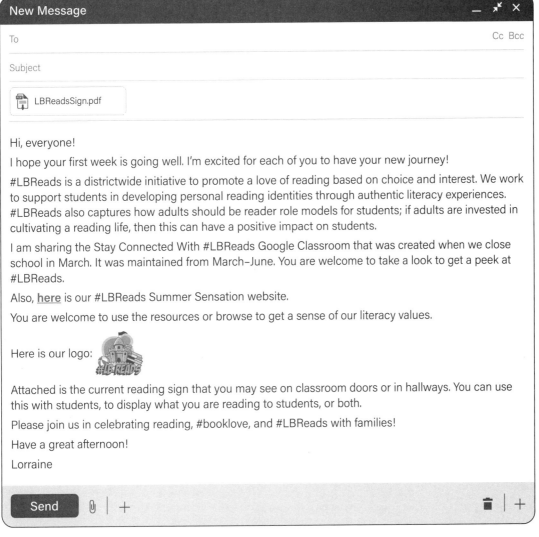

FIGURE 1.9: An email to new staff to explain the #LBReads campaign and encourage participation in the reading celebration.

- **Anticipate your context will evolve and prepare to continue to cultivate your reading campaign:** When teachers began creating new instructional material in response to the COVID-19 pandemic, many used Google Slides (https://google.com/slides/about) to create virtual literacy centers, virtual classrooms, and online spaces for students to interact with digital resources. Visit www.lorrainemradice.com/blog to view images of a virtual classroom and a virtual library that feature the #LBReads logo. The #LBReads campaign supported efforts to connect students to reading in virtual space. Even when our approach to schooling changed, the commitment to reading culture remained in spirit, but evolved in practice. Chapter 7 (page 165) is shows you how to continue to prioritize reading culture when introducing other initiatives or circumstances.

Once my district shared the vision and rationale of the #LBReads campaign with the adults in our schools, the campaign blossomed in unexpected ways. Teachers began to use the hashtag on student work. The hashtag also appeared on bulletin boards that shared what students were currently reading.

Consider adding your campaign logo to your school email signatures as a way to identify it as part of the school reading campaign. Alongside the logo, you can also include a book you are currently reading (read more in The Currently Reading Sign section in chapter 3, page 81).

Engage in Community Outreach Through Your New Campaign

Part of the vision for a reading campaign is to honor and extend literacy beyond the school walls to reach families and communities. Literacies form through social and cultural experiences (Clinton, Jenkins, & McWilliams, 2013; Gee, 2010; Heath, 1983; Jenkins, 2009; Jenkins & Kelley, 2013; Street, 1993, 1995, 2016; Taylor, 1997). While one dimension of literacy is acquiring academic skills in the classroom, literacy is also situated in the social practices that students participate in beyond school hours (Street, 2016). Students develop various literacies through interacting with family, community, and social groups that may influence their academic literacies and reading identities (Gee, 1999). The social experiences students participate in expand their worldview as they acquire knowledge and contribute to cognitive processes and schema while reading for meaning (Richgels, 1982). Educators honor this in schools by developing a shared responsibility in supporting the literacy development of students with community members and community organizations.

A reading culture does not grow in isolation; it spreads through the commitment of multiple stakeholders who normalize and value authentic reading experiences for students. Drawing on the community literacy work of experts Shirley Brice Heath (1983, 2010), Heath & Milbrey W. McLaughlin (1994), Brian Street (1993, 1995, 2017), Denny Taylor (1997), and Taylor & Catherine Dorsey-Gaines (1988) when planning my campaign, I embraced the communities outside the school building and knew they would be an important contributor to the meaning of #LBReads. In this section, I share examples of read-aloud experiences brought into community spaces outside the school buildings. Think about the community spaces that contribute to the academic and social development of young people, and when during the year branching out into community spaces may support the reading culture and students as readers.

During the first summer of the #LBReads campaign, our district conducted a series of community read-alouds to keep students engaged in reading throughout the summer months. We invited students and families to attend these read-alouds district and school administrators hosted. The read-alouds were held at various places in the community and at different times of the day to offer as many opportunities as possible for families and students to participate (see figure 1.10).

SAVE THE DATES!

Long Beach Community Reads
Summer 2019

Date	Location	Time
July 10, 2019	Long Beach Public Library	4:30 p.m.
July 17, 2019	Lido Complex	9:15 a.m.
July 24, 2019	Earth Arts	4:30 p.m.
July 31, 2019	Círculo de la Hispanidad *Bilingual Read-Aloud	3:00 p.m.
August 7, 2019	Martin Luther King Jr. Center	10:00 a.m.
August 14, 2019	Lindell Elementary School	9:15 a.m.
August 21, 2019	East School Playground	4:30 p.m.
August 28, 2019	Long Beach Public Library	4:30 p.m.

GUEST READERS FROM THE LONG BEACH SCHOOL DISTRICT WILL READ THEIR FAVORITE BOOKS AT EACH OF THESE LOCATIONS. WE LOOK FORWARD TO SEEING YOU THERE!

FIGURE 1.10: A schedule of community read-alouds.

You should strongly consider the geographic locations of community events (like the summer read-alouds) when building a schedule. Prioritize access for families. Consider limiting the need for transportation to participate, and honor people's connections to community groups.

- **Embrace outdoor spaces on school grounds like playgrounds, fields, courts, or gathering areas:** These spaces are convenient and familiar, allowing families to access their neighborhood school to participate. At the Long Beach summer community read-aloud events, an administrator from each school signed up to read at the school and then students played on the playground after. One principal read *The Recess Queen* by Alexis O'Neill (2002) in the school's playground.

- **Partner with community youth programs:** The influence of community programs as a critical development context for youth was highlighted in a 2002 National Research

Council report, *Community Programs to Promote Youth Development* (Eccles & Gootman, 2002). Heath and McLaughlin (1994) argue educators should consider their relationships with youth-based organizations, as they create and maintain highly educational institutions that are preparatory for workplace and career pathways. Schools have resources and human capital (people who really care about students) to offer youth-based organizations—all to benefit the growth and development of young people. Consider visiting community organizations to read with young people. You may also consider hosting a book donation and distributing books for students to take home.

Heath (2010) discusses the importance of the preposition used when explaining family literacy events, noting the difference between literacy events *to* young people and literacy events *with* young people. The preposition *to* implies one-way giving—the adult is giving opportunities to a child. However, the preposition *with* implies the adult and the child experience an event together for mutual benefit to exchange talents, skills, ideas, and laughter. Consider this notion when visiting camps and local community centers for literacy events.

In addition to reading, my district engaged students in an activity related to the reading to demonstrate how books can inspire inquiry in various topics, like learning new talents or hobbies. For example, at the local Martin Luther King Jr. Center, my colleague and I invited students to participate in an interactive read-aloud to learn how to practice yoga. My colleague read *Good Night Yoga: A Pose-by-Pose Bedtime Story* by Mariam Gates (2015) as I demonstrated the poses. The students followed along with the demonstration and practiced the poses. After, we engaged in a conversation about why to practice yoga and the benefits it can bring to one's life. This led to discussion about mindfulness, stress management, physical fitness, and overall health. To conclude the experience, we provided each student with a book to take home after receiving donations of gently used or new books from families, the PTA, and book fair sponsors.

Reading Culture in Action
Reflections From Those Who Are Making It Happen

Throughout the summer following my first year as director of instructional technology, administrators hosted read-alouds throughout the district. As a former English language arts teacher at the secondary level, early childhood reading events were very unfamiliar to me. I wasn't sure what to expect or how to prepare. I signed up to read with my colleague at a community center's summer camp. Walking in, the campers' energy was electric... and we had a calming book about yoga for them. As I read *Good Night Yoga*, we modeled the poses and the students copied. Total fixation replaced the frenetic energy! We tree-posed; they tree-posed. We cat-posed; they cat-posed. These young readers saw the potential connection between reading and physical activity; many clutched the handouts of poses we had prepared for them, eager to perform the poses at home. (P. Kiley-Rendon, former director of instructional technology, personal communication, June 27, 2022)

- **Connect with local camps:** You can host read-alouds during camp sessions at your local community center or at camps that may be held in or near your school. Connecting with camps students attend provides you exposure to a population of students during the day and may alleviate potential pressure working caregivers may feel to attend the community reading events. Caregivers don't need to arrange for additional transportation or attend because the read-aloud is part of the camp experience students already attend.

- **Engage your local multilingual community:** Connect with organizations that support multilingual communities. A bilingual read-aloud was held at a local not-for-profit organization called *Círculo de la Hispanidad*, which works to improve the lives of families through social service, education, recreation, cultural development, economic development, and social justice programs. The read-aloud was in English and Spanish to honor the language identity of the students affiliated with the community organization. Two administrators read—one in English and one in Spanish—page by page. The administrators encouraged students to engage in conversation about the book and shared their reactions, questions, and connections. This provided an opportunity for students to practice their English language skills as well as the behaviors for participating in a learning community. After, students received books to take home for summer reading.

- **Partner with your public library:** Libraries can be community partners and are a great place to grow the reading lives of students when they are not in school. Libraries may have multipurpose rooms you can utilize as a space to host read-aloud sessions, and students can peruse the bookshelves to search for their next read. In Long Beach schools, all students receive a library card application when they enter kindergarten. Consider contacting your public library director to share your campaign details and summer reading plans.

- **Contact local restaurants as a source of commuity partnership:** Soon after our district launched #LBReads, our schools partnered with a local pizzeria to sponsor an #LBReads event. The owner agreed to give a free slice of pizza to students who brought in the book they were currently reading or students who were able to tell an employee at the pizzeria about the book they were currently reading. Students were invited to complete a reading reflection to submit as a raffle ticket as another way of participating in this event. Raffle winners won a free book delivered to them days later in school. A list of books with a pizza theme was also sent home with the invitation to the event to build excitement and emphasize the importance of books in the reading campaign (see appendix A, page 181). An event like this not only highlights the reading campaign but also invites community members and commercial businesses to join the schools in their efforts to promote reading.

When local partners engage in this work, it becomes less about the reading campaign and more about the connections you make with the community. Consider the identities within the community and the important places people gather. Use reading as a pathway to form relationships with the people and places that make up your school community and that ultimately influence students' reading lives.

Maintaining a reading campaign during the summer months in a beach community is not an easy task. The families in my school community have sand in their shoes all year long and are waiting to hit the ocean, soak up the sun, and embrace their beach community. I don't blame them! The challenge as a literacy leader is to figure out how to integrate reading into community values and not exist in the status quo of what the summer traditionally looks like in the community (Brown, 2018). It's OK to redefine what has been defined for so long.

While not an abundant number of students and families attended the #LBReads summer read-aloud event, those who did connected with their school community and engaged in a meaningful reading experience. Literacy culture events not only promote the importance of reading but also create spaces for people to participate and gain a sense of belonging within the school community. Keep this in mind while reading the ideas I share in this book. If participation rates vary among events at the beginning of your journey, reflect on the factors that could contribute to high- or low-participation rates. Solicit feedback from stakeholders you invite to participate as well. Involving class or school community members in the conversation about the culture will help create a clear direction for your work.

All initiatives have to start somewhere. Capitalize on your initial investors because they are the foundation for your reading culture to build on. Celebrate any and all participation. Culture builds over time. Early adopters act as the roots to what will eventually grow.

Summary

This is the beginning of your journey. Celebrate what you have started!

Promotion and advertisement are normed in society. How do you know about a great restaurant or eatery in your community? People probably talk about it or you may have seen a sample menu online. How do you know about a new show or movie about to debut on a streaming platform or in theaters? You probably have seen a commercial or an advertisement on social media. Promote your learning communities' values—particularly your reading or literacy campaign—in similar ways! Have fun with your logo, slogan, and hashtag. Lean into positive uses of technology and social media. Use people's ubiquitous hyperconnectivity in positive ways to spread word about the importance of reading and commitment to it in your school community.

A strategic launch of your campaign with a clear vision and purpose is crucial to the sustainability and success of the work. Stakeholders need clarity. When messaging is clear, it allows for deeper understanding and participation in the work.

Additionally, literacy work is about the collective efforts of a community. It doesn't exist in a vacuum. Build an inclusive campaign where community members (in and outside the school) fill various roles and make contributions. Spread joy through how you engage community members and capitalize on how they can help spread the message about the importance of reading.

The reading culture work is to engage and inspire students, but the work begins with rallying the adults in the learning community. In the next chapter, you will find ways to engage adults in reading culture events so they can be reading champions for students!

Reflection Questions

On your own or with a collaborative team, answer the following questions.

1. What is the current state of engagement in reading among adults and students in our community?

2. What is the current level of commitment among students to read in and outside of school? Are students reading? Are students excited about reading?

3. Is this the right time to commit to reading being the center of the school or classroom culture? Are we ready to promote this work regularly? What action plans do we need to create to include multiple stakeholders?

4. What is the vision for our reading campaign? Why is the campaign important?

5. What are the talents and interests the adults can contribute to the success of the campaign? Is someone skilled in art or graphic design? Is someone skilled in social media use?

6. How do we plan to reflect on the work of the campaign so it stays relevant and accessible to the reading community?

CHAPTER 2

Developing Reading Role Models
How to Rally Adults to Explore Their Reading Lives

This Chapter Features...

Ways to Rally and Invite Adults to Explore Their Own Reading Lives

- Plan a book swap (page 32).
- Design a newsletter (page 39).
- Facilitate book clubs for adults (page 43).
- Collaborate on a book recommendation video (page 54).
- Host a book tasting (page 55).

School leaders cannot shift a school's culture alone. Every person in a school community has both an opportunity and a responsibility to lead students (DuFour & Marzano, 2011). This chapter leans into leader and educator John W. Gardner's (1993) idea to share ways to build a school's reading culture. Gardner (1993) writes, "Every great leader is clearly teaching and every great teacher is leading" (p. 18). Educators can integrate the ideas I present in this chapter into schoolwide and classroom communities, including *all leaders are teachers and all teachers are leaders*. All adults in a school community can build their capacity to lead students to a robust reading life. Everyone is important.

In this chapter, I consider two literacies that develop as a result of leadership practices framed around the sociocultural perspective of literacy. The first is the literacy that emerges among the adults in the school community because of the culture-building work. The cultural practices among adults in the school begin to define how the school community grows together in its commitment to fostering the reading lives of students (Gee, 2010). Adults talk about books, provide time for reading in school, and prioritize the reading culture in their learning communities. Language and thinking about reading are common. As a result of this change in school culture and the mindsets of their teachers, a second literacy evolves among students. They begin to identify themselves as readers and learn the importance of spending time reading material of their choice to cultivate engagement and achievement (Allington & McGill-Franzen, 2021). In summary, the literacies among the adults impact the literacy (specifically reading) lives of students. This begs the question: How do you create shared reading culture literacies among adults so they exercise those literacies to impact the reading lives of students? One way is to rally adults to explore their own reading lives so they can become reading role models for students.

The Roots of This Work

In their research to reimagine schools, Jacqueline Grennon Brooks and Martin Brooks (2021) argue that for any change to take hold in a school, the structures and norms that frame the organization's culture must support the change. When alignment among these elements is tight, a powerful and seamless message about what is valued ripples through the system. A commitment to collaboration among all school community members to prioritize reading helps to solidify a culture that sustains progress and conveys a message about the value held to reading.

As daily teaching and learning practices are focused on developing the reading lives of students, students become immersed in a culture that celebrates a commitment to reading and honors personal reading identities. It is alarming that the voluntary reading of books has dramatically declined in the last half-century (National Endowment for the Arts [NEA], 2007; Schaeffer, 2021), but hopeful to consider that increasing students' motivation to read influences their long-term reading habits (De Naeghel, Van Keer, Vansteenkiste, & Rosseel, 2012). A collective effort among all adults in a school community can be a force to positively influence student motivation and the volume of books students read.

Professor and director of the Melbourne Education Research Institute John A. C. Hattie (2012) reiterates and expands on this notion in his work on making learning visible to maximize the impact on student learning. Hattie (2012) claims the school's culture is the essence of sustained success and "improvements relate to building a collective capacity of teachers in a school to show success" (p. 150). As a result of his research, Hattie (2012) concludes that teachers are among the most powerful influences on student learning, and school leaders and teachers must create school environments where teachers can feel safe to learn, relearn, and explore knowledge and understanding.

When I began to focus on schools' reading cultures, I embraced Hattie's (2012) research about the importance of the teacher and expanded on his findings by inviting all adults in the school community to engage and identify with reading. While teachers control the environment and practices in the classroom, they should recognize students' reading identities can evolve in all spaces within a school community. Librarians, administrators, nurses, teaching assistants and aides, custodians, food service workers, and performance area teachers (art, physical education, music) can all contribute to a student's reading life. All adults in a school community are teachers in some form; teachers are just the ones who are in the classroom with students for the majority of the school day teaching reading, mathematics, or science. The strategies in this chapter help literacy leaders nurture how all types of teachers can identify, learn, and grow as readers themselves so their attitudes, beliefs, and commitments can positively impact the reading lives of students (Hattie, 2012).

Focusing on literacy development, specifically the commitment to developing students' reading lives, requires the efforts of the entire school team to make a lasting impact on students. The adults become the source of inspiration for students. People need to believe in the work to rally behind reading and feel part of developing the school culture. This is your work as a leader in your school or classroom. Don't worry; while it may seem that you are the one with the biggest pom-poms at the start of your cheerleading for reading effort, you will see the squad grow over time!

Understanding Why Social and Cultural Experiences Influence Literacy Development

Reading culture–building events set out to influence teachers' attitudes and beliefs, as well as their pedagogical practices for reading in the classroom. Educators should consider the factors that contribute to how teachers develop their pedagogical practices when planning and engaging in this work. Coauthors Michelle M. Gemmink, Marjon Fokkens-Bruinsma, Ietje Pauw, and Klaas van Veen (2021) find teachers' social-professional relationships empower their professional spaces and, therefore, strengthen their pedagogical practices. If teachers don't perceive shared goals with colleagues and there is strain on professional dialogue and spaces, teachers feel negative pressure in the workplace. This idea of a social-professional relationships is at the heart of the leadership strategies I describe in this chapter. Through social literacy events for adults in schools, there are opportunities to build adult reading lives with colleagues.

Research about teacher pedagogy and school improvement acknowledges the importance of social-professional relationships with shared goals (Gemmink et al., 2021; Hamre, Hatfield, Pianta, & Jamil, 2014) and connects to how the reading culture work I outline in this book is grounded in sociocultural literacies research. Sociocultural literacies research suggests that literacy changes as culture and context changes. Language use is an example of this. The language people use may vary depending on the group they are engaging with. Dialects vary among community groups. Also, the language students and adults use in an academic space like a classroom may be different from the language they use in a restaurant or on a playground. Literacy practices reflect the cultural norms of the context in which individuals participate, a concept known as the *new literacy studies* (Gee, 1990, 2010; Street, 1997, 2016) and also referred to as *literacy as a social practice* (Street, 2016). Street (2016) explains that literacy practices are particular ways of thinking about and conducting reading and writing in cultural contexts. Literacy practices are constructions of particular social groups rather than attributable to cognition alone. The values and practices of different social and cultural groups determine how people read and write specific groupings of text.

Literacy has become plural because there are many different social and cultural practices that incorporate literacy (Gee, 2010). The way people gather, the content of conversations, the ways people speak about topics, and their overall attitudes and beliefs are examples of literacies that develop within larger groups of people. Literacies become shared visions and discourses among a group of people (in this case, educators).

Professor Len Unsworth (2008), research director of Educational Semiotics in English and Literacy Pedagogy at the Australian Catholic University, explains multiliteracies by asserting that new literacies integrate multiple meaning-making systems, such as language, image, sound, and movement, as well as multiple text–generation devices like digital cameras, scanners, computer software, and handheld devices. Under this framework, multiple literacies include functions people use to make meaning: "In multiliteracies pedagogy all forms of representation, including language, are regarded as dynamic processes of transformation rather than processes of reproduction" (Baker, 2010, p. 70). As you provide various opportunities to engage in school reading events through different modalities (I mention throughout this book), participants construct meaning about their own identities as readers and how they can support students in the classroom.

Embrace the concepts of the new literacy studies and literacy as a social practice when building a school reading culture. Consider the literacies that develop among students and staff through the work you do in schools. While students develop core language competencies and content literacies in various disciplines, adults grow their literacies as they refine their teaching and learning practices and introduce new initiatives, and as the identity of the school evolves over time. School leaders have a lot of influence on the literacies the school community embraces.

The natural social aspect of school helps develop a culture that engages the adults in literacy practices of their own. Specific social conditions like faculty meetings, grade-level meetings, professional development, a book club, a book fair, an assembly, or a field trip always construct a variety of literacy practices (Luke, 1994). School leaders need to design social conditions in the school so it acts as a hub for interaction, connection, and sharing—all in an effort to build reading culture together. Hattie (2009) developed a checklist for inspired and passionate teaching as a result of his research. He claims when teachers do things with certain attitudes or belief systems, they truly make a difference. Two items on Hattie's (2009) checklist are:

> All adults in the school community recognize that all are vigilant about building expertise to creative positive effects on achievement for all students. [Further,] the school has convincing evidence that all of its teachers are passionate and inspired—and this should be the major promotion attribute of the school. (pp. 23–24)

Creating opportunities for adults in the school community to make a personal connection to reading allows them to consider the importance of reading and prepare for ways to bring a dynamic reading culture to the classroom. Building reading culture through social interactions for adults in the school community serves as a source of inspiration for learning, planning, and reflection. Teaching is personal; if people can see themselves in the culture, then the culture becomes the impetus for change.

Learning From Literacy Leaders in the Field

These ideas also stand on the work of accomplished literacy teachers and leaders. In her book *In The Middle: A Lifetime of Learning About Writing, Reading, and Adolescents*, Global Teacher Prize winner Nancie Atwell (2015) shares the importance of teachers acknowledging their own reading identities, specifically noting their identities can impact the way they provide reading instruction in the classroom. Atwell (2015) recounts how teachers design traditional secondary reading instruction, which relies heavily on texts referred to as *literary canons*. Those reading experiences are mostly assigned and somewhat contrived. As a result of this reflection, Atwell (2015) concludes that her own personal processes as a reader did not match what she asked her students to do in her classroom. Her process lacked authenticity. She explains how her own process was riveted with choice, personal routines, and spaces to talk about books, authors, and reading with others (Atwell, 2015). She then learns to demonstrate her own reading identity to her students and realizes she needs to authenticate the reading practices in her classroom (Atwell, 2015).

When I began building a reading culture, one of the first books I reread was *The Book Whisperer* by Donalyn Miller (2009), who explains her love for books and strong reading identity:

> My obsession with books and reading defines my life, and . . . I walked into my classroom convinced I would share this passion with my students. No matter what else I had to offer them, I could offer my enthusiasm for books. (p. 11)

Miller's (2009) work validates how important it is for adults in a school community to have their own reading identities. Think about the adults in your school community who aren't avid readers, don't identify with reading, or may incorporate reading with students because it's part of their job and not what they intrinsically believe in or connect to. Their attitudes and beliefs about the act of reading, as Hattie (2009) would reference, are not truly inspired. Think carefully about these folks when planning reading culture events. The goal is not to turn every adult in the school community into a reader; the goal is to encourage every adult to reflect on their reading identity and, if there isn't a strong connection to reading, to acknowledge it. There is strength in knowing what you don't like or connect to as a teacher because you can then think about the implications of that void when working with students. It's part of how you develop a belief system about what you put forth to students in the classroom.

The ideas I share in this chapter are in response to several factors: the research and theoretical perspectives of literacy, what I've learned about the important role adults play in the reading lives of students, and the impact reading culture events can have on the adults in a school community. Any adult can be a reading role model for students. Providing experiences for adults to transform their attitudes and beliefs by exploring their reading identities and to celebrate their reading lives sets the intention for what educators can do with students. Experiential, social approaches contribute to the development of culture; excitement builds, and the adults start talking about how much they enjoy the opportunities they have to share about reading and connect with other adults through social reading experiences.

How to Make It Happen

Teachers often ask students to reflect on their reading habits, behaviors, and preferences at the beginning of and throughout the school year. Interviews and surveys serve as an informal assessment to help teachers get to know their students as readers. This is a practice you can transfer to adults when getting ready to build reading culture. One of the first reflections adults can engage in is a survey to identify where they are as readers. Pose the question, What kind of reader are you? and provide the following five responses. People may identify with one or several.

1. I always read and carry my book with me.
2. I really want to read, but I have laundry to do.
3. I read short bursts of text (articles, blogs, sports recaps).
4. I read and have gone completely digital.
5. Hmm . . . I think I last read *The Outsiders* in middle school.

If you are a teacher who is building reading culture in your classroom, use this question to self-assess your own reading life and think about how the response impacts your work with students. If you are planning to engage many adults in reflection, consider the following practices.

- Share a digital survey form like a Google Form (https://google.com/forms/about) with the group and ask them to complete it knowing you will look at their responses. Use the information to inform next steps in building reading culture.

- Create small groups of adults to discuss the question, What kind of reader are you? at a faculty or department meeting. Ask them to consider how their responses impact their work with students.

- Engage the large group in a gallery walk at a faculty or department meeting. Put each of the five responses on a piece of chart paper and arrange them in different spaces around a room. Invite people to walk over to the statement or statements they identify with most so they can converse with peers who have similar reading identities. People appreciate the camaraderie and how the conversation pushes their thinking about how their current reading identity influences, or doesn't influence, their work with students.

This type of reflection, whether done individually or collaboratively, acts as a precursor to the work to support the reading lives of students.

Plan a Book Swap

A *book swap* is an opportunity to create a social space where adults rally behind the excitement of reading, develop their social and professional relationships, and influence pedagogical practices. It is both a social event and professional learning opportunity as well as a way to bring people together, develop relationships, and engage colleagues in an authentic practice of avid readers. For colleagues with rich reading identities, it is a place to find the next great read (and mingle with coworkers). For colleagues who may have read their last book in eleventh grade English class, it is a place to spark inspiration for their reading identities (and mingle with coworkers). What all colleagues gain are ideas and resources to bring back to their classrooms and workspaces to help develop the reading lives of students. A book swap is a literacy event that can benefit the culture of a school in and out of the classroom.

Mark the Calendar

Schedule the book swap at a time that works best for the adults in your school community. Consider the time of year and time of day. You may know the availability of staff, or you may survey folks to gauge their availability for participation in school events. You may also schedule the book swap during a designated meeting time, like a faculty or department meeting. I choose to capitalize on two times during the school year: (1) the holiday season and (2) the end of the school year with summer approaching. I make a connection to books as gifts when hosting during the holiday season, and I make a connection to finding a great summer beach read when hosting as summer approaches. The calendar markers support my planning because they contextualize the event and may encourage participation.

Send an Invitation

Hosting a book swap is like hosting a party. As a literacy leader, you are creating an experience for school community members to be excited about and look forward to. These positive party vibes can elevate morale and help spread joy among colleagues as they place books at the center of the school cultural experience. While an invitation could be a standard email, it's exciting for folks to receive an invitation that looks different from what regularly hits inboxes. The invitation can be similar to a flier that is emailed to colleagues or placed in office mailboxes (see figure 2.1). I choose to include an RSVP because it is helpful for planning. A bit of caution: twenty people may RSVP *yes*, but only five people may show up. This is OK. Celebrate your first investors and, over time, participation will increase.

Plan With Students in Mind

A book swap can help bring merriment to your school community and also shift the culture in classrooms, as teachers bring their experiences back to their students and build excitement about reading. A book swap is the perfect opportunity to model ways for staff to engage students in choosing their next great read.

It's helpful to utilize a similar structure each time you host a book swap event: as community members arrive, welcome them with displays of book love. Gather several books to put in thematic displays to showcase how to avail books to students in the classroom, as well as to introduce new titles to those in attendance. For a *Read the Rainbow* display, find seven books, each with a

FIGURE 2.1: Book swap invitations—a print flier (left), and a digital invitation (right).

cover dominated by a color in a rainbow. Here is an example of a Read the Rainbow display featuring middle grades and young adult titles.

- **Red:** *Monday's Not Coming* by Tiffany D. Jackson
- **Orange:** *Rebound* by Kwame Alexander
- **Yellow:** *Supernova: A Graphic Novel (Amulet #8)* by Kazu Kibuishi
- **Green:** *Sunny* by Jason Reynolds
- **Blue:** *Anger Is a Gift: A Novel* by Mark Oshiro
- **Maroon:** *With The Fire On High* by Elizabeth Acevedo
- **Purple:** *Guts* by Raina Telgemeier

This display promotes factors teachers should consider when sharing books with students. For example, the book choices in the display intentionally represent a diverse group of authors, themes, and formats to appeal to a variety of readers. It's important for school and classroom libraries to be inclusive and reflect the options available to young readers. Many adults may fall in love with these book choices and, in turn, share their newfound loves with students.

Another display idea is called *Intrigued by the Lead*, in which you choose to feature books with an intriguing lead character (see figure 2.2, page 34, for a list of ideas). Type up the first few lines of the book, wrap the book in wrapping paper, and then tape the first few lines on the wrapped cover. Select books that are diverse in topic, genre, and format, and span a K–12 grade-level audience. Participants then read each of the book introductions and enter their name into a raffle for the book most appealing to them based on the lead. You can raffle off the books during the book swap. Winners receive new books, and all participants learn a methodology for sparking excitement about reading in the classroom.

Book Title	Author	Excerpt to Paste on the Front of a Wrapped Book
The Bad Beginning (first book in *A Series of Unfortunate Events*)	Lemony Snicket (1999)	"If you are interested in stories with happy endings, you would be better off reading some other book." (p. 1)
Baby-Sitters Little Sister #1: Karen's Witch	Ann M. Martin (2019)	"Hi. I am Karen Brewer. I'm six going on seven years old, and I think I'm very lucky." (p. 1)
Diary of a Wimpy Kid (first book in the series)	Jeff Kinney (2007)	"First of all, let me get something straight: this is a JOURNAL, not a diary." (p. 1)
Fly Away Home	Eve Bunting (1991)	"My dad and I live in an airport." (p. 5)
Holes	Louis Sachar (2000)	"There is no lake at Camp Greenlake." (p. 3)
Hood	Jenny Elder Moke (2020)	"Isabelle took great pride in herself that she did not cry once during the whole wretched, messy ordeal." (p. 1)
My Life As a Potato	Arianne Costner (2022)	"I don't know what I did to deserve it, but the fact is clear: I, Ben Hardy, am cursed by potatoes." (p. 1)
Rita and Ralph's Rotten Day	Carmen Agra Deedy (2020)	"In two little houses, on two little hills, lived two best friends." (p. 1)
Sing With Me/Canta Conmigo: Six Classic Songs in English and Spanish (Spanish and English edition)	José-Luis Orozco (2020)	"THE ABC (THE ALPHABET SONG)" (p. 1) EL ABC (CANCIÓN DEL ABECEDARIO)" (p. 3)
Spaceman (adapted for young readers): The True Story of a Young Boy's Journey to Becoming an Astronaut	Mike Massimino (2020)	"During my first week as an astronaut, my astronaut classmates and I got lucky." (p. 1)
The Winter Duke	Claire Eliza Bartlett (2020)	"The night could be worse, considering. The likelihood of a public death was low." (p. 1)

FIGURE 2.2: Intrigued by the Lead book ideas.

Reading Culture in Action
Reflections From Those Who Are Making It Happen

One the ways we built our reading culture was through organizing a book-gifting experience at one of our task force meetings. Every member brought a wrapped book and wrote a very brief note about the book or just the book's genre on the wrapping. We went around the room selecting and unwrapping books (it is always fun to open a present!) and then shared the books we chose. The book I received was *Salt, Fat, Acid, Heat: Mastering the Elements of Good Cooking* by Samin Nosrat (2017). The book is meant to inspire the next generation of cooks about how to make good decisions in the kitchen and prepare delicious meals anytime, anywhere, with the best ingredients (Nosrat, 2017). I was definitely inspired by the book, and at our next meeting I prepared *kuku sabzi* (Persian herb frittata) to share with the group. It was delicious! I have never made anything like this before, and the dish received rave reviews as we ate and worked to plan events to celebrate book love in Long Beach. I have made the recipe a few times since for family and it is always a hit. For me, each time I take a bite of the dish, it takes me back to the people I was with that day and the book I received that inspired me to try something new! (P. Romanelli, former assistant superintendent for curriculum and instruction, personal communication, June 15, 2022)

First-line fascinations resonate with teachers and become a way to boost engagement in reading with students. A middle school English teacher asked her students to capture the first lines of their independent reading book to display on a bulletin board as an initial reading engagement invitation. The title of the bulletin board was *First Lines of Books: Exploring Beautiful Language in Our Independent Reading Books*. Across town at the high school, an English teacher created a chart titled Fantastic First Lines. She photocopied the first page of six different books she wanted to recommend to students for independent reading and highlighted the first line on each page. The chart became a reference point for book recommendations for students.

Another useful and engaging display is the *Genre Jar*. This jar serves as a book recommendation tool for readers who are looking for their next reading adventure. In the jar are a variety of book covers mounted on different color cards; the card colors represent the different genres. For example, a yellow card might represent a graphic novel, and a blue card might represent nonfiction. If a reader is looking for a graphic novel, the reader would pull a yellow card from the jar, and on that yellow card might be the book cover for *Best Friends* by Shannon Hale and LeUyen Pham. In the classroom, you can do the initial setup and then invite students to contribute to the jar as they finish books and want to recommend titles to classmates. After the librarian at my high school attended one of the book swaps, she created a Genre Jar for the high school library. Students now use it as a source for book recommendations.

Get People Talking About Their Books

Conversation is a way to build relationships and cultivate joy. Before swapping books, provide people time to talk about the books through a game-like experience. Your approach for this portion should be responsive to the people who attend the book swap. Choose a way for people to share based on the personalities and interests of the group.

One way to invite conversation is through *Lift a Line* prompt cards (see the reproducible, "Lift a Line Conversation Cards for an Adult Book Swap," page 64) from *The Reading Strategies Book* (Serravallo, 2015). Figure 2.3 shows sample cards.

FIGURE 2.3: Examples of Lift a Line prompt cards for adults to use to talk about books.

Participants each draw a card and find a line in the book they brought that matches the prompt on the card. For example, a card may have the following prompt: *Something you would say to introduce yourself* or *Something to avoid saying at a business meeting*. While lines from the book may or may not exactly match the prompt, Life a Line is a way to get people sharing book content. This method of sharing usually sparks a lot of laughter and inquiry in groups. The lines people share generate interest in the books for when it comes time to swap. You can use this strategy in classrooms as a way to invite students to talk about their books or respond to their reading.

Another way to structure conversation is to distribute a list of book discussion questions participants can choose from (see the reproducible, "Book Discussion Questions List," page 65). When using this list, I ask participants to introduce the book they brought to swap and then choose a question to respond to from the list (which may or may not relate to the book they brought for the book swap). Here are examples of questions on the discussion list.

- If you could join any fictional character on the character's journey, quest, voyage, or adventure, who would you choose?
- One morning, you open your closet to discover it is actually a portal into the world of one of your favorite books. Which literary world is it?
- What book have you least enjoyed? Why did you read the book in the first place?
- Name a character from a book you really disliked. Why?
- If you were going on a road trip in your own world, which literary character would you choose to be your companion?

The purpose of this list is to get people talking about books and thinking about all the reading adventures they may want to share with a community of other readers. I want the adults to experience the joy that can result from these types of conversations about books and stories.

Beach ball–inspired conversations are fun ways to incorporate movement into conversations about books. You could use this approach when the book swap is tied to a summer theme (toward the end of the school year). Write one book discussion prompt on each of the colored stripes of a beach ball. As participants throw the ball to one another, they respond to the prompt most visible when they catch the ball. This as a way for adults to share about the book they brought to the book swap. The prompts are as follows.

- Share something about your favorite character.
- Share something you love about the book.
- Share something you don't care for in the book.
- Share the major problem or tension in the story.
- Share what the story makes you think of or connect to from your personal experiences.
- Share something you learned from reading.

If you are interested in purchasing a product designed for having conversations about books, there are many available for booklovers that support these types of experiences in schools, including the following.

- *Table Topics Book Club: Questions to Start Great Conversations* (https://tabletopics.com/products/book-club)
- *Bring Your Own Book: A Game of Borrowed Phrases* (https://www.bringyourownbook.com)
- *Lit Chat: Conversation Starters About Books and Life (100 Questions)* (www.abramsbooks.com/product/lit-chat_9781683352013)

Get Ready to Swap

The way you choose for people swap their books may be dependent on the number of people who attend your event.

For a smaller crowd, you may consider a *White Elephant Gift Exchange*, similar to a gift exchange you may see at a holiday party, where participants bring a generic gift for grab bag game. With this approach, put all the books in the middle of a table. Put numbered cards into a bag or basket; be sure you have the same number of cards as participants. Each participant draws a number. Those numbers become the order in which participants will choose a book from the middle of the table. You can vary this game by allowing *steals*, in which participants can "steal" a book someone else has already taken, but each book can only be stolen once. Then, the person who is stolen from chooses a new book from the pile. Ultimately, the person who picks the highest number is in the best position to choose the "just right" book.

For a larger crowd, you may consider creating book categories in which people place the book they brought on a table for each category. Examples of book categories include: If You Want to Laugh, A Real Tear-Jerker, Learn Something New Here, Self-Discovery, Professional Learning, and so on. With this method, participants can browse the tables (similar to browsing in a bookstore or library) and take a book most appealing to them.

Reading Culture in Action
Reflections From Those Who Are Making It Happen

Departmental book swaps have become a tradition; teachers can share their more recent reads or their favorite all-time reads. I pick the last department meeting date before the December break for our departmental book swap. Teachers are encouraged to bring a book they recommend. When teachers come by after school, I try to have tablecloths on the tables in our meeting space, festive music playing, and treats to eat. At the book swap, I asked all teachers to pick one card that communicated some statement about gratitude. On the back of each card was a number. We used these cards as a way into the event as volunteers read statements that resonated with them. Then, we got to book swapping!

This book swap event is modeled after the White Elephant Gift Exchange. Teachers laugh and talk the whole time, and this is mixed with gasps and sighs as the books they are interested in are picked. Invariably, everyone walks out with something they want, and often there are post-swap, unsanctioned trades where participants can get books on their way out the door. Each year, several teachers ask to do this. The feedback I get is, "That was the best department meeting ever."

As a leader, it is great for me to see people sharing a bit about themselves as they share their reading choices. We see many models of book talks, and we put our reading lives at the front and center of our work. And we stop to celebrate our work, our department, and our reading lives. (J. Anisansel, director of English language arts and reading, 6–12, and director of English as a new language, K–12, personal communication, June 20, 2022)

Memorialize This Joyous Event for Your School

As the party begins to wind down, be sure to capture the smiles so your school community members can remember the happiness they felt and the experiences they can bring back to students in the classroom.

Invite participants to take a picture with their new book! Schools have incorporated new technology, and you can absolutely take advantage of this. One new tool is a green screen. Work with technology staff members to set up an iPad and a green screen at one of your book swaps so people can add an image to the background of their photos. They can choose to add a book cover or their favorite reading spot as the background. Share the photos with participants after the event.

Make an effort to take a group photo at every event. In an image-driven society, it's important to document the elements that contribute to your school culture. Then, share this image as part of school news or on social media posts, and add all the images to a portfolio to demonstrate the ways your school values reading culture.

Share a Thank-You

Great leaders demonstrate gratitude. After all, if you host a book swap during noncontractual time, the people who attend are giving up their own time to attend a work function. Time is precious, and it's important to honor and acknowledge the people invested in their school community and their own reading lives. Shortly after the book swap, send a thank-you card with the group photo to each participant. It's rewarding to see the thank-you card hanging up in classrooms and offices around the school community. A visual reminder of this cultural experience helps sustain the commitment to reading and adults as reading role models.

A Classroom Connection

As a result of a staff book swap event, a teacher invited me to partner in bringing this activity into her classroom. The lesson we planned together taught her third graders that a *book swap* is an authentic way for readers to discover new books to read by talking and sharing with other readers. We designed the classroom experience similar to the adult book swap. The teacher asked students to bring a book from home they were willing to give away. If a student did not bring one, the teacher had a book previously read in the classroom ready for the book swap.

On the day of the book swap, we rallied the students to share the teaching point and to explain that a book swap is a fun practice of avid readers. We then divided the students into small groups and invited them to share their thoughts about their book through the beach ball conversation game. Afterward, the students swapped books using the White Elephant Gift Exchange method on the carpet, excited to share and "steal." Seeing all the books in the center of the carpet sparked even more conversation about the book choices, as students reached their turn to pick a new book.

This classroom connection illustrates the power of rallying adults to explore their reading lives and the impact it can have on working with students in the classroom. There is no better place to be than in a classroom working with students as they marvel over books!

Design a Newsletter

You can learn a lot about building a positive reading culture by studying the marketing strategies of bookstores. While bookstores are in the business of selling books for profit, school literacy leaders find ways to amplify the significance of books. One of the marketing strategies in my local bookstore is the volume of recommendations made in various categories on digital newsletters. I see catchy promotions like *Our Staff's Top Picks, Recently Reviewed, Fiction Favorites for Mom, These Books Will Put a Spell on You*, and *Nonfiction Favorites From Our Booksellers*. You can use promotional strategies similar to those bookstores use to create a newsletter and solicit book recommendations from adults in your school community.

The newletter should be a space for the adults in the school community to share book recommendations with colleagues. It can unite people through books and motivate them in a practice that cultivates their own reading lives. For example, the introduction to my newsletter says, "Welcome to the Long Beach Book Batch, a place where members of the Long Beach School community share their enthusiasm for books and curiosities for their next great reads!" Consider dividing your newsletter into three categories (or niches) of recommendations, such as Featured Classroom Collection, Personal Picks, and Professional Pack. The *Featured Classroom Collection* can appeal to a wide audience because the books are available in classrooms for all subject areas. The *Personal Picks* category appeals to the adults who read for pleasure and adults who are looking to further develop their own independent reading lives. *Professional Pack* books appeal to those who read professional books as part of their own professional development and are enthusiastic to contribute to the learning of others. I was surprised to find I received recommendations for all niches; one wasn't more popular than the other. I learned adult reading lives vary, something important to keep in mind as a literacy leader.

Solicit Book Recommendations

In preparation for the first fall issue of your newsletter, send an email to all school community members to invite them to share a book recommendation. In the invitation I send at the beginning of the year (see figure 2.4), I explain why the newsletter exists and how it can become a resource for personal and professional practices. I also share the three niches for which people can submit books, and assure colleagues that whether or not they share a recommendation, the newsletter is an effort to engage all adults in the school community. It is helpful to provide a format for people to use when submitting the recommendation, along with examples of each type of recommendation (see figure 2.5). The standardization of this text will reduce the amount of time you need to revise for publication.

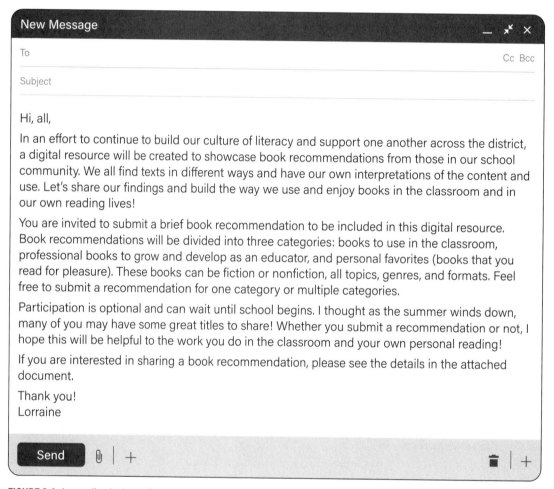

FIGURE 2.4: An email to invite staff to submit book recommendations for the newsletter.

Create Your Newsletter

Think of a title that captures the purpose of your newsletter and appeals to readers. The title you choose should fit with the name of your school—it will soon become a staple in your school culture. Decide how often you will compile a newsletter, which can help with naming the issue. You can produce a new issue each season (for example, *Fall Edition*), or you may choose to name each issue by month and year (for example, *February 2022 Edition*). These details professionalize the newsletter, which can contribute to the excitement when it is published.

Thank you for your interest in submitting a book recommendation! See the following details.

Please send the following in an email to me (Lorraine):
- ☐ The category of the recommendation (classroom, professional, personal)
- ☐ Title of the book
- ☐ Author of the book
- ☐ A brief recommendation

When your recommendation is published, your name will be attached to your recommendation. If you do not want your name included, please indicate when you send me the recommendation.

Following are examples of how you can craft your recommendations. These are just samples. Please share your recommendations how you see fit!

Classroom:
The Pigeon Has to Go to School by Mo Willems (2019)—This story takes you on the pigeon's thought-journey as he anticipates going to school. He names his fears and worries but, in the end, he discovers what an exciting opportunity going to school can be! This is a fantastic read-aloud that addresses jitters students may feel about coming to school in a humorous way. You and your students can giggle your way into a conversation about all the great things going to school has to offer! This is not only perfect for the beginning of the school year but also all year long.

Professional:
Heart Maps by Georgia Heard (2016)—This book provides practical explanations and samples of student work to illustrate show readers can use heart maps to develop a writer's life across multiple genres. Use this book as a resource for all grade levels! I love how there are *heart maps* (that is, visual reminders of what you love and care about) to motivate writers with all different interests! It helped me to reflect on how I engage students in the beginning stages of the writing process.

Personal:
Breathe (https://breathemagazine.com)—*Breathe* is a magazine available digitally or in print. The November 2019 issue focuses on the science of how and why people feel stress. The authors use simple language to help understand complex ideas about stress. There are also practical strategies for practicing mindfulness, prioritizing life events, and being your best you! This helped me decompress throughout the summer. You can find additional issues online with similar content and themes.

FIGURE 2.5: Suggested format for a book recommendation submission.

Choose a platform with which you are most comfortable. There are many platforms available for newsletter creation: Canva (https://canva.com), smore (https://smore.com), Google Docs (https://google.com/docs/about), Google Slides (https://google.com/slides/about), and Google Sites (https://workspace.google.com/products/sites). After deciding on the aesthetics and title, divide your newsletter into the niches you selected when soliciting book recommendations. When compiling your colleagues recommendations, include the cover of the book, the written recommendation, and the name of the school community member who shared the recommendation (with permission).

Share Your Newsletter

When your newsletter is ready, send a link or attachment via email to the members of your school community. Encourage them to read the newsletter and embrace the recommendations your colleagues made for both personal and professional use. I must admit, when I first decided to share a newsletter, I worried there would be some reaction of disapproval from colleagues, especially from those who don't like to receive an abundance of emails and who would think soliciting book recommendations is another burden. The reality is, when you are working to develop a positive culture, you will be uncomfortable because people's reactions and enthusiasm levels will vary. Prepare to work through the discomfort and uncertainty. There are people in the school community who want to participate, belong, and contribute to a joyful environment that celebrates reading because a positive culture is good for students. The newsletter serves as a visual reminder that the adults in the school are united in many ways, including via books. It signifies community and togetherness with hope of leading to more joy among students and staff.

A Classroom Connection

Many teachers facilitate students sharing book recommendations and make their recommendations a visual artifact of their classroom reading communities. Teachers invite students to share their reviews of books they read, and students encourage fellow readers to use the recommendations area as a resource for finding new books to read. Here are some ways to make this classroom connection.

- One teacher posts book recommendations on a large bulletin board in her classroom. She prints recommendations on paper she pins to a string so she can easily add and rotate titles throughout the year.

- Another teacher posts book recommendations on clipboards mounted to the wall. The clipboard is another option that teachers can easily rotate recommendations throughout the school year.

- A high school teacher works with her students to create visual representations of books to recommend to peers. Each visual representation has a QR code that leads to a written recommendation, similar to the adult recommendations in your staff newsletter. The school library houses and shares the recommendations with the school community.

Reading Culture in Action
Reflections From Those Who Are Making It Happen

After over twenty years of teaching, I had yet to find the perfect reading log. I called mine *the reading lie* because students inflated their minutes and even forged signatures. My reading log served students who were already readers and demoralized those who struggled. I needed something universally accepted—with no lies!

Then came Padlet (https://padlet.com). The first iteration of a digital reading log was monthly Padlets for every student. This allowed students to record their reading on a weekly basis. It was weakly received.

The following year, I created one Padlet for the school year for each student; each student would then record their reading on a monthly basis. Students took pictures of themselves with their books and shared their reading recommendations. Once a month, I'd view selected Padlets and invite students to elaborate on their posts. Impromptu book clubs popped up. I enhanced shared reading. At the end of the year, students created top ten lists and discovered a pattern with *Mentimeter word clouds* (https://mentimeter.com/features/word-cloud)—humorous graphic novels were the favorite genre, among the many represented genres.

As a result, the students digitally encapsulated a visual representation of their reading lives. They saw their growth from September to June. They harvested books, took reading risks, veered from their go-tos, and grew together because they had many shared reading experiences.

Finally, I had found a reading log that wasn't tossed into the trash at the end of the year because completing it was drudgery. These new reading logs will live forever and serve as a source of pride. (D. Cupani, elementary teacher, personal communication, June 16, 2022)

Reading Culture in Action
Reflections From Those Who Are Making It Happen

One great way my students and I love to build a reading community in the classroom is to have a book recommendations display. After finishing a book, a student completes a book recommendation form. This form has a large square for students to create a cover of the book (it can be the same cover or a cover of their choice if they choose to redo it), as well as a rating scale and lines to write a recommendation. The students and I worked very hard on what we should write on these recommendations, such as *If you loved Harry Potter, you would love this* or *This is a must-read if you like nonfiction*.

This practice provides students a sense of closure when they finish a book, and a sense of excitement about completing a book recommendation form! It also supports conversations about their love of reading and books in the classroom.

Another way we use this display is for students to book shop. When students are book shopping, they know they should be taking a glance at the book recommendations display in addition to looking in the class library to see if there is anything that interests them.

Having a display up all year long provides a sense of inclusion (or *student say* in the classroom). The students are excited to see their work on the bulletin board and know their voice and opinions matter. You can also modify this practice for any grade level. I will continue to make a student book recommendations display part of my classroom community each year. (J. Donato, elementary teacher, personal communication, June 17, 2022)

Facilitate Book Clubs for Adults

A book club is an effective way to invite adults to identify as readers. If your school district provides opportunities for staff to earn professional development credits, participating in a book club can be a way for staff to earn credit. If participation for credit is not an option, you may choose to host optional book clubs or book clubs during designated meeting times.

One of the goals for a book club is to invite teachers to read what their students read so they can bring books back to their classroom libraries and share them with other students. When I first decided to host a book club, I felt like I was in uncharted waters. I was unsure about the target audience, when to meet, which books to read, how to select books, and most of all, if colleagues would be interested in participating. After all, reading takes time!

I started by inviting middle level English and reading teachers to participate in a middle grades novels book club. Since I was a literacy teacher at the middle level for many years, middle grades novels are familiar to me (and my favorite). I felt my leadership in this new endeavor would be stronger if I led with material comfortable for me. I would branch out later. I also used previous research and theory about readers' response, literature circles, and grand conversations to help me plan (Eeds & Wells, 1989; Rosenblatt, 1968). Key elements like choice-in-response formats, text selection variety, student-directed discussion, teacher-as-facilitator roles, journaling, and student self-evaluations guided my work with teachers (Jocius & Shealy, 2018).

Four teachers signed up to participate. This was another moment of discomfort and uncertainty. I suddenly felt discouraged and thought about canceling the book club knowing just four people were interested in reading and talking about books their students may want to read. But again, I worked through what was uncomfortable and learned that *just four people* can be the catalyst to start something powerful in a school community.

When the COVID-19 pandemic shut down our schools, the book club continued to meet via videoconferencing. I will never forget the first time four squares framed my computer screen. There was worry in our hearts and disbelief on our minds, but it was the connectedness through conversations about books that strengthened us as educators and readers. Whether it is a pandemic or another monumental challenge, there will be encounters along the way that present as reasons not to prioritize reading. School leaders adapt to context; the challenge for leaders is to be innovative in building culture in ways responsive to how the context evolves.

Decide Your Intent

Books clubs invite adults to connect with their reading identities. Use the following questions to consider your intentions when planning your book club.

- Is there a theme or idea you want to encourage community members to think about?
- Are there new books you want to advertise to put in classroom and school libraries or curriculum materials?
- Do you want to use the book club as a forum to build relationships with staff?

Knowing your intent will aid in the book-selection process.

Choose a Structure

Following are three structures to consider when designing book club experiences. Determine which structure to use based on your intent because it impacts the book-selection process.

One Book, Several Meetings

Reading one book in a book club is impactful when the content is complex, long, or both. Similar to students, teachers should dig deeply into the text and think broadly, with frequent opportunities to think within, across, and beyond the text (Jocius & Shealy, 2018; Leland, Lewison, & Harste, 2013). Working with one book supports a deeper level of thinking. It's important to consider the time participants have to dedicate to reading. Packing too much content into one experience risks lacking depth in the conversation. Topics that may warrant this type of consideration are books about mental health, social justice, equity, social media use among young people, artificial intelligence in the classroom, or innovations relative to the future of schools. Consider how the book club can support reflections on these ideas and how to approach conversations or work with students in the area you choose to read about. Divide the chapters or sections of the book across three to five meetings, and invite participants to engage in journaling along the way to prepare for conversation.

Clubs Within a Club: Multiple Books, Multiple Groups

You can make book club experiences thematic and tailor them for a large number of participants (twelve or more). I use the *club within a club* structure when my intent is to expose participants to the diversity within a specific genre, format, or author, and when I want to provide choice in the book club experience.

Dedicate the first club meeting to becoming acquainted with the titles to choose from. Begin by sharing a book talk about each book so participants can choose one that appeals to them. After the book talks, survey the top three choices of the participants (Google Forms are helpful for this). When creating the clubs, balance the number of people in each to support the conversation. Do your best to give everyone their first book choice. Between the first and second meetings, notify participants about who is in each smaller club (see figure 2.6, page 46), and ask each club to make a reading plan for their remaining club sessions. Ask each group to honor the timing of book club sessions so everyone is reading at a similar pace. Start the next session together in a large group, and then move the smaller clubs into breakout rooms to have their specific book conversations. As the facilitator, I visit each club to listen and contribute to conversations.

A graphic novel study works well in a club within a club structure. There is a lot of variety in graphic novels, and they are increasingly popular among young readers. In fact, there was a 56.2 percent increase in the number of graphic novels published for children in 2018, and graphic novels for children and teenagers are dominating the graphic novel market (Middaugh, 2019).

I hosted a graphic novel study with the following titles using a club within a club structure with middle and high school teachers.

- *Almost American Girl: An Illustrated Memoir* by Robin Ha
- *Class Act* by Jerry Craft
- *Hey, Kiddo: How I Lost My Mother, Found My Father, and Dealt With Family Addiction* by Jarrett J. Krosoczka
- *New Kid* by Jerry Craft
- *Superman Smashes the Clan* by Gene Luen Yang
- *When Stars Are Scattered* by Victoria Jamieson and Omar Mohamed

Graphic novels written for a younger audience are often part of a series. Consider these titles for a book club with elementary teachers.

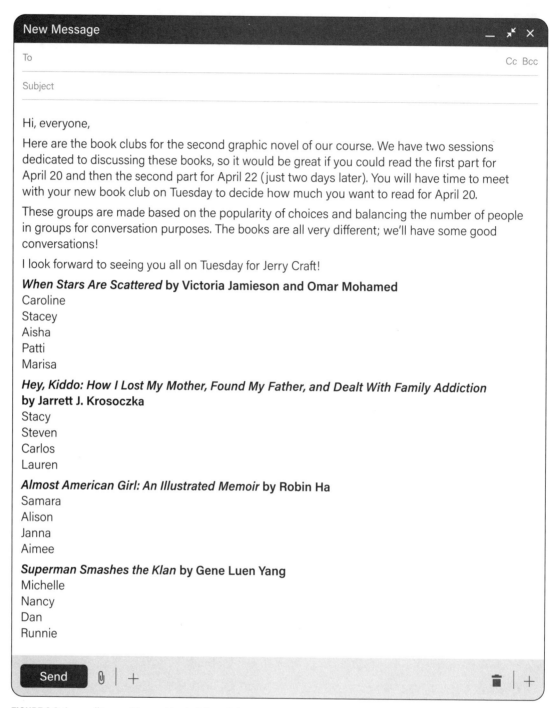

FIGURE 2.6: An email to graphic novel book club participants.

Grades 1–3:

- *Dog Man #1* by Dav Pilkey
- *Baloney and Friends* by Greg Pizzoli
- *Bug Boys* by Laura Knetzger
- *Narwhal and Jelly #1: Unicorn of the Sea* by Ben Clanton
- *Pea, Bee, & Jay #1: Stuck Together* by Brian "Smitty" Smith

Grades 3–5:
- *Amulet* series (nine books) by Kazu Kibuishi
- *El Deafo* by Cece Bell
- *I Survived* series (ten books) by Lauren Tarshis
- *Smile* by Raina Telgemeier
- *Twins #1* by Varian Johnson

I also use the club within a club structure when my intent is to engage adults in an author study and sometimes pair it with a visit from the author. For example, I hosted clubs within a club using books by Jerry Craft, the first author to ever win a John Newbury Medal for a graphic novel (as cited in de León, 2020). Participants chose to read *New Kid* and *Class Act*, and Craft visited the graphic novel book club during its last session to share his experience as an author and illustrator of graphic novels. I explain further on ways to connect with authors in chapter 5 (page 123).

Several Books, Several Meetings

I launched the original middle grades novel book club with a *several books, several meetings* structure. This structure is best when the intent is to expose participants to a variety of titles, and is designed for participants who are willing to read multiple books in a relatively short amount of time. I typically choose three books to read in one book club experience that spans five weeks. Teachers have diverse readers in their classrooms, and the variety of books they read within an experience gives them options to recommend to students, in addition to their own personal reading enjoyment. Notify the book club participants of the book list prior to the start date and share the reading schedule at least two weeks before the experience begins. A typical reading schedule follows (see the reproducible, "Reading Schedule for a Book Club," page 66).

Meeting 1: Come prepared to discuss book one in its entirety (you'll read the entire first book prior to our first meeting).
Meeting 2: Read the first half of book two (to page 112).
Meeting 3: Read the second half of book two (to page 245).
Meeting 4: Read the first half of book three (to page 120).
Meeting 5: Read the second half of book three (to page 268).

I recommend sending a note to all participants about honoring the reading schedule. Because this book club (see previous schedule) divided books two and three in half for reading, it is helpful if participants don't read ahead. I know sometimes it's tough, but the meeting conversation will include wonderings, predictions, and so on.

Reading Culture in Action
Reflections From Those Who Are Making It Happen

I didn't realize how much I loved young adult and middle grade books until I was introduced to them through our book club. I especially appreciate it when you assign recently published books that are current with the themes our students experience in everyday life. When I

> listen to my peers discussing the experiences they share with the characters in the books we read together, I get to appreciate their testimonies as prime sources. The books become that much more vivid because I see how others relate to similar situations in their own lives, and I can relate to them more as well.
>
> This helps me to have more empathy for my peers and students. We can see what we have in common on the surface, but through book clubs, we get a deeper look into each other. Reading the same book together, then sharing our thoughts and experiences creates this bond or culture that would not otherwise exist. I am very thankful for this culture because it reminds me that readers have their own interpretations of the same text due to their own backgrounds. For this reason, we need to keep an open mind with our students. (C. Morales Hauser, world languages teacher, personal communication, August 19, 2022)

Choose Your Audience

The way you invite people to participate will depend on your role in the school community. Because I am a district leader and work in multiple schools, there are times when I design book clubs for teachers of specific grade levels. However, most of the book clubs I host are open to all adults in the school community. I advertise the book club to all adults via email and include the book titles or the genre of books that participants will read. Colleagues participate according to their interests. If you work in one school, you may consider book clubs for specific grade-level or content-area teams, or you may host an experience open to the whole faculty.

Choose a Meeting Time

Similar to other events I describe in this book, you'll want to consider the availability of your staff and colleagues. Consider surveying staff for the time of day that works best. If you transition the meeting space to Zoom (https://zoom.us), you broaden the availability for folks. There is less travel time, and people can participate from home. Choose a time that gives colleagues time to transition to or from the school day.

Host Your Book Club

Once you finalize the logistics, be careful not to overplan the book club sessions (Vygotsky, 1978, 1986). *Social constructivism* designates the concept of people constantly learning, acquiring, and building new knowledge in social context through observation and external interactions (Vygotsky, 1978, 1986). Through sharing thoughts, questions, and new ideas during a book club discussion, participants construct their own knowledge first through an efferent or aesthetic reader response, and then as a result of the social interaction with peers (Rosenblatt, 1968). If you overplan the book club experience, you run the risk of compromising the authenticity of the peer group discussion.

During the first session, share ideas for book club members to consider when reading and when engaging in discussion to support their reflections on their reading identities. See the reproducible "Book Club Launch Presentation Slides" (page 67) for a sample presentation to help launch your book club. Professor emerita of education Rudine Sims Bishop's (1990) notion of books as mirrors, windows, and sliding glass doors is a powerful idea to frame conversations. Encourage members to read through these lenses so they can consider their own identities when reading and, in turn, talk with students about how personal identities impact how readers make meaning of text. Figure 2.7 utilizes Bishop's (1990) idea of books as mirrors, windows, and

Books as Mirrors	Books as Windows	Books as Sliding Glass Doors
Reading a book that is a *mirror* means that an aspect (or several aspects) of the book reflects the reader's personal experiences and understandings.	Reading a book that is a *window* means that an aspect (or several aspects) of the book serve as an invitation to learn a new perspective. Experiences portrayed in the book are not relatable to the reader.	Reading a book that is a *sliding glass door* means that an aspect (or several aspects) of the book reflect a combination of real experiences the reader can relate to and imagined experiences that the reader cannot relate to.
Questions to consider while reading: Do you see yourself represented in this story? Are parts of your identity portrayed in the story? How is this story similar to your life experience? How is this character's perspective similar to yours? What is your personal relationship with this story, the characters, and the conflict? What are you learning about yourself through reading?	**Questions to consider while reading:** What types of identities are represented in this story that are different from yours? How is this character's perspective different from yours? How is the character's life circumstance different from yours? How is the setting different from environments you have experienced? Is your own perspective influenced by this new perspective? How does this story help you empathize with others?	**Questions to consider while reading:** What is it about this world you can step into and feel part of? What is it about this world that is similar, yet different from your own? What aspects of this story make you feel comfortable and uncomfortable? At what points in the story do you feel your connection shifting while reading? How does the duality impact your understandings and meaning-making?

Source: Adapted from Bishop, 1990.

FIGURE 2.7: An outline to explain books as window, mirrors, and sliding glass doors with questions to consider while reading.

sliding glass doors and poses questions for book club members to think about when reading and talking. See "Books as Mirrors, Windows, and Sliding Glass Doors Thinking Chart" (page 71) for a reproducible version of this figure with space for book club members to record their thinking while reading.

Provide an example of books that are mirrors, windows, and sliding glass doors for you and demonstrate your thinking process to model considerations for conversation. When selecting books for the book club, aim to have a diverse selection so there are opportunities for book club members to think through several of the questions.

In addition to providing a framework for reflection, engage the book club participants in establishing norms and agreements (see figure 2.8, page 50, for an example, and "Norms and Agreements," page 72, for a reproducible). Ask, "What is important to you as we establish our reading community?" One way to gather responses is to share a digital document all book club members can edit. On the document, ask participants to respond to the question individually and then compare answers and discuss the commonalities with other members. It's powerful for everyone to see the thinking of the group. The document provides an inclusive way for you to amplify all

What is important to you as we establish our reading community?		
Name	**Roles for students**	**What are your personal expectations for our community?**
Patti	High school librarian	Insights and respect; listening and thoughtful comments; have an open mind (no judgment)
Lorraine	Director of literacy	I want to be able to say I'm not sure about something or don't have a lot of experience in an area and want to learn more.
Deb	Bilingual social worker	Hmm . . . I didn't really join with a specific expectation other than to listen to other folks' perspectives and to share some of mine. I assume we will all be respectful and open minded.
Lauren	Middle school Spanish teacher	Respect and empathy; it's OK to disagree, but it's not OK to be disrespectful.
Marisa	High school English as a new language and English language arts teacher	Come with an open mind to everyone's ideas and respect and empathize with others even if there is a difference of option.
Carlos	Special education teacher	Respect, welcoming other people's views and perspectives
Justin	Third-grade teacher	Openness and respect so everyone feels comfortable to make personal connections or express opinions
Patrick	Middle school librarian	Listen to each other's points of view and being OK with not being on the same page; being open minded.
Stacey	Social worker	Respect and allowing different perspectives
Alistair	High school reading teacher	The ability to talk about different perspectives in an open-minded environment to help me better understand new ideas.
Aimee	High school Spanish teacher	Respect for each other's opinions

FIGURE 2.8: An example of norms and agreements all book club members share in a Google Doc.

voices—especially those who may not be as comfortable sharing their ideas verbally—and establish norms and agreements. You can also implement this practice in classrooms with students.

After establishing norms and agreements, transition to talking about the reading. I belong to a book club in my personal life, and no one creates a lesson plan for when we gather to talk about the book we just read. The best part about being in a book club is the natural conversation that emerges and the meaning made by each individual through reading and in response to the conversation. I carry that practice into my work-related book clubs and rely on the natural conversation to influence the construction of learning. There are references to books as mirrors, windows, and sliding glass doors (Bishop, 1990) in addition to in-depth explorations of characters, conflicts, themes, and wonderings. The conversation usually lasts about forty-five minutes. The book club meeting concludes with reviewing a plan for the next meeting, which often includes deciding on the next reading is due and introducing some ideas to think about and make connections to while reading to support future conversations.

Ask for Feedback

Ask colleagues for feedback about their experiences. If your intention is to inclusively build a school reading culture, your colleagues' insight is an important component to leadership and future planning. Share a survey or a space for participants to share narrative feedback.

Reading Culture in Action
Reflections From Those Who Are Making It Happen

It's good to practice the things I often ask students to do. You see what works and what you may want students to do differently when asking them to read. I noticed how I struggled with the last book we read in book club and thought about how I try to not have students abandon books. However, I can see how difficult it is to finish a book when you struggle to connect at first. I will try some new strategies if students want to abandon now.

I would like to find books that may not be what students expect to read. It was interesting for me to read a book that I didn't think was for me, but I ended up liking. Students often stay with the same genre when given free choice. I would like to open their minds to some new styles of writing.

We all bring things to the table when discussing a book. Different teachers have connections and experiences that make the book conversations so interesting. We, as a school community, can connect to students. I think it's even better when you have adults that students do not normally see reading engage in book talks with them. Whether it's the security guard or the nurse, students can learn so much from different adults. A school community is not just the classroom teachers but also *all* the other adults, as seen from the variety of adults who participated in in our book club. (S. Steier, reading teacher, personal communication, August 20, 2022)

Reading Culture in Action
Reflections From Those Who Are Making It Happen

Hearing the perspectives of my peers helps me remember my students also have these perspectives and come from many different backgrounds. This helps me as their teacher: I can keep an open mind and allow my room to be a safe space. (D. Stuono, middle-levels English teacher, personal communication, August 19, 2022)

You may be wondering, "But what about the people who *don't* participate? How does that help build a culture that is committed to reading?" I ask myself these questions all the time. My advice is to trust your process and capitalize on the participation you *do* receive. Reading culture builds in bits and pieces over time. Sometimes, it takes one teacher who participated in a book club to go back to his classroom library to add the books he read, and then his colleague notices and sparks a discussion about availing new titles to students. Sometimes, it's what you're not directly involved in as a leader that makes the most impact. Coauthors and literacy professors Cathy Burnett and Guy Merchant (2020) explain this to be *literacy-as-events*, where meaning-making can often be unpredictable. A book club helps to ignite a fire, but then it spreads in ways you don't control. That is what you hope for!

A Classroom Connection

Book clubs are a part of my district's grade-level reading curricula in almost every grade from grades 2–11. Clubs did not emerge in curricula because of the adult book clubs. The connection to the classroom is the teachers' desire to add new and diverse titles to existing book club units of study and to classroom and school libraries after reading them in the adult book clubs. There was a new enthusiasm about the importance of diverse literature in the classroom, with characters and themes representative of the identities of students as a result of book club conversations. Participants genuinely liked the books and appreciated the ones they didn't personally connect to.

Participants also enjoyed exploring the complex ideas the text offered in our conversations. They saw value in bringing the materials into the classroom. This is another example of literacy-as-events, where the teachers who participate in a book club experience can influence those who don't participate (Burnett & Merchant, 2020). Teachers serve as professional resources for one another and can spread the learning in ways beyond what you facilitate as leader.

Figure 2.9 is a list of some of the books that are in our school libraries, classroom libraries, or curricula as a result of book club experiences.

Middle Grades Books	Young Adult Books
• *A Soft Place to Land* by Janae Marks • *A Rover's Story* by Jasmine Warga • *Closer to Nowhere* by Ellen Hopkins • *Dear Sweet Pea* by Julie Murphy • *In Your Shoes* by Donna Gephart • *Maybe He Just Likes You* by Barbara Dee • *Shouting At The Rain* by Lynda Mullaly Hunt • *Stuntboy, In The Meantime* by Jason Reynolds • *The 47 People You'll Meet in Middle School* by Kristin Mahoney • *The Beatryce Prophecy* by Kate DiCamillo • *The List of Things That Will Not Change* by Rebecca Stead • *The Midnight Children* by Dan Gemeinhart • *The Remarkable Journey of Coyote Sunrise* by Dan Gemeinhart	• *Almost American Girl* by Robin Ha • *Clap When You Land* by Elizabeth Acevedo • *Dragon Hoops* by Gene Luen Yang • *Eleanor and Park* by Rainbow Rowell • *Free Lunch* by Rex Ogle • *One of Us is Lying* by Karen M. McManus • *Patron Saints of Nothing* by Randy Ribay • *Poisoned* by Jennifer Donnolly • *Stepsister* by Jennifer Donnelly • *The Playbook: 52 Rules to Aim, Shoot, and Score in This Game Called Life* by Kwame Alexander • *With The Fire On High* by Elizabeth Acevedo

FIGURE 2.9: Books added to school libraries, classroom libraries, or curricula after teachers read them in adult book clubs.

In addition to diversifying text choices in curricula and libraries, the adult book club experiences encouraged teachers to create their own book clubs with colleagues. In one instance, two teachers facilitated a book club with *Stamped: Racism, Antiracism, and You* by Jason Reynolds and Ibram X. Kendi (2021). Additionally, another teacher facilitated book clubs with *Uncomfortable Conversations With a Black Boy* by Emmanuel Acho and *Genesis Begins Again* by Alicia D. Williams. All participating teachers wanted to continue discussions about inclusivity with other school community members. It was illuminating to see others facilitate developing reading culture through conversations about humanity.

Reading Culture in Action
Reflections From Those Who Are Making It Happen

My colleague and I decided to start a summer book club for the middle school teachers, staff, and administrators to reflect on how to make classrooms more equitable. We used a book by Jason Reynolds (who is always a hit with our students) and Ibram X. Kendi. The authors write this book in such a way that readers, no matter their background, are brought on a journey through time, sprinkled with relatable, kid-friendly anecdotes.

We decided to meet five times over the course of the summer for one-hour sessions over Zoom to discuss sections of the book. During the sessions, we divided ourselves up into smaller breakout rooms and discussed prompts about the topics in the various chapters. We found ourselves lingering on Zoom for longer than the required one hour. It was evident that these discussions were important and needed to continue. The participants shared openly and honestly their experiences as educators, but also as complex human beings living in the world. I am grateful to have so many colleagues who were asked to be vulnerable and share their perspectives and for the colleagues who practiced deep listening to understand a different point of view. By celebrating differences, listening to students and their families, and making shifts in the way we approach our pedagogies, we can create atmospheres where students thrive. (K. Smith, middle-levels reading teacher, personal communication, June 17, 2022)

Reading Culture in Action
Reflections From Those Who Are Making It Happen

Book clubs have always held a special place in my classroom. Students love to read a book with friends and share and discuss their ideas with one another. As a teacher, I share with my students that I am in a book club too. I bring up different experiences and ideas from my book club and connect these experiences to my students. This helps students understand that reading is a lifelong process and they are starting to begin the reading work now adult readers engage in! Book clubs allow students an opportunity to learn accountable talk, grow ideas from text, analyze character choices, set realistic reading goals, choose books they love, and reflect on themselves as readers. Listening to students talk about a book's

> characters and storyline and think deeply about why events are occurring or characters are responding in a particular way brings me so much joy! We are setting up our students for a successful reading future if they can fall in love with reading through their book clubs today. (E. Cain, elementary teacher, personal communication, June 24, 2022)

Collaborate on a Book Recommendation Video

Every year poses a new challenge of stimulating excitement about summer reading for students. An unfortunate reality is some students will not pick up a book during the summer months and need to rebuild their reading muscles when they return to school in the fall. According to Scholastic's (2019) *Kids and Family Reading Report*, 32 percent of teens ages fifteen to seventeen said the number of books they read over the summer was zero in 2018, a percentage increase from 22 percent in 2016. The percentage of students ages nine to eleven who read zero books over the summer in 2018 doubled since 2016 (7–14 percent). This is not all students. Some students will read because an adult in their life creates space for them to read, as parental awareness about *summer slide* (the tendency of some students to lose some of the academic gains they made during the previous school year) is increasing (Scholastic, 2019). And some students will always have a book in their hands—whether at the beach, the park, or sitting outside in front of their home.

Toward the end of my first year of my reading culture mission, I collaborated with a group of teachers to develop summer reading opportunities for students. One motivational tactic was to invite the adults in our school community to be reading role models for students and demonstrate they could read *anywhere* throughout the summer. We decided to use our new green screens in the school's computer labs to create a staff video to share with students before they sailed off into summer. Adults chose a place to read they wanted to show in the video and selected an image of that place. The image became the background to their video portion (using a green screen), as they showed a book they were looking forward to reading over the summer. The video was a book recommendations resource and a way for students to see the adults in their school as summer readers. It was also a reminder to our community about the importance of reading. After all, if your principal or teacher is sharing a book with you in a video, it must be something special.

Find Your Technicians

While my group wanted to showcase new technology, a green screen is not necessary for this project. You will need a device to film short video clips of staff, like a phone or tablet camera, and then a program to put the video clips together, like iMovie (https://apple.com/imovie). Background music adds a nice touch to the video. You may need to find someone in your school who can help with the technical aspect of this project if you aren't familiar with certain digital tools.

Invite Adults to Participate

Invite all the adults in your school community to participate in the video. Request they choose a book to recommend to students. We also asked participants to decide on a place they wanted to showcase in the video as their green screen background using the theme, *Remember that you can read anywhere this summer!* Provide several options for days and times to visit participants to film their short video clips.

Create and Share the Video

After filming is complete, access a movie-making program to put your video together. Add background music (with permission and credits, if needed) and publish the video.

To ensure students view the video, show it in classes during one of the final days of the school year. In addition to showing the video in class, share a link to the video on your school or class website or in your communication with families about summer reading opportunities.

A Classroom Connection

The following school year, teachers worked with students to incorporate the green screen into their responses to reading and when writing book reviews. Students stood in front of the green screen knowing a picture of a book cover would be behind them. They posed as if they were part of the book cover to help tell the story. They wrote a response to the literature in addition to designing with the technology!

Host a Book Tasting

A *book tasting* is a great way to introduce books to students as they make choices for independent reading or participate in a book club unit of study. It is designed similarly to how one would engage in a food tasting—sample a small portion and decide on a first impression. As students sample portions of multiple books throughout a book tasting, they can then decide on what book or books they want to read next as a result of their first impressions. An aspect of being a reader is getting to know yourself as a reader through opportunities where you have access to an abundance of books and are encouraged to make personal choices about reading (Allington & Gabriel, 2012; Wilhelm & Smith, 2016). A book tasting provides opportunities to develop into readers as participants experience excitement about reading, learn about new titles, gain strategies for making appropriate book choices, and make choices about independent reading routines.

As a teacher, I collaborated with my school's librarian to host at least four book tastings during the school year, with one tasting at the beginning of each quarter. When I became a school leader, I wanted to bring this practice that I have seen influence the reading lives of so many young readers into my leadership work with adults. I wanted to provide an active professional learning experience for teachers, packed with book tasting ideas and resources. It is important for teachers to experience the book tasting themselves and connect with their own reading identities and practices *before* making plans for students.

One day, I (nervously) introduced myself to teachers and building leaders as the new director of literacy while wearing a chef's hat and an #LBReads chef's apron. I explained I would take them through an experience designed to bring the best out of young readers . . . chef's hat, apron, and all!

Prepare the Learning Space

The conditions of the learning space are crucial in generating interest and enthusiasm. I hosted the book tasting during a faculty meeting before school. As teachers and building leaders arrived, they were met with a table of treats (three kinds of muffins, cookies, and candy), as well as two books with titles about food: *Charlie and the Chocolate Factory* by Roald Dahl and *Cloudy With a Chance of Meatballs* by Judi Barrett. (See appendix A, page 181, for more titles about food.) The table was lined with a plastic red and white checkered tablecloth, which helped introduce the restaurant theme to the book tasting. The rest of the tables also had plastic red and white checkered tablecloths, and in front of each chair was a book, so participants each had one book in front of them when they sat down.

Prepare the Materials

Decide what kind of books you want teachers to "taste" and gauge your access to the books. Education professors Jeffrey D. Wilhelm and Michael W. Smith (2016) assert that pleasure is at the heart of engaged reading and multifaceted for readers. Readers read for different reasons: play, intellectual, social, and inner (psychological and spiritual) exploration. You can carry out this notion in preparing for a book tasting.

Do you want teachers to preview books their students read? Do you want teachers to preview professional books that may inform their practice? Do you want teachers to preview adult fiction to read for pleasure? Put out a variety of books during a book tasting and designate variations by table. For example, you might set one table with professional books to preview. At another table, put bilingual books written in both English and Spanish, and at another table put early chapter books or those first in a series. Other ways to organize the book tasting are by series, genre, author, format, topic, theme, student recommendation, a mixture of types, or something special, like books made into movies. Share this with teachers so they can start thinking about how to organize their book tastings for students.

When working with adults, much like when working with students, think about what may be interesting and new to those attending the book tasting to tap into the pleasure aspect of reading (Wilhelm & Smith, 2016). Consider people who attend, their roles in the school, and what types of books may appeal to them. If social workers are attending, perhaps offer books that address social-emotional learning themes. If English as a new language teachers are attending, perhaps offer books in multiple languages or bilingual books. If grade 5 teachers are attending, feature new middle grades novels. Relevance of material is important in capturing teachers' attention.

Many of the books I use for these experiences are my own. If you don't have a lot of books that represent what you want to share with teachers, visit your school and local libraries, or ask colleagues to loan their books. Teachers do not actually take home any books they preview during the book tasting; this is the one difference in procedure between a teacher and student experience. Rather, teachers have an opportunity to read each book for five minutes during the tasting and track their initial thoughts on a menu (see "Dig In! Facilitate the Book Tasting," page 58), so they can refer back to the menu to follow up on what they learn. When implementing a book tasting with students, the goal is for them to take a book for their next read.

Great professional learning experiences provide teachers with relevant ideas and materials to use with students almost instantly. Teachers should practice using materials they could potentially provide to their students. There are two versions of book tasting materials: one version fit for students in primary grades (see figure 2.10) and one version fit for students in upper-elementary or secondary grades (see figure 2.11). Encourage teachers to change material to suit the needs of their students. These figures are available in the reproducibles "Book Tasting Recording Sheet, Primary" (page 78) and "Book Tasting Recording Sheet, Upper Elementary and Secondary" (page 79).

Developing Reading Role Models 57

Book Tasting
What do you fancy?

Book Title	Author	First Impression			Explain Your Rating
		😊	🤔	😟	
		😊	🤔	😟	
		😊	🤔	😟	
		😊	🤔	😟	

Reflection:
What did you think about as you sampled the books at your table?
How can this influence the ways you engage students in reading?

Source: © 2018 by Lorraine M. Radice.

FIGURE 2.10: Use this book tasting menu for primary grades like a placemat.

Menu Option

Book Title:
_____

Author:
_____

Genre:
_____

My First Impression: 😊   🤔   😟

Explain your first impression of this book:
_____
_____
_____

What are you wondering about this book?
_____
_____
_____

Welcome to a

Book Tasting!

Name: _____

Date: _____

FIGURE 2.11: Fold and use this book tasting menu for upper-elementary and secondary grades.

Share the Benefits of a Book Tasting

Sharing the *why* behind a practice when promoting literacy work is important to understand the potential for influence on students' reading lives. While book tastings can be helpful to teachers in availing new titles, the practice is ultimately to engage them in thinking about how to design the literacy experience for their students. The following are benefits of a book tasting.

- Students are exposed to a variety of books and can choose from a diverse selection that may present as windows, mirrors, or sliding glass doors (Bishop, 1990).
- Students have opportunities to talk about books and their book choices with peers. Conversation contributes to understanding, construction of knowledge, and reading identities (Vygotsky, 1978, 1986). Use this time when students are working with their peers to promote active listening and accountable talk.
- Students practice handling books and navigating ways to preview an unfamiliar text—for example, read the back blurb, inside cover, first few pages, and so on (Serravallo, 2015).
- Students become familiar with how books are organized.
- Students practice strategies for choosing a new book (Hiebert, 2014).
- Students learn how to form initial opinions or first impressions of books, and how they may influence the book-selection process. During the tasting, students write or express their opinions with reasonings.
- Students make choices about their reading lives. Choice can promote intrinsic motivation to read more (Pruzinsky, 2014).

Dig In! Facilitate the Book Tasting

You are ready to begin the tasting when participants are sitting at tables with colleagues, have books in front of them, and each participant has chosen a book tasting menu to use. You can use the reproducible "Book Tasting Presentation Slides" (page 73) to introduce the activity. Explain to participants they will sample all the books on their table. They start with the book in front of them and have five minutes to "taste" the book. Demonstrate and explain ways readers may *taste a book*—read the back blurb, inside front cover, about the author and illustrator, the first few pages, and so on. After five minutes, prompt teachers to stop and add information about the book to the menu, along with their first impressions. There are different ways to record depending on the menu type you use. For example, when using figure 2.10 (page 57) and the reproducible, "Book Tasting Recording Sheet, Primary" (page 78), the primary tool for recording the first impression is an emoji. When using figure 2.11 (page 57) and the reproducible, "Book Tasting Recording Sheet, Upper Elementary and Secondary" (page 79), there are spaces to explain your first impression and jot wonderings.

After the first tasting round, prompt participants to pass the first book they tasted to the person sitting to their right to start a new round. Repeat this process two or three more times, depending on how many people are sitting at each table. Participants should "taste" a total of three or four books in one sitting. After participants preview all books at their table, invite them to discuss their first impressions with one another to elevate the book talk.

Ask for Feedback

At the end of the book tasting, distribute a feedback card to each participant. Ask participants to rate their experience and provide any narrative feedback. Figure 2.12 is an example of a feedback card.

Developing Reading Role Models 59

Are your professional development taste buds fulfilled? Please complete this feedback card and place it in the "salad bowl" in the middle of your table.

4 = Delicious! I'll be back to this restaurant next week.

3 = Tasty! I am going to come back.

2 = Good, but not for me. Maybe I will recommend to someone.

1 = Yikes, what's in this dish? I'll never be back.

Please complete the feedback card to share your thoughts about the book tasting experience.

FIGURE 2.12: A feedback card to distribute after the book tasting experience.

Consider Purchasing Books

You may design the book tasting so teachers preview professional books or books for students. You may also consider purchasing popular books in the tasting to follow up the experience. Add professional books to the school's professional library to support teachers and their work in the classroom. Purchase books students may read (and teachers really liked) for classroom or school libraries. You may team up with your school librarian or other leaders in the school community to help with funds for purchasing. Participants will be thrilled to see some of their favorites appear in the school as a result of the book tasting.

A Classroom Connection

Book tastings have become part of the reading experience in many classrooms. Teachers fall in love with the process, the restaurant theme, and how this practice avails many new titles and conversation to readers. Many teachers use the material the adult book tastings provide while adding their own ideas to the classroom experience. Autonomy in carrying out the literacy events contributes to their success and connects to Gemmink and colleagues' (2021) research about how positive social-professional relationships and autonomy strengthen teachers' pedagogical practices.

One second-grade classroom adapted a book tasting at the *Starbook Café*. The teacher placed paper plates on tables for students to put the book they were tasting, and provided bookmarks to remind students of authentic practices for previewing books. You can view photos of their experience at my blog (www.lorrainemradice.com/blog).

Teachers also connected book tastings to a holiday experience, anticipating students wouldn't be in school for several days. Students engage in a book tasting a day or two before a holiday recess, so they can choose a book to take home to continue their commitment to reading. One teacher created a "Thanksgiving feast of books" for students to taste. This teacher continued the practice during the COVID-19 pandemic with students tasting at least six feet apart with masks on.

School libraries can be a place to host book tastings. The librarian can be a helpful resource for determining which books to include in the tasting as well as for access to books. Perhaps new books just arrived in the library. A tasting can be an experience to avail those books to students. Students could be entering a research unit of study where they will access the library. A book tasting can be a way to sample research topics with the librarian's support. The tasting can also be a way for librarians to introduce practices for previewing and handling books in the school library. Pictures of a book tasting set up in a middle school library are available at www.lorrainemradice

.com/blog. This tasting featured laminated placemats, table numbers, and a menu recording sheet on each table, along with four library books for students to taste. You may consider encouraging a partnership between teachers and librarians to explore the possibilities.

Reading Culture in Action
Reflections From Those Who Are Making It Happen

There is something enchanting and inspiring about beginning each new cycle of independent reading with a book tasting. Asking students to pick up and briefly examine various novels in a given class period is a practice I've noticed brings a simultaneous joy and determination to the process of finding that next "right" book. "I'll try this one," "This one looks cool," "Look at the cover!" "I'm actually really excited to read this one." Without fail, these are the kind of murmured buzz I can typically expect to surface during a book tasting. And that's why we always start [each new independent reading cycle] this way.

My eleventh-grade students engaged in a book tasting that started in our school library and continued the next day in our classroom. I love bringing my classes to our school library first; the options are seemingly endless, and the students get to hear about great books from someone besides me [that is, the librarians]. This particular time, the librarians spent a few minutes giving book talks, and I got to witness my students' piquing interest. "That movie was a book *before* it became a movie? Can I take that one?" (Students literally had to play rock-paper-scissors to determine who got to take out certain books first—an absolute joy for an English teacher to watch!) Then, it was time to scatter based on interest: realistic fiction, fantasy, historical fiction, horror . . . students moved throughout the library and began informally tasting possible titles. The growing excitement was palpable.

The next day, students engaged in a book tasting of independent reading titles in our classroom. Students rotated around the room, readers' notebooks in hand, ready to add to their *To Read* lists based on book stacks I'd placed throughout the room. They read back covers, inside covers, blurbs, and checked out audio excerpts on their devices. Book tastings are magical to witness because students get invested. They take ownership of their interests and subsequent reading choices. I truly believe starting a new cycle of independent reading this way renews students' belief that there are great books everywhere; they just need the time and resources to look. (J. Scheel, grades 9–12 English teacher, personal communication, June 15, 2022)

Teachers can create virtual book tastings using Google Slides to set up independent reading routines, as well as to launch book club units of study in the curricula (see figure 2.13). As students progressed through the Google Slide deck, they tasted a series of books. Each book cover image was hyperlinked to a book trailer or a review of the book. After watching the trailer or reading the review, students recorded their initial impressions on a Google Slide (see figure 2.14). At the end of the book tasting, students completed a Google Form to notify their teacher which book from the tasting they would like to read.

Developing Reading Role Models 61

FIGURE 2.13: Images from a virtual book tasting in a high school English class.

Book title: *Patron Saints of Nothing* by Randy Ribay		
What was your initial impression, the first "bite," when looking at the book cover?	After reading the review and a few pages, how did this book "taste"? What are your initial thoughts?	How would you rate this book at first glance? How many stars?
I am kind of confused on what the title means; I'm not sure why there is light coming out of his hands.	I find this book interesting. I like books that have to do with coming of age, mystery, and murder novels, so this might be a book for me.	★ ★ ★ ★

FIGURE 2.14: A space for students to record initial impressions of books during a virtual book tasting experience.

While the restraints of the COVID-19 pandemic prompted virtual book tastings, this practice continues. Teachers report the virtual version acts as a book log students refer back to for book recommendations. Students also learn how to preview books on a digital platform; reading online is a popular way to engage with text. Book reviews websites, like Goodreads (https://goodreads.com) and Amazon (https://amazon.com), invite readers to engage in authentic practices for learning about new books, and provide ways for them to practice as readers outside the classroom.

A Goal to Personalize Culture

Effective leaders realize they cannot accomplish great things alone (DuFour & Marzano, 2011), especially when considering the new literacy studies (Gee, 1990; Street, 1997) and how literacies develop in social practices (Street, 2021). Community participation in culture building is essential, so the will to work and lead are intrinsic.

The leadership actions I share in this chapter honor what Burnett and Merchant (2020) distinguish as literacy-as-event:

> *Literacy-as-event rests on three related ideas: 1. event is generated as people and things come into relation; 2. what happens always exceeds what can be conceived and perceived; and 3. implicit in the event are multiple potentialities, including multiple possibilities for what might materialize as well as what does not. (p. 49)*

Literacy-as-event implies meaning-making is often unpredictable, and the results of an event or material could far exceed your initial plan. You approach the work asking, "What else is going on?" This leaves room for constant growth and acknowledges how meaning-making is not standard. Literacy development is unique to the person participating in the culture. Reading culture–building through a literacy-as-event lens allows participants to own the outcomes, which can positively impact the pedagogical practices and how school culture evolves. There is room for personal expression of the shared vision and goal. This is helpful when developing your mindset about culture building. You may plan an event or design an activity for others to participate in with a desired outcome, but as the commitment evolves and you foster creativity in culture building, participants develop their own contributions to the vision. For example, a teacher shared his idea with me of creating a Spotlight Book of the Month celebration to highlight the traits the school district identified as important in the profile of a graduate from high school (hardworking, critical thinker, open minded, and so on). A book was chosen for each graduate trait and shared in elementary classrooms each month of the school year to engage in conversation about the traits with young readers. This is an example of personalizing culture; a teacher is looking to promote reading and literacy events in ways the administration did not initiate and define. Read more about making connections between literacy and school initiatives in chapter 7 (page 165).

It is important to allow members of the literacy community the space to make personal what is ultimately supporting a universal vision about reading or another aspect of literacy.

Summary

Culture building is about cultivating the hearts and minds of the people in the learning community. By promoting reading and reading-related events as a social practice, you develop collaboration and shared experiences among the people in the reading community. This can bring positive energy and commitment to your vision on the importance of reading.

The ideas in this chapter serve to invite adults to reflect on their own reading identities so they can incorporate this personalized work into ways they engage students in reading communities. Whether an adult identifies as a reader or not, both positions, and those between, can become important to the ways students engage. You can conduct the activities in this chapter with students. Events like book swaps, book clubs, book tastings, book recommendations videos, and book recommendations newsletters are all ways to invite students to get excited about reading and experience the joy of belonging to a literacy community.

In many ways, the ideas I describe in the chapter are participatory and make your learning communities' commitment to reading visible. These ideas are rooted in literacy as a social event. If you lead or teach adults, consider the importance of adults participating in reading events as a way to move the culture work forward. If you are a teacher, engage in your own self-reading reflection (as I outline in this chapter) and embrace the activities I describe with the young readers in your classroom.

In the next chapter, I will explore how permeating participation, celebration, and visibility of messaging can be when building culture and a commitment to reading.

Reflection Questions

On your own or with a collaborative team, answer the following questions.

1. What structures are in place to support adults participating in reading culture–building events? Are there contractual meeting times? Are there opportunities to provide professional learning credit for participation so staff can earn hours or compensation for attending an event held outside of school hours?

2. Invite school community members to write a description of *themselves as readers* as an initial reflection. Engage in conversations to determine how these descriptions may or may not influence the way adults talk with students about reading.

3. Survey the adults in the school to gauge reading interests and preferences. This information can help when planning reading events.

4. What identities of staff and students should we consider when choosing books to read in book clubs, peruse in book tastings, and so on? How can we diversify book choices to be inclusive of the identities of those participating in the reading events?

5. What talents, skills, and creativity exist among staff contribute to the planning and implementation of social reading events? What ideas in this chapter can we modify or mold to fit our school community to represent staff strengths?

6. Which social reading event will have the most significant impact on classroom culture? Start planning this event and develop ways to support transfer to the classroom.

Lift a Line Conversation Cards for an Adult Book Swap

Lift a line . . .

Something you would say to introduce yourself

Lift a line . . .

Something to never say on a first date

Lift a line . . .

Something you would never say to your best friend

Lift a line . . .

Something you would say to share positive vibes with someone

Lift a line . . .

Something you would share with someone who needs inspiration

Lift a line . . .

Something you say to make someone laugh

Book Discussion Questions List

Please feel free to use these as they are or modify them to fit the needs of your specific grade level, your students' interests, and where you are in the curriculum.

Questions that address literary opinions and creative responses to reading:
- What book would you love to see as a movie or television series? Who would you choose to be in the cast?
- What book would you recommend for someone who is sad?
- What book would you recommend for someone who loves magical adventures?
- What book would you recommend for someone who needs to feel inspired?
- What book has a character that is similar to you or a storyline that is similar to the events in your life?
- What is your favorite book title and why do you like that title?
- Is there a book you've read that made you want to travel to where the story took place? What was that place and why did you want to go there?
- Name a character from a book that you really disliked and why.
- Share your thoughts about a book that you felt compelled to read because you knew a lot of people who were reading it. What do you think it is about the book that captured the attention of many readers?

Questions that address personal connections to literature:
- If you could join a friend group from any book, which one would you join and why?
- If you could join a magical world in a fantasy book, which world would you join?
- If you could be on a deserted island with one literary character, who would it be and why?
- If you could be best friends with a literacy character, which character would you choose?
- If there was a literary character that would really challenge you in some way, which character would it be and how would the character challenge you?
- If you could pick a literary character to be your study partner, which character would you choose?
- If you could live in a house from any story, which house would you choose to live in and why?
- If you could rewrite the title of any book that you have read, which book would you create a new title for? What would the title be?
- If you could be the main character in an existing story, which story would you want to be the main character of?

Source: Adapted from Book Riot. (2017). Lit chat: Conversation starters about books and life (100 questions). New York: Abrams Noterie.

Reading Schedule for a Book Club

Meeting Date	Book Title	Read to Page . . .

Because we divide some of our books into parts, it is helpful if you don't read ahead (I know sometimes it's tough!), but the conversation will include wonderings, predictions, and so on.

Book Club Launch Presentation Slides

Welcome to Book Club!

SLIDE 1

Books as Mirrors, Windows, Sliding Glass Doors (Bishop, 1990)

- Mirror: a reflection of your own life, understandings, perspectives
- Window: an invitation into a new perspective
- Sliding glass door: a combination of real and imagined experiences for the reader

SLIDE 2

It Starts With Your Own Reflection

- Books as Mirrors:
    - *How is this story similar to your life experience?*
    - *How is this character's perspective similar to yours?*
    - *What is your personal relationship with this story (that is, the characters, the conflict, and so on)?*
    - *Do you see yourself in this story?*

SLIDE 3

It Starts With Your Own Reflection

- Books as Windows:
    - *How is this character's perspective different from yours?*
    - *How is this character's life circumstance different from yours?*
    - *Does this new perspective influence your perspective?*
    - *How does this perspective help you empathize with others?*

SLIDE 4

It Starts With Your Own Reflection

- Books as Sliding Glass Doors:
    - *What is it about this world you could step into and feel a part of?*
    - *What is it about this world that is similar but different from yours?*

SLIDE 5

Reflect:

- What are your identities?
- How do your identities impact your meaning-making and understandings of text?
- How do these reflections influence your conversations with students?

*Provide a personal example of a book as a mirror and a book as a window to share with book club members to model thinking and reflection.

SLIDE 6

Norms and Agreements

- What is important to you as we establish our reading community?
- What is important to consider as we engage in conversation about a variety of social issues?

SLIDE 7

Think About:

- What is your reading identity?
- Are you comfortable with exploring social issues with students?
  - *What makes you comfortable?*
  - *What makes you uncomfortable?*
- Do you believe readers should read material they don't relate to?
- How do you support readers as an English or reading teacher?
- How do you support readers as if you are not an English or reading teacher?
- What do you believe about reading?
- What do you believe about reading instruction?

SLIDE 8

Source: Adapted from Bishop, R. S. (1990). Mirrors, windows, and sliding glass doors. Perspectives, 6(3), ix–xi.

Books as Mirrors, Windows, and Sliding Glass Doors Thinking Chart

Book Title:		
Books as Mirrors	**Books as Windows**	**Books as Sliding Glass Doors**
Reading a book that is a *mirror* means an aspect or several aspects of the book reflect the reader's personal experiences and understandings.	Reading a book that is a *window* means an aspect or several aspects of the book serve as an invitation to learn a new perspective. Experiences are portrayed in the book that are not relatable to the reader.	Reading a book that is a *sliding glass door* means an aspect or several aspects of the book reflect a combination of real experiences the reader can relate to and imagined experiences that are not relatable.
Questions to consider while reading: Do you see yourself represented in this story? Are parts of your identity portrayed in the story? How is this story similar to your life experience? How is this character's perspective similar to yours? What is your personal relationship with this story (that is, the characters, the conflict, and so on)? What are you learning about yourself through reading?	**Questions to consider while reading:** What types of identities are represented in this story that are different from yours? How is this character's perspective different from yours? How is the character's life circumstance different from yours? How is the setting different from environments you have experienced? Does this new perspective influence your perspective? How does this story help you empathize with others?	**Questions to consider while reading:** What is it about this world you could step into and feel a part of? What is it about this world that is similar but different from yours? What aspects of this story make you feel comfortable and uncomfortable? At what points in the story do you feel your connection shifting while reading? How does the duality impact your understandings and meaning-making?
My Thinking:	**My Thinking:**	**My Thinking:**

Source: Adapted from Bishop, R. S. (1990). Mirrors, windows, and sliding glass doors. Perspectives, *6(3), ix–xi.*

Norms and Agreements

What is important to us as we share ideas and responses in our reading community?

Name	Roles for students	What are your personal expectations for our reading community?

Book Tasting Presentation Slides

Welcome to a Book Tasting!

SLIDE 1

Our Plan for Today

- Enjoy some treats (food and then books)
- Book tasting experience
- Reflect on ways to incorporate this engagement in classrooms
- Share feedback on this workshop

SLIDE 2

Book tasting menu for younger readers.

Book Tasting
What do you fancy?

Book Title	Author	First Impression			Explain Your Rating
		😊	🤔	☹️	
		😊	🤔	☹️	
		😊	🤔	☹️	
		😊	🤔	☹️	

Reflection:
What did you think about as you sampled the books at your table?
How can this influence the ways you engage students in reading?

SLIDE 3

Book tasting menu for older readers.

Menu Option #1

Book Title: _____

Author: _____

Genre: _____

My First Impression: 😊 🤔 ☹️

Explain your first impression of this book:
_____
_____
_____

What are you wondering about this book?
_____
_____
_____

Menu Option #2

Book Title: _____

Author: _____

Genre: _____

My First Impression: 😊 🤔 ☹️

Explain your first impression of this book:
_____
_____
_____

What are you wondering about this book?
_____
_____
_____

SLIDE 4

Let the Back Blurb Help You Decide

Look for:

The character and the problem

The genre

A theme or an important plot idea

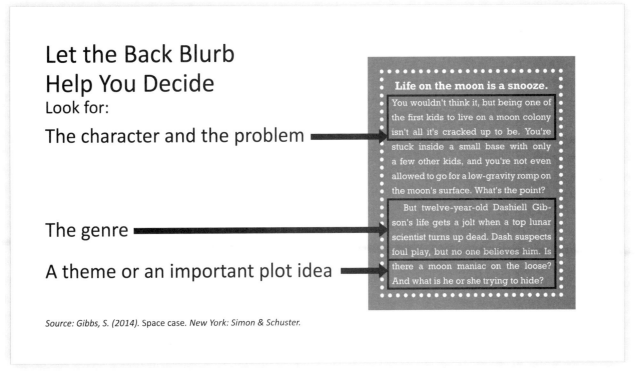

Source: Gibbs, S. (2014). Space case. New York: Simon & Schuster.

SLIDE 5

How are the books on the tables organized?

- Professional
- Celebration of women
- Graphic novels
- Who is . . . series (biography)
- Early reader chapter books
- Bilingual and celebration of diversity

SLIDE 6

Ways to Organize Your Tasting

- By series
- By genre
- By author
- By illustration type
- By topic
- By theme
- By something special (examples: books made into movies, change in format)
- By student recommendation
- Randomly

SLIDE 7

The Benefits of a Book Tasting

- Students are exposed to a variety of books and can choose from a diverse selection that may present as windows, mirrors, and sliding glass doors (Bishop, 1990).
- Students can talk about books and their book choices with peers. Conversation contributes to understandings, construction of knowledge, and reading identities (Vygotsky, 1978, 1986).
- Students practice handling books and navigating ways to preview an unfamiliar text—read the back blurb, inside cover, first few pages, and so on. (Serravallo, 2015).
- Students become familiar with how books are organized.
- Students practice strategies for choosing a new book (Hiebert, 2014).
- Students learn how to form initial opinions or first impressions about books and how those may influence the book-selection process.
- Students make choices about their reading lives. Choice can promote intrinsic motivation to read more (Pruzinsky, 2014).

SLIDE 8

Your Feedback Is Important

- Are your professional learning taste buds fulfilled?
    - 4 = Delicious! I'll be back to this restaurant next week.
    - 3 = Tasty! I am going to come back.
    - 2 = Good, but not for me. Maybe I will recommend to someone.
    - 1 = Yikes, what's in this dish? I'll never be back.

Please complete the feedback card to share your thoughts about the book tasting experience.

SLIDE 9

Source: Bishop. R. S. (1990). Mirrors, windows, and sliding glass doors. Perspectives, 6(3), ix–xi; Hiebert, E. H. (2014). Frank views on literacy and the Common Core. Accessed at https://textproject.org/wp-content/uploads/books/Hiebert-2014-Frank-Views-on-Literacy-and-the-Common-Core.pdf on March 30, 2023; Pruzinsky, T. (2014). Read books. Every day. Mostly for pleasure. The English Journal, 103(4), 25–30; Serravallo, J. (2015). The reading strategies book: Your everything guide to developing skilled readers. Portsmouth, NH: Heinemann; Vygotsky, L. S. (1978). Mind in society: The development of higher psychological processes. Cambridge, MA: Harvard University Press; Vygotsky, L. S. (1986). Thought and language (Rev. ed.). Cambridge, MA: The MIT Press.

Book Tasting Recording Sheet, Primary

 **Book Tasting** *What do you fancy?*

Book Title	Author	First Impression			Explain Your Rating
		😊	🤔	😟	
		😊	🤔	😟	
		😊	🤔	😟	
		😊	🤔	😟	
		😊	🤔	😟	

Reflection:

What did you think about as you sampled the books at your table?

How can this influence the way you engage students in reading?

How does this experience impact the ways in which you engage students in making choices about reading?

Leading a Culture of Reading © 2024 Solution Tree Press • SolutionTree.com
Visit **go.SolutionTree.com/literacy** to download this free reproducible.

Book Tasting Recording Sheet, Upper Elementary and Secondary

Menu Option #1

Book Title:
_____

Author:
_____

Genre:
_____

My First Impression: 😀 🤔 😕

Explain your first impression of this book:
_____
_____
_____

What are you wondering about this book?
_____
_____
_____

Menu Option #2

Book Title:
_____

Author:
_____

Genre:
_____

My First Impression: 😀 🤔 😕

Explain your first impression of this book:
_____
_____
_____

What are you wondering about this book?
_____
_____
_____

Menu Option #3

Book Title:
_____

Author:
_____

Genre:
_____

My First Impression: 😀 🤔 😕

Explain your first impression of this book:
_____
_____
_____

What are you wondering about this book?
_____
_____
_____

Menu Option #4

Book Title:
_____

Author:
_____

Genre:
_____

My First Impression: 😀 🤔 😕

Explain your first impression of this book:
_____
_____
_____

What are you wondering about this book?
_____
_____
_____

Leading a Culture of Reading © 2024 Solution Tree Press • SolutionTree.com
Visit **go.SolutionTree.com/literacy** to download this free reproducible.

Welcome to a Book Tasting!

Name: _____

Date: _____

Leading a Culture of Reading © 2024 Solution Tree Press • SolutionTree.com
Visit **go.SolutionTree.com/literacy** to download this free reproducible.

CHAPTER 3

Sustaining the Culture
How to Make the Culture Visible, Participatory, and Celebratory

This Chapter Features...
Ways to Make Reading Culture Visible in the Community, Participatory for Community Members, and Something for All to Celebrate

- Make reading and reading identity visible (page 83).
- Host community reading events in online spaces (page 87).
- Declare your own celebratory month (page 94).
- Have a kindergarten reading parade (page 96).
- Build a book fair (page 98).

Trends in fashion and on social media signal what's popular in a moment in time. They can be hot items or topics for a few months and then eventually something new comes along that attracts interest—like a new season or a new story. Be careful of those types of trends in education—like buzz words, the next big thing, the pendulum swinging, an initiative here today and gone tomorrow. Educators know exactly what I'm referring to. Building reading culture is not a trend—I repeat, *not a trend*. Building culture is about traditions. It is not something packaged you can purchase. It is an ongoing embedded commitment in your school or classroom and daily functioning. Sustainability is important for all stakeholders, especially students, as the commitment to reading is part of the identity of your learning community.

Chapter 1 (page 9) introduced ideas to consider when launching a reading campaign and getting started with your exciting new endeavor. In this chapter, I share ideas for traditions and sustainability. While some ideas may be reoccurring and some may be special features during the school year, creating a visible, participatory, and celebratory culture invites everyone in the school community to contribute to the ongoing commitment to reading. The reading campaign is launched, and now all community members can discover ways to build momentum in the messaging.

The Roots of This Work

The sociocultural perspective of *new literacies* signifies that literacy changes as culture changes (Gee, 2010; Street, 2016). Literacy practices reflect the norms of society. While this idea refers to the experiences students have outside of school—experiences with media, family, and social communities—schools and classrooms are also societies of their own. Ultimately, educators strive to design learning communities to reflect society outside the school doors, so students learn the skills and competencies they need to be productive members of the global community. You can bring the ideas of new literacies (Gee, 2010; Street, 2016) into schools and classrooms; the practices my district brings to our schools and classrooms to elevate reading become the norms of the school community.

One factor to consider when building reading culture is the *visibility* of reading in the learning community. What do students see that signals reading is important? How are adults making reading visible so students know it is a norm in the learning community? What you choose to make public and visible in your school signals what you value. The environment contributes to the messaging about the importance of reading.

Making reading visible as part of building culture leans on research about the influence of environmental print on emergent and early literacy development. When young students are in their developing stages of literacy, extrinsic factors can encourage or hinder their learning and motivation (Neumann, Hood, Ford, & Neumann, 2011). In their review of research on the role of environmental print on literacy development, Neumann and colleagues (2011) suggest adult-child encounters and interactions with print greatly influence a child's intrinsic motivation to participate in print-related activities. Also, the more interested a child is in environmental print, the more likely they may be to ask what something means and, thus, initiate literacy interactions at home and in school. Research inspires many of the practices I outline in this chapter. While the research focuses on early childhood literacy, the concepts are easily transferable to older readers and adults when considering the influence extrinsic factors have on motivation and engagement. Think about a time you were driving along a road and saw multiple signs to advertise a restaurant or your favorite ice cream shop. Did you find yourself feeling hungry? This idea of external influences on behavior and thinking is not unique to young children.

A guiding principle under the new literacies framework is that literacy is *participatory* (Clinton et al., 2013; Jenkins, 2009). The increased use of media among tweens, teens, and adults is partly responsible as to why the definition of literacy practices continues to evolve (Rideout et al., 2022; Schaeffer, 2021). Literacy now includes print and media skills and the choices people have in exercising those skills for meaning-making (Jenkins, 2009). Technology allows for greater connectivity and increases access to information and online spaces. Clinton and colleagues (2013) provide a rationale for why literacy practices have moved toward a more participatory culture:

> Over the past several decades, our culture has undergone a period of profound and prolonged media change, not only a shift in the technical infrastructure for communication but shifts in the cultural logics and social practices that shape the ways we interact . . . . These shifts point us toward a more participatory culture, one in which everyday citizens have an expanded capacity to communicate and circulate their ideas . . . these shifts require us to reimagine the nature of literacy itself. (p. 7)

Reimaging literacy to include acts of participation is part of building and rebranding reading culture in schools and classrooms. The ideas I share in this chapter value the participatory nature of building culture through practices to brand the importance of reading, some in online spaces and some in the school building.

One of the "simple" ideas I share in the introduction (page 1) is *joy in schools is important*. School is a place where students and adults should want to be. School or class literacy communities provide opportunities to norm joy and *celebration*. Students often celebrate new learning by creating a class museum or sharing a presentation. Students also share and celebrate their published writing pieces. Schools may hold schoolwide celebrations of particular cultural events or holidays. Integrating reading into the ways you cultivate joy across a school or class community can have a positive impact on morale, as well as attitudes and behaviors toward reading.

Literacy is complex. There are several perspectives and ideologies on how people develop literacy skills and the factors that specifically contribute to students' engagement in reading. In literacy leadership, consider several perspectives and areas of research and use the information to influence the needs of your school or class community. Throughout this book, each chapter features different aspects of literacy development. Consider each of these aspects when developing creative practices to instill a culture that celebrates and is committed to reading.

How to Make It Happen

The following are ways to make reading culture visible, participatory, and celebratory among students and adults in a school or class community.

Make Reading and Reading Identity Visible

Literacy leaders work to create schools and classrooms where adults and students share in making their reading identities and reading lives visible. By sharing this responsibility, the community commits to participating and making reading visible. The adults can lead in this charge; students will follow.

The Currently Reading Sign

Educators and other staff in the school building may choose to display a *Currently Reading* sign, which provides a visual indicator of what that adult is reading at a particular moment in time. To encourage staff to use this sign, follow these steps.

- **Distribute signs to all adults in the school:** Share a digital copy of a Currently Reading sign with all adults in the school community. Ask them to display the sign near their doorway or inside their classrooms or office spaces (see figure 3.1, page 84, for an example email, and figure 3.2, page 84, for an image of a Currently Reading sign). After the first year of embracing this practice as a school community, I began sending a file showing all of the creative ways teachers used the Currently Reading signs to share their own reading lives, as well as the reading lives of their students. This file serves as a resource for how others can utilize this tool.

- **Begin group conversations (meetings, lessons, and so on) by asking participants to share what they are currently reading:** Have blank copies of the sign available to start conversations. Ask participants to share what they are currently reading as a way to connect in the meeting space. If you are leading a conversation with students in the classroom, encourage students to share what they are currently reading as a way to share reading identities and perhaps connect to something students are working on in a lesson.

    If you are leading a meeting with adults, the Currently Reading sign helps build relationships among adults and sets up a soft start to the meeting. There may be certain meetings throughout the year when this is especially important. For example, when meeting with new teachers for the first time at the start of the school year, invite them to fill out a Currently Reading sign and share what they are reading. Encourage the use of this practice in the classroom. As you invite people to share what they are currently reading, assure them that text like emails, blogs, articles, and even takeout menus are all viable options to include on their Currently Reading sign. The reality is that not all adults are readers of fiction novels, nor do they have to be. This is an opportunity to encourage diversity in reading experiences, which is beneficial for students to learn about the adults they interact with.

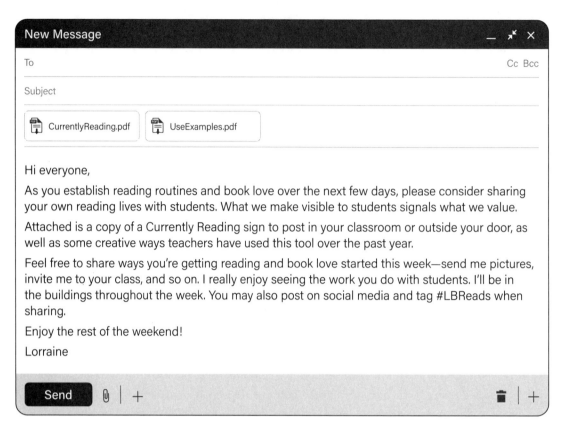

FIGURE 3.1: An email to staff encouraging the use of the Currently Reading sign.

Visit go.SolutionTree.com/literacy for a free reproducible version of this figure.

FIGURE 3.2: The school nurse shares what he is currently reading.

Visit go.SolutionTree.com/literacy for a free reproducible version of this figure.

- **Encourage using signs for reflection:** By the middle of the school year, students will have read several books and should aim to have a list of future books to read (gained from their peers, teachers, or librarians). A quick reading reflection can capture a favorite book, the book the student is currently reading, and the book to read next. Figure 3.3 is a different version of the Currently Reading sign to share during the middle of the school year to capture this reflection. Some teachers display this student work on bulletin boards to celebrate their reading lives and accomplishments.

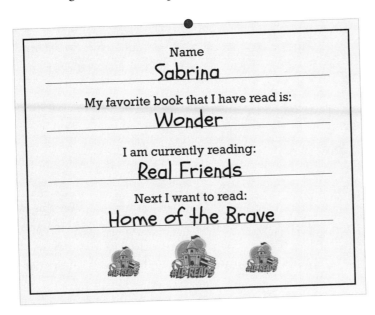

FIGURE 3.3: A student's Currently Reading sign with reading reflection.

You can also place reading signs in plastic sheet protectors and hang them on a bulletin board. Students use dry-erase markers to update their reading signs as they finish books as part of the reflection process. Some students also attach a book review to their reading sign when they complete a book to act as a reading record so all the books they have read are on display. You can see several versions of how to use this tool to engage students in reflection by visiting my blog (www.lorrainemradice.com/blog).

- **Share a reading life through book covers:** As an alternative to a Currently Reading sign, share your reading life, the reading lives of students through displaying book covers, or both. In kindergarten classes, teachers created a #BookADay challenge and read one picture book per day throughout the year. Teachers and students recorded these readings as part of their reading lives on a board displaying each book cover outside their classrooms. This is another way to make reading visible. Pernille Ripp (2018), a teacher, speaker, author, blogger, and education advocate, shares a similar idea in her book *Passionate Readers: The Art of Teaching Reading and Engaging Every Child*, in which she recommends sharing a board filled with covers of books you have read. Ripp (2018) includes a count of how many books she reads during the school year to share with her students. Ripp (2018) writes, "Making our reading visible through posters, displays, and even book challenges is a sure way to show students that we are readers in both word and action" (p. 9).

Make Books Part of You and Your Routines

Think about your daily school routine—tasks you typically complete and your overall responsibilities. In what ways can you integrate a book into what you already do each day? The following are suggestions on how to make reading and books part of the ways you represent yourself and your work.

- **Make a book an accessory:** There are items educators carry around school buildings throughout the day: a school ID card, classroom or office keys, a cell phone or walkie-talkie, and a class list, among others. Add the book you are currently reading or have just read to your list. When walking students to art class, grab your book to walk in the hallway. When visiting a teacher's classroom or walking to a meeting, grab your book before you go. Carrying your book signals you are a reader and may even spark a conversation with another adult or student when you walk around the building. I must admit that while I love accessories, having a book with me that is visible to others is not something I always remember to do. Educators are busy, spending most of the day on their feet and managing a lot in their minds. I suggest making a book as an accessory when you can. When I do make it a priority, there is always a conversation about the book in my hand, and I make a mental note about how beneficial this practice is. Note to self: *remember to take the book!*

- **Start with a book talk:** Whether facilitating a meeting with staff or starting the day or class period with students, begin with a book talk. Book talks take just a few minutes and signal to your audience that reading is important to you. You may also inspire someone's next great read or new genre to explore. I try to begin most of my meetings with adults and interactions with students by saying something like this:

    > *I am reading this really great book. It's about _____. If you're interested in _____ then you should check it out.*

    I keep it short, as I don't want to extend the duration of the meeting. While I am conscious of meeting time with adults, I usually have to (politely) bring the focus back to the meeting because the book talk inspires ongoing conversation about books!

    You may also challenge adults and students to share at the start of a meeting through a *ten-word book talk*. This activity is challenging because it invites the reader to consider what is most important or universal in the book they are reading or have recently read by summing it up or quoting from the book using just ten words. Here is an example of a ten-word book talk about the must-read, *Stepsister* by Jennifer Donnelly (2019): "Beauty is not binary. Beauty is fierce, smart, brave." By sharing the book cover and ten words, readers get a sense of what the book is about.

- **Establish First Chapter Fridays:** Every Friday, introduce a new book to students by reading the first chapter aloud. You can also do this with a picture book by reading the first few pages to hook students' interest. Reading the beginning of a new book each week exposes students to a variety of titles they may choose to read in the future. Consider diversity in genre, author, character, setting, theme, and so on when choosing books to expose to students. You may collaborate with colleagues in selecting books to ease your workload. Choose books inclusive of the identities of the students in the class or school, so First Chapter Fridays become opportunities for students to see themselves and others in books you expose to the whole class.

- **Introduce staff or a class through a reading directory:** School or class websites typically have a directory to introduce members of the learning community. In addition to information like the person's name, email address, phone number, room number, class name, and so on, list a favorite book as part of their contact information and identity. You can do this for administrative teams, teacher teams, support staff, and student groups.

Host Community Reading Events in Online Spaces

Using technology to communicate, learn, and gather people is now a societal norm. While the use of technology and media increased as a result of the COVID-19 pandemic (Rideout et al., 2022), it was on the rise during the years prior (Anderson & Jiang, 2018; Common Sense Media, 2020). The challenge for educators is how to embrace technology in ways that make school relevant to the social practices of students and adults outside of school. If educators ignore the growing use and popularity of media among young people, they risk appearing antiquated and disconnected from students' interests. In this section, I will share ways to leverage technology as a tool to build reading culture.

Technology and media can be assets to developing reading culture. "Given the huge amounts of time children give to media, it's all the more important to elevate quality media by creating and highlighting the shows, games, apps, and books that engage, inspire, and provide positive representations" (Rideout et al., 2022, p. 43). You can elevate quality media use through building reading culture practices. Capitalize on the opportunities technology and media provide as a way to make reading culture participatory and at the center of what the school community values.

Bringing reading to online spaces may bring it a new dimension and be a catalyst to spark interest in reading. There is often a participatory culture in navigating online spaces, with opportunities to engage in social media platforms and comment on print and visual texts in shared spaces. New learning is available that young people can explore through the participation (Bilton, 2010). This type of activity can contribute to how people's reading identity develops. If educators consider *literacy* a set of communicative practices social groups and the tools they use shape, both analog (such as paper and pencils or pens) and digital (such as computers, cameras, or microphones), then they broaden what it means to be a reader, build a reading identity, and participate in social groups in online spaces committed to reading (Dooley, Ellison, Welch, Allen, & Bauer, 2016).

The media activity young people enjoy most is watching online videos. According to Rideout and colleague (2022), 64 percent of tweens (ages eight to twelve) report they watch online videos every day, and 61 percent report they watch online videos a lot. Seventy-seven percent of teens (ages thirteen to eighteen) report they watch online videos every day, and 62 percent report they watch online videos a lot (Rideout et al., 2022). In 2021, YouTube and TikTok were among the most popular platforms for viewing online videos (Rideout et al., 2022). It is important to consider this information when making decisions about the type of reading events to host in online spaces. What media activity do young people enjoy most? How can educators connect popular media activity to messaging about the importance of reading? I used this information and explored the participatory aspect of literacy development when deciding to host reading events in online spaces.

Rally Behind a Read-Aloud: A Chapter Book

A read-aloud is a way to bring people together. It provides an opportunity to engage in conversation and share perspectives. With each read-aloud, communities strengthen. Read-alouds also set up conditions for adults to model reading behaviors and support students' thinking about a variety of topics in text selections. While read-alouds happen in individual classrooms, technology offers opportunities to bring read-alouds to larger communities.

When the COVID-19 pandemic started, one of my greatest responsibilities as a literacy leader was to inspire connection and hope in a time of isolation and fear. Reading and stories helped to do just that. My colleague, a fellow reading enthusiast in another school district just a few minutes away, invited me and my school community to join a community reading event where we both read a chapter book aloud on Instagram Live (https://help.instagram.com/292478487812558) for students and families in our own school communities each day. We read between fifteen and twenty minutes each day of the week (one or two chapters) for three weeks. At the culmination of the book, the author joined us for a book talk via Google Meet (https://apps.google.com/meet). Adults and students joined this reading celebration as a way to stay connected through reading. While this event was born during a pandemic, distance and struggle do not have to define the event. Our two school communities learned through this difficult time just how powerful a community reading event via any digital platform can be. Since watching online videos is the media activity of choice among tweens and teens (Rideout et al., 2022), literacy leaders can marry students' interest in watching online videos with providing live readings from familiar faces at school for them and their families to watch. The school reading community can become part of the media activity students and families engage in outside of school.

- **Choose a book that will capture a wide audience:** Choosing a book is perhaps the most challenging aspect of this practice of building reading culture. There are many factors to consider when choosing a book to expose to a large community: age of students, maturity of content, representation, interest level, length of book, genre, and theme.

  Mystery books work very well for community read-alouds because the unknowns in the story entices listeners. The following list of middle grades mystery novels are conducive to a read-aloud format and will appeal across audiences with different age groups.

  - *Escape From Mr. Lemoncello's Library* by Chris Grabenstein
  - *Finally, Something Mysterious* by Doug Cornett
  - *Finally, Something Dangerous* by Doug Cornett
  - *Space Case* by Stuart Gibbs
  - *The Secret Letters* by Margaret Peterson Haddix

  Consider the following questions when selecting a book to share with a wide audience.

  - Is this a story most people can find some joy in no matter their age or grade level?
  - Is there a universal message most people can connect to?
  - Are there likable characters readers or listeners will find entertaining, funny, intriguing, or interesting?
  - Is there material that could be offensive?
  - Is there material inappropriate for a read-aloud without follow-up conversation?
  - Is there a hook to the story that will keep readers or listeners coming back the next day?

- **Create a reading schedule:** After selecting the book, plan out how long the read-aloud series will be. Look at the number of pages or chapters and divide them among how long you would like the read-aloud series to last. This will help in your advertising to the school community.
- **Select a time to host your chapter book read-aloud:** Choose a time that fits the context and availability of your school or class community. The time of year may dictate when you decide to host the community read-aloud experience. Here are some theme structures you may want to consider.
  - Read live in the morning or evening during a summer month as a summer reading experience.
  - Read live each evening during a holiday month to celebrate the gift of reading.
  - Read live each evening in the fall as a way to welcome students and families back to school.
- **Choose a platform to read on:** Consider the access to technology students may have via school-issued devices (for example, iPads or Chromebooks) or personal devices. The following are user-friendly and accessible platforms that help facilitate read-alouds in a school community.
  - *Videoconference*—Zoom or Google Meet
  - *Livestream or webinar style*—YouTube Live or Google Meet
  - *Social media sites*—Instagram Live or Facebook Live (Students will need support from caregivers for this option.)

If reading aloud live presents challenges, you may choose to record your readings and post them on a secure school-related space (for example, a Google Classroom; https://classroom.google.com). Invite community members to watch the videos and respond to the chapter or section of text you read in a comment area.

- **Advertise your read-aloud series:** Put on your public relations hat again (recall chapter 1, page 9) and advertise your read-aloud event. Use your reading campaign to promote this event and advertise in spaces where staff and families will see it often: fliers sent home, school website posts, emails, and social media postings (see figure 3.4 for an example). Consider what the research shows about adult use of social media: 72 percent of the public uses some type of social media, and Facebook, YouTube, and Instagram are among the most common social media platforms for adults (Schaeffer, 2021). By integrating the use of media with your already existing forms of school communication, school community members will be informed (and excited) for your reading event!

FIGURE 3.4: Social media advertisement for the chapter book read-aloud.

- **Provide opportunities for responses to reading:** Since people often read chapter books over time (in this case, several weeks), provide spaces for participants to leave comments and responses to the reading along the way. Inviting reading community members to contribute to an online discussion forum honors the participatory culture of contemporary literacy development (Bilton, 2010; Gee, 2010; Jenkins, 2009; Mills, 2015). The following are ways to engage reading community members in online text discussion spaces.
    - *Utilize Flipgrid (www.flip.com)*—Invite people to post video responses to the read-aloud on a password-secured Flipgrid site. Participants can listen to one another's ideas about the book.
    - *Use a Comment feature*—Depending on which platform you choose to read on, invite participants to leave a comment on a thread (for example, YouTube Live or Facebook Live).
    - *Use a live chat or Comment feature*—If you choose to read on a videoconferencing platform or social media site, you may enable participants to comment or chat during live read-alouds. Many platforms allow the host to control the chat feature, so you may choose if and how participants access it to respond.
    - *Post questions on a learning management system*—Post a question after each read-aloud session on a learning management system like Google Classroom. Participants can share their response on the stream and comment on others' responses (if you choose to allow that access through the settings).
    - *BAND app (https://band.us/home)*—The BAND app is a platform to streamline communication among a group of people. It is free, but you need an email and password to log in. Create a thread on this app to invite read-aloud participants to engage in a chat in an online space.
- **Celebrate with a culminating event:** At the end of the read-aloud series, invite participants to join a book talk to discuss the book. Host the book talk via an online space (like Zoom or Google Meet) for a live verbal discussion, or host the book talk in person at the school. Engaging in dialogue in a shared space builds reading culture and community.

Please note: access to devices and the internet are important to consider when planning reading events online. You may consult your technology department colleagues as thinking partners to maximize and actualize the potential of technology for reading culture. You can conduct the plans I outline in this chapter in a variety of ways—during school hours in the school building, after school hours when students are at home, or via recordings and postings on a school website. Every context is different. Consider these plans as seeds to ideas you may adapt for your class or school community.

Use Picture Books to Gather and Share Community Values

If you walk around an elementary school and some secondary schools, you will most likely see displays of picture books and read-alouds happening on a carpet or in a classroom gathering area. When building reading culture, literacy leaders can leverage the power of picture books by broadening the read-aloud from the classroom to the larger school community. While the chapter book read-aloud series requires a commitment of several weeks, live picture book read-alouds in online spaces can be sporadic throughout the school year to sustain the momentum of reading culture–building and accommodate the schedules and availability of participants. You can strategically select read-alouds to share learning community values.

A priority of school and class communities is to create inviting spaces where all feel welcome and celebrated. A school is a place where different people come together and unite in shared values and goals on inclusivity, harmony, and cooperation. Adults support young people with learning experiences that internalize those ideas so students can share them in their communities outside of school. Books can help to reinforce the core values and expose the reading community to diverse authors, topics, interests, characters, and themes. Students should have opportunities to see themselves in the books they read and learn about the lives of others to gain new perspectives. Recall how Bishop (1999) captures this idea of books as mirrors and windows—books as *mirrors* of your own life, and books as *windows* look into the lives of others. You can use technology to engage school or class communities—students, staff, and families—in being intentional about the diversity of books you share with the community. Create an inclusive environment where the books represent different populations and what those people share and discuss in the larger school community.

A significant aspect of literacy leadership is elevating the importance of diversity by providing reading material inclusive of the populations represented in schools and global communities. Technology and a reading campaign are tools that help you share this message. As part of a summer reading experience, I used the #LBReads reading campaign to advertise a *Read Around the World* experience for students, families, and staff. I used Instagram Live to read a diverse group of picture books across six weeks, one book per week. I chose each picture book to represent an author or character from a different part of the world. I used social media sites to advertise the read-aloud schedule and to do a weekly reveal of the book I read online (see figure 3.5). My *reveal* was to add a surprise element to attending the read-aloud.

I read the following books during the Read Around the World summer reading experience. See appendix A (page 181) for more book suggestions to celebrate diverse identities and communities.

- *Along Came Coco: A Story About Coco Chanel* by Eva Byrne
- *Fry Bread* by Kevin Noble Maillard
- *Islandborn* by Junot Díaz
- *My Papi Has a Motorcycle/Mi Papi Tiene una Moto* by Isabel Quintero
- *Saturday* by Oge Mora
- *The Proudest Blue* by Ibtihaj Muhammad and S.K. Ali

FIGURE 3.5: Social media advertisement showcasing the book reveals for the Read Around the World read-aloud series.

Tips for sharing community values through literacy follow.

- **Choose a value or message you want to represent and select your book list:** Think about what you want your reading community to value in the school or classroom, and select a book (or books) that illustrates that value. Values may include community, connectedness, kindness, empathy, friendship, perseverance, innovation, and so on. See appendix A (page 181) for book recommendations.

- **Decide on a structure for the community picture book read-alouds:** There are several ways to integrate live read-alouds into the school reading community. The following are options to consider.
    - Schedule live picture book read-alouds throughout the school year. Consider hosting them after school hours so staff and families can join from home.
    - Host live picture book read-alouds as part of a thematic series, similar to the Read Around the World experience. Choose a time of year to host the series and create a calendar of the read-alouds.
    - Share a live picture book read-aloud as a bedtime story during the evening.
    - Integrate live picture book read-alouds as part of a summer reading experience to promote summer reading and keep staff and families connected to school.
    - Schedule live picture book read-alouds in school during school hours. You may have an administrator, teacher, or guest reader read a book live from a location via an online platform. Teachers can log into the online platform and the class can watch the read-aloud on a screen or SMART Board.
    - Make a read-aloud part of an assembly or schoolwide event. Choose a book that matches the event content.

- **Choose a platform to read on:** Similar to preparing for a chapter book read-aloud series, consider the access to technology students have via school-issued devices (iPads, Chromebooks) or personal devices when planning to do a live picture book read-aloud. Videoconference tools work well for this type of reading event. The reader can control options for viewer participation; the option to share the screen is helpful if a digital version of the book is available and the reader wants to show it (instead of holding up a print book). The reader can read-aloud while showing participants the illustrations digitally. In chapter 7 (page 165), you will see why after reflecting on the Read Around the World experience on a social media site, I moved to using videoconferencing platforms for sharing picture book read-alouds.

- **Advertise, advertise, advertise:** When hosting events outside the school day, the advertisement is an essential component to its success. It's important for staff and families to be aware of the great experience you are providing. Shared reading events are powerful because of the gathering and participation, and online spaces afford educators ways to bring a large group of people together in the same space to build reading culture. Use a variety of tools to advertise—social media, the school website, print fliers sent home, emails, and reminders from teachers. The more school community members see and hear about the events, the greater priority they become. Be sure to also advertise the online platform you will use, and share directions and access information for how participants can join. Plan to send the information out several times during the weeks leading up to the read-aloud. My district created the advertisement figure 3.6 features on the PicCollage app (https://piccollage.com) and posted it on school social media sites each day leading up to the read-aloud event. Once you have a template, you can use it for future events as well.

- **Host your read-aloud:** During the live event, consider sharing about the book and author to open the session. You may share about why the author wrote the book and any special features. You may also share the author's biography from the book. Discuss why you chose the book to read and provide an idea for listeners to think about while you are reading. When you are finished, state a message you want participants to leave with and how the message can have a positive influence in your school and classrooms moving forward.

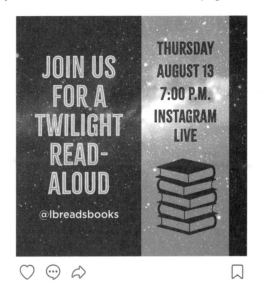

FIGURE 3.6: Social media advertisement for the Read Around the World read-aloud series.

During my experiences in online spaces, I did not have verbal interaction with my participants. They tuned in on Instagram Live and watched me talking and reading as if they were watching a video. Prior to me starting the read-aloud, participants were able to comment, often saying "hello" as they entered the live session. I disabled the comments when I started reading to limit distractions. If you choose an online space with no verbal interaction, it may feel strange (or as if you are talking to yourself), but don't worry—your school community members who join are there to celebrate the reading experience with you. They are just on the other side of your screen!

I realize that while literacy leaders can embrace technology during the school day to simultaneously reach large audiences, most of this section about community reading events in online spaces is about events you may hold outside the school day. It's important to consider your time, contractual parameters, and ability to manage additional events outside the school day. Consider revisiting the traditional events on your school calendar; you may want to update or change to reflect new work in your building. You may choose to add read-alouds to existing traditional school events. For example, if you have a fall festival or fundraising event, a read-aloud that matches the event theme can be a new addition to the schedule. Online read-aloud events may also take the place of a typical night event at your school. If working during the summer is part of your job description, you may embrace these events as part of your summer work since there aren't school hours to consider. Also, read-alouds do not have to be lengthy to be effective; they can even be fifteen-minute events—an introduction to the reading and the read-aloud, whether a chapter from a book or a picture book. Celebrate gathering school community members together to share in a reading experience. This is part of the culture you are building, and every event matters. Families and staff also have busy lives so don't feel the need to overextend the time. Brevity can still be impactful. If you choose to explore community reading events in online spaces, choose a structure appropriate and manageable for your role in your school community.

Declare Your Own Celebratory Month

Celebration is an important part of school life. School communities celebrate common events like seasons, holidays, birthdays, graduations, and academic successes. They also celebrate events unique to the school community like spirit weeks, sporting events, performances, and concerts. There are monthly observances schools highlight like Black History Month in February, Women's History Month in March, Mental Health Awareness Month in May, and National Bullying Prevention Month in October. Add reading as something to intensely celebrate at certain times of year. While educators should not only acknowledge what is being celebrated during a designated month but also use monthly observances to raise awareness on the importance of a topic or issue they should celebrate and acknowledge all year long.

What educators choose to celebrate in schools is part of what defines the culture. I chose the month of February as the time of year when my district honors books and reading in similar ways to how schools celebrate holidays. The February theme in my schools is: *Fall in Love . . . #booklove*. I invite all school community members to celebrate reading and books with extra emphasis at this time of year. There are several ways to elevate a book love month in a classroom or school community.

- **Select a month to declare as your book love month:** Determine a time of year when your class or school community can dedicate time and energy to decorating the halls with book love. Review your school calendar and plan to declare an annual book love month celebration. School community members will anticipate this month just like a holiday, the first day of spring, or another spirit event as a hallmark of your school.

- **Promote the event to students, families, and staff:** Create an image to advertise book love month. Post fliers or posters in classrooms, in the windows of offices, and in hallways. Make book love celebrations the focus of what is visible in the school community during that month. Consider offering students the opportunity to design the advertising posters. Figure 3.7 shows a poster a student designed. As digital tools became necessary during the COVID-19 pandemic, I used Canva (https://canva.com), a free online graphic design tool, to design an image to promote book love month (see figure 3.8).

- **Plan ways to celebrate book love month:** There are a variety of ways to celebrate book love month. You may organize events for the school community or groups. Here are ways you may choose to celebrate during your book love month or use to plan within the context of your community.

    - *Schoolwide or grade-level read-alouds*—Bring students together with others not in the same class to engage in a read-aloud. Consider suggestions from earlier in this chapter about the

FIGURE 3.7: Promotional poster for book love month a student artist designed.

use of technology to assist in such an event (page 87).

- *Schedule guest readers*—Invite guests to read to students. Extend an invitation to administrators, caregivers, community members, or local businesspeople. If you work in a high school, consider inviting people who represent different career paths and have them read from a book or online source about career choices or paths after high school. This is relevant to any high school community and contributes to reading culture.

FIGURE 3.8: Online promotional material for book love month.

- *Host an author visit*—Authors bring the reading and writing experience alive for students. Whether talking about a specific book or their life, this a valuable experience for students to listen to authors discuss their thinking process and perseverance through the writing process. See chapter 5 (page 123) for more details on author visits.

- *Host a book fair or book swap*—Book fairs and book swaps are ways to engage groups of people behind a love of books, but these events may be different from typical classroom book events. Refer back to chapter 2 (page 27) for book swap ideas. More content about book fairs appears later in this chapter (see the Build a Book Fair section, page 98).

- *Create book displays in classrooms and hallways*—Fill bulletin boards and walls with book covers and student work related to reading. Highlight the Currently Reading signs, post book reflections, and hang pictures of students holding books and reading. Decorating with pictures of books and students reading can transform the aesthetics of your classroom and school and signals it's a month of celebration in the community.

- *Build creative writing invitations about reading*—Engage students in creative writing about reading during book love month. Dedicate class time to creative writing or share writing invitations as a challenge for the month.

- **Encourage school community members to design their own ways of celebrating:** When communicating about this reading culture event, provide options for how to celebrate and, in the future, provide examples of how school community members have celebrated in years prior. Providing them pictures of celebrations from prior years as examples serves both as a resource as well as evidence of interest among others in participating in the culture building.

You may also share potential ways for school community members to celebrate when sharing information about your book love month (see figure 3.9, page 96). It's important to

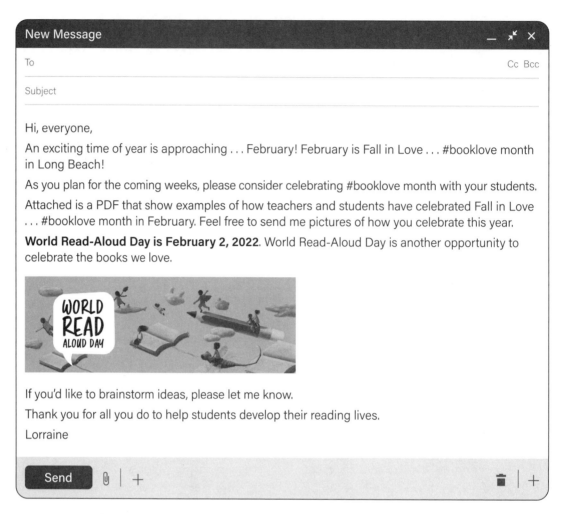

FIGURE 3.9: An email to staff inviting them to celebrate Fall in Love . . . #booklove month.

give people agency in how they participate in culture building. While scheduling activities adds structure and brings emphasis to the reading culture event, sometimes it is the work teachers in individual classrooms or smaller teams take that perpetuate the culture because they are making their own decisions about participation and activities. When you first introduce this new celebration, staff and students will join in on the celebration in ways you may not have thought of. If you are a leader, you must give yourself permission to let the culture grow beyond yourself.

- **Capture the momentum and stay committed:** Fall in Love . . . #booklove month was not a trend, but rather a new tradition that remains on the district's yearly calendar. Take pictures of how you celebrate book love each year and post them on your class or school website and social media, and in the school building. What you make visible exemplifies what matters. Reading culture matters, and a homegrown holiday is an interactive way to get all involved.

Have a Kindergarten Reading Parade

Parades are opportunities for people to gather behind something celebratory—like holidays, winning a sporting event championship, and now, reading! A kindergarten reading parade is an opportunity to reinforce the importance of the growing the reading identities of students, as well as to provide time for play-oriented learning. Plan for kindergarten students to make hats and carry books, instruments, and pom-poms to march in a school parade to celebrate themselves as readers. Teachers often face challenges implementing play-based pedagogy while also addressing academic standards (Pyle & Bigelow, 2015). This example of play-based learning is a way to honor both (Hirsh-Pasek & Golinkoff, 2008; Van Oers & Duijkers, 2013; Weisberg, Hirsh-Patek, & Golinkoff, 2013).

Students' identities begin to mold in response to all the new experiences they have in kindergarten. They learn routines in a classroom, how to navigate a school, ways to socialize and make new friends, and amazingly, their beginning steps to become a reader. The world opens up to kindergarteners through their access to different types of books—informational books, alphabet books, story books, decodable books, pattern books, and picture books. They learn that written words are a pathway to sharing and discovering meaning. They begin to develop their reading identities and the statement *I am a reader!* Becomes powerful. This is something to celebrate with a parade and publicize in a school community. Kindergarten is the start of it all, and a parade provides an opportunity to acknowledge that milestone.

While the parade is for kindergarteners, you can include other members of the school community in this event. Invite older students, caregivers, teachers, and administrators to join the celebration of the kindergarteners and their teachers.

- **Work with the kindergarten team to schedule a time for the parade:** You could attach a kindergarten reading parade to a curriculum unit of study or let it stand on its own. Schedule the parade during an appropriate time during the school year. Consider hosting the parade in the fall after kindergarteners have been in school for a few months. After initially exposing these students to a variety of books and reading experiences, plan for the parade as an event to celebrate that the kindergarteners are now readers. This emphasis on reading identity for emergent readers will pave the way for a school year focused on reading. Students will internalize what it means to be a reader in kindergarten. You may also schedule the reading parade near a holiday and bridge a holiday celebration with a reading theme that features kindergarteners—the school's newest readers!

- **Plan the parade with props and garb:** Elevate joy in the reading parade by having kindergarteners make hats or crowns that say, "I am a reader!" Invite them to march in the parade carrying a favorite book. Kindergarten teachers can be parade leaders and march carrying pom-poms and signs, and wearing special T-shirts. Make signs for display with statements of encouragement—*Keep reading!* Or *Way to go, readers!*—and covers of books the students have read in the classroom. Play music over the loudspeaker and pump up the positive energy for celebrating kindergarten readers.

- **Invite the school community to watch the parade and cheer:** While kindergarten readers feature in this reading culture event, it is also a time for the school community to gather for a reading celebration, which is a reminder of the importance of reading and reading identity. You may choose to invite caregivers, administrators, and other students and teachers to spread the joy. Work with teachers of other grade levels in the school to plan and attend the kindergarten parade. Older students can line the hallways of the school or station themselves outside to cheer on the kindergarteners as they march through the school hallways, outside in a recess area, or both. Invite older students to make signs to bring to the parade that say: *Way to go, readers!* Or *Reading in kindergarten rocks!* Or *Keep reading!* Or *Congratulations, readers!* You may also invite students now in their secondary years—middle and high school—to attend the kindergarten parade; they can serve as role models for younger students as they begin their reading journey. You may even schedule time for older and younger students to read together after the kindergarten parade to end the celebration. If you work in a middle or high school, consider reaching out to a colleague in an elementary school to build connections among older and younger readers. These types of planned interactions make the reading culture permeate throughout a school district and an individual student's journey across schools.

Build a Book Fair

A *book fair* is a reading event where school community members can find their next great read. Students can make choices about their reading lives, and adults can find books for themselves, their children, other family members, and friends. School book fairs are typically held in a central location inside a school. The visibility of the fair represents how the school values reading, which helps build culture. While companies have built their businesses on the legs of book fairs (for example, Scholastic), there are alternate ways of hosting a book fair that don't require partnerships with companies or monetary transactions. Whatever type of book fair you plan to host, your school reading culture will reap the benefits.

- **Decide on the type of fair:** There are planning items to consider when deciding on the type of fair to host: access to books, your audience, and the time of year to schedule.

    - *Access to books*—You may partner with a company to provide books to sell to students and staff and caregivers or company employees work at the fair (similar to a Scholastic book fair). You may also host a book fair with new or gently used books donated to the school and sell them as part of fundraiser to raise money for a school cause. Or you could display the books as available for students to choose from and take at no charge. These events can be schoolwide or in a classroom where a class participates in a class book fair.

    - *Audience*—Book fairs are traditionally held in elementary schools as a way to promote excitement about reading and get books into the hands of young students. A slightly less common audience is middle school students. This is ironic because as students age, there are more external factors calling their attention—extracurricular activities, sports, friends, social media, and gaming—and time for and interest in reading gains competition. Educators must consistently promote reading to older students. Older students are not too old or mature for a school book fair. Encourage a book fair in the secondary schools in your community. Older students may reminisce about when they may have visited a book fair in elementary school; they may be excited to have the opportunity to shop for books later in their school careers. Hosting a book fair for older students also signifies you value reading and making choices about reading at the secondary level. Reading is not something reserved for only the youngest readers.

- *Be intentional about when you host your book fair*—Consider hosting the fair at times of the year when you may need to emphasize book access. You might hold your fair early in the school year to launch into reading, before a holiday recess when students will be out of school for an extended period of time (without access to a school or classroom library), or as the school year comes to an end to promote summer reading. You may also choose to host a book fair during your celebratory book love month (see the section Declare Your Own Celebratory Month, page 94). A unique idea is to host a school book fair during a summer month when school is not in session. Doing this can sustain the reading culture at a time when school is not a focus of students' lives.

  As a result of the reading campaign and efforts to build reading culture in my school community, a group of caregivers approached me to host a summer book fair as a way to continue to provide students access to books. The summer book fair has become an annual event. Our community hosts the fair at a central school location or at a location close to where many students attend camps or summer learning programs.

- **Bring student creativity into book fair promotion:** The more students are involved in efforts to build reading culture, the more opportunities they have to internalize the importance of reading and build reading identity. Invite students to join the advertising team for the book fair to generate excitement and create space for them to integrate their talents into a school reading event.

  - *Create a news broadcast*—Share announcements about the book fair through a news broadcast. You can do this through a student-created video you share with the school community, a morning announcement broadcast, or a school news team segment. Some schools are beginning to explore live streaming options for school announcements inside buildings; this is a great opportunity to promote reading events.

  - *Invite students to design bookmarks*—Students can design bookmarks to give out at the book fair. Have students submit designs on cardstock, and then print them and cut them into the shape and size of bookmarks. Students will be excited to see their artwork on display at the fair. You can see high school students' artwork turned into bookmarks at www.lorrainemradice.com/blog.

  - *Recruit the musicians to promote reading*—Invite a small group of musicians in your school to play music as students arrive at school the morning of the fair. If the fair is a schoolwide event, the ensemble can perform at the site of the fair or at the entrance of the school. If the fair is a class event, there may be musicians in the class who can perform a celebratory song to kick off the event.

  - *Recruit the art and technology departments to promote reading*—Invite art and technology teachers to encourage students to create posters, design fliers, or both to display throughout the school hallways and classrooms. Beautify the school and promote reading at the same time. View examples of such posters at www.lorrainemradice.com/blog.

- **Notice what students choose to read:** Use the book fair to gauge patterns about students' reading lives and interests. According to the *Kids and Family Reading Report*, 52 percent of children ages six to seventeen want a stories that make them laugh, and 40 percent want books that allow them to explore places and worlds they have never been to (Scholastic, 2019). Knowing the type of books your students are interested in will help move your reading culture work forward. Notice what books attract students and what excites them. These are indicators of the types of books that should be available in school and classroom libraries. You may also host raffles during the fair by putting books on display for students to enter to win (see figure 3.10). Organize by genre, author, theme, or topic and notice which raffle bucket students put the most entries in.

FIGURE 3.10: Raffle advertisement at the book fair.

The Importance of Shared Planning

There is a lot of planning involved in making school and class events visible and participatory. If you are designing culture events to appeal to a larger audience, may increase the pressure on you or stretch your time commitment. The ideas I share in this chapter don't all have to happen right away or even during one school year. Reflect on the context of your school or classroom environment and think about which reading event may appeal to your school community or is needed to cultivate reading culture. What would be most impactful to elevate the importance of reading? You may also consider developing a committee to organize and promote celebratory reading events. If planning for schoolwide culture, a committee of adults and older students can work together. If planning for class culture, a committee of students and the teacher can work together.

While there is choice in some of the ideas I share in the chapter, there are also ideas that require stakeholders' time. For online read-alouds held outside the school day, consider offering credit hours to staff who participate. For a kindergarten reading parade, host grade-level meetings for teachers to discuss and solicit planning ideas so you gain a commitment from the team and the event is not a directive. Cooperation and a shared commitment are essential to elevating reading culture. Shared decision making will help move the work forward.

Summary

Commitment requires forward thinking because you design plans for making reading part of a class or school plan for the year. You may notice that many of the events I describe in this chapter are annual commitments; they reserve a place on the calendar! In August, print out your Currently Reading signs and get them ready for display. Also, start thinking about your community read-aloud before the school year begins so you can plan ahead and prioritize calendar space. Mark the end of a kindergarten reading unit to plan the parade. Choose a month of the school year to dedicate to book love. Know when you will organize the book fair so you can plan other school or class events around it.

Reading culture is not a trend; it should grow into something your school or class community is continuously building and contributing to. Learning communities thrive when there is sustainability and consistency in vision and messaging. Not only will school or class culture transform in time as you commitment to prioritizing reading and literacy events but also reading and literacy commitment will become part of how others identify your school or class.

With all of the buzz about reading in your school or class, some students are bound to want to become part of the literacy leadership, similar to how athletes want to join the school team or how performers want to participate in the school musical. In the next chapter, you'll explore ways to position students as literacy leaders in your school or class community.

Reflection Questions

On your own or with a collaborative team, answer the following questions.

1. What are ways people already participate in school events in our school community? How can we bridge current ways of participation to new reading culture events?
2. List spaces in our school where we could host shared events or promote student reading culture displays.
3. What available digital tools can we integrate into celebratory reading events?
4. What access to technology do families have (or lack) that may influence hosting reading events in digital spaces?
5. Are there opportunities for staff to earn professional learning hours or credit for participating in reading culture events during hours outside the school day?
6. How can various departments or disciplines—art, technology, music—support aspects of reading culture events as we invite students to bring their talents into celebrations?
7. What kind of participatory event should we prioritize based on the needs of our students and school culture? Why?
8. What kind of participatory event may be a long-term goal that we do not prioritize right now? Why?

CHAPTER 4

Helping Students Become Literacy Leaders
How to Rally Students to Plan Reading Events

This Chapter Features...
Ways on How to Position Students as Leaders of Reading Culture Work

- Form a team of student reading ambassadors (page 105).
- Host a student-led schoolwide book talk (page 107).
- Host student-led book talks in the classroom (page 114).
- Launch a Readers as Leaders program (page 114).

Students are part of the literacy leadership team in a school or class community. Students can contribute to building reading culture in ways that engage their peers and adults. Providing opportunities for students to be literacy leaders offers several benefits.

- Students can further develop their own reading identities by expanding their identities to include leadership.
- Students can explore an area of passion, interest, or both.
- Students discover new areas of learning through leadership activities, such as planning, organization, communication, decision making, and creativity. Learning while leading can help build students' self-efficacy—or confidence in believing they have the capacity to make their learning happen (Hattie, 2012). This, in turn, can impact their confidence in other academic or social areas. Self-efficacy is a global consideration for literacy educators (Fisher, Flood, Lapp, & Frey, 2004).
- Students will find reading culture events more relevant when they organize the events for other students.
- Students can have a lasting impact on school and reading culture. Student leadership teams can inspire younger students to be literacy leaders in the future. This supports the sustainability (and avoids trends) of reading culture in a school community.

In school, students have opportunities to find a niche where they feel comfortable and thrive—an academic group, a sports team, a theater guild, a musical ensemble, an art club, a writing community, a gaming league, and so on. Creating conditions for students to plan and execute reading culture events provides opportunities that balance engagement and empowerment. Educator and author Bill Ferriter (2014) distinguishes between *engagement* and *empowerment* by explaining, "Engaging students means getting kids excited about our content, interests, and curricula," whereas "empowering students means giving kids the knowledge and skills to pursue their own passions, interests, and future." You do both when you invite students to be literacy leaders; they are engaged in and contribute to the reading culture mission that school leaders set and empowered because they lead projects tied to their interest in reading and, in some cases, their future. This student leadership may lead to new and innovative ways to develop reading culture.

Reading Culture in Action
An Anecdote About Students Who Made It Happen

Jasper and Laika were literacy leaders in their high school's first ever schoolwide book talk. Because of their passion for reading and interest in planning a school event, they volunteered to be part of a team that would host a discussion of the novel they selected: *Long Way Down* by Jason Reynolds. Jasper and Laika, who also enrolled in an honors-level film class, worked with their film teacher to design a documentary project about the schoolwide book talk experience and how they were working to build book love in their high school. They filmed segments of the planning process and interviewed teachers and students about their thoughts on reading. They went on to submit their documentary about their high school's reading culture to a film festival through their film class. Jasper went on to pursue the arts in college.

Adults can serve as a resource for students, setting up the opportunities for them to lead and make choices about how to celebrate reading in the school or their class. Teaching students by example to be self-starters and to continuously evaluate how they may improve helps them learn how to effectively learn. The adults act as *guides on the side* when they encourage students to discover their own plans and solutions (Couros, 2015).

The Roots of This Work

Recall figure 1.1 (page 11), which shows the percentages of students at the elementary, middle school, and high school levels of a school district who say they read for fun almost daily. These percentages have dropped from nearly a decade ago and are at the lowest levels since the mid-1980s (Schaeffer, 2021). With advancements in technology, media, and extracurricular activities, there are more contenders vying for the attention of young people. Reading may have been one of a few choices for how students spent their time in the 1980s; reading is now one of many choices of how students spend their time. In mainstream culture and media, *connectedness* is the epicenter. People connect through gaming networks, social media platforms, and reality television shows' viewer voting. Solitary acts like reading have less promotion and may diminish due to the array of options to occupy people's time.

This is not necessarily a reason or suggestion to pry students away from media culture and personal interests. Research shows there is a positive relationship between reading volume and achievement (Allington & McGill-Franzen, 2021). So, how do you create conditions where students have a personal investment in their reading to create more balance in how they choose to spend their time, both in school and at home? How do you bring reading back into focus and encourage reading for pleasure? One way is to capitalize on the power of student agency; invite students to lead this charge by becoming reading role models for their peers.

Agency is the cornerstone of effective literacy practice (Pressley, Allington, Wharton-McDonald, Block, & Morrow, 2001). It is the ability to influence and create opportunities in the learning context through intentions, decisions, and actions related to the social context (Vaughn, Jang, Sotirovska, & Cooper-Novack, 2020). It's the power to choose what to read or write, explore the ideas meaningful to oneself, and filter texts through a personal lens, leading to meaning-making and understanding. Agency is a common denominator in all I share in this book. The work of literacy leadership is to create circumstances for school community members to act with agency to elevate the reading culture. Reflect on instruction and culture events to ensure they include opportunities for empowerment, agency, and direct learning (Gitomer & Bell, 2016). The culture thrives on the agencies of school community members.

Educators and coauthors Margaret Vaughn and colleagues (2020) did a review of the literature regarding student agency in literacy and developed a model for educators to use when designing experiences for students. Agency incorporates the following.

- **Self-perception:** How individuals perceive their roles as readers, writers, and individuals capable of performing actions
- **Intentionality:** How individuals use ideas in their work while making decisions within social contexts and influences
- **Choice making:** The individual's willingness to make choices and decisions to influence the environment
- **Persistence:** The individual's propensity to persist through obstacles and challenges
- **Interactiveness:** How individuals interact and exist within contexts, and their ability to influence, alter, and expand opportunities within social contexts

These ideas are important to integrate into your plans for student leadership in building reading culture in a school or class. They include components about decision making, taking action, and influencing the social context. Just as I've explored creating social opportunities for adults to celebrate their reading lives to build culture, I will now explore ways to cultivate student agency so students are operational in creating social experiences about reading for peers and adults.

How to Make It Happen

Students can become a part of the literacy leadership team. As you read about these ideas, think about the grade levels of the students you work with and what will work best in your own school or class community. Students may be leaders in carrying out some steps in each event or they may be leaders (under the guidance of an adult) in all steps.

Form a Team of Student Reading Ambassadors

Committees or focus groups are often part of a school or class structure where people gather together for a cause or to work on a project to benefit the learning community. Contribute to building your reading culture by forming a team of student reading ambassadors to lead the reading culture charge throughout the year. This team may be schoolwide or for a particular class or grade-level community. Students who have an interest in reading and leadership can volunteer to join the reading ambassadors team to plan reading culture events. Just as musicians play in a band or orchestra, artists display their work at art shows and in the hallways, singers sing in a chorus, actors perform in plays or musicals, and athletes play on teams, readers will have opportunities to connect with other readers and plan events for their school or class. You may even form a student journalism team or a student media literacy team in charge of information and content creation about the school. Add new niches to your school identities.

- **Reflect on the opportunities students have to join the school community and build on those structures:** Begin this process by reflecting on the structures you may already have in place to create a reading ambassadors team. By inventorying how you already invite students to participate in the school community through extensions, you may want to avoid creating another area you have to manage. Here are examples of how to integrate a reading ambassadors team into your school or class community.

    - *Schoolwide*—Are there clubs students join at your school? Add a reading ambassadors club.

    - *Schoolwide*—Is there an existing literacy-themed club that needs a makeover? Make it a literacy and reading ambassadors club to include some of the activities already in place.

    - *Schoolwide*—Are there existing enrichment programs or extended learning opportunities before or after school? Add a reading ambassadors class where students receive instruction about becoming leaders and integrating their passion for reading. Part of the class could include the field work experience of the reading events.

    - *Schoolwide*—Are there committees or focus groups for adults in your school? Consider dedicating the work of one committee or focus group to a reading ambassadors committee and invite students to join. Students and adults can work together to plan reading events.

    - *Grade level*—Is there free time during a lunch period when students could want to be productive for the betterment of the school? Form a reading ambassadors team. Consider this option for older, independent students who just need a guide on the side (a grade-level teacher or administrator) while planning events (Couros, 2015).

    - *Class*—Is there an existing structure for roles and responsibilities in a class? Make a reading ambassadors team and student leadership team to plan reading events for the class. These teams may even extend the opportunities to other classes in the school.

    If there isn't an existing structure for student involvement in your school or class community, consider creating one. Students who want to be involved can meet with administrators and teachers during the school day (for example, during a lunch period or before or after school). Consider exploring stipends for adults who participate in this work with students.

- **Coach the reading ambassadors team on the components of building agency and orient members to the leadership work:** While students are leading the charge, the adult who works with them serves an important role—a facilitator of conversations to coach students in developing their agency in the group: planning, organizing, working through challenges, and making decisions that will influence the school's social context (Vaughn et al., 2020). The role of the adult is to outline a process for students, and students choose reading events to engage in the process.

- **Prepare resources in your own leadership tool kit to support the students in developing ideas:** While students may be excited and ambitious to begin their leadership in building reading culture, they may not have a lot of experience in how to do so. This is OK! When meeting with students, come prepared with ways to support them so they learn about effective ways to plan and advance the work in a timely manner. Here are resources you may want to include in your tool kit when working with students.
    - A list of ways to build excitement about reading in a school or class that student leaders can manage, choose from, or add to with original ideas
    - A planning time line for a reading event
    - A list of ways to advertise reading events to peers and adults
    - Book lists by topic or theme

    See the reproducibles "School Resources Tool Kit" (page 118) and "Advertise Your Reading Event!" (page 120) for sample resources to include in your tool kit.

- **Introduce the reading ambassadors team to the school or class community:** Celebrate the reading ambassadors team by introducing members to students, staff, and caregivers through email, morning announcements, a school news team report, or other existing methods of communication in the school or class community. Make sure others know who the members are so their peers and adults can share ideas to take to the leadership team and promote to the school community that reading is important enough to have its own reading ambassadors team.

Host a Student-Led Schoolwide Book Talk

A schoolwide book talk can bring the school community together. Stakeholders gather to discuss a story they read independently and celebrate reactions and ideas about the text in conversation with other readers. This reading culture event is different from the read-alouds via virtual platforms ideas in chapter 3 (page 81). A schoolwide book talk can happen in a physical or virtual space, typically occurs after participants read the book on their own, and focuses on the discussion about the story. Adults also host the ideas I share in chapter 3 (page 81). A reading ambassadors team could host a schoolwide book talk. If there isn't a reading ambassadors team, students interested in planning and hosting a schoolwide book talk could host one.

- **Recruit student leaders to join the planning committee:** Advertise the opportunity to plan and host a schoolwide book talk to students. Collaborate with teachers to promote the event in the classroom, create fliers, make announcements, and share information with caregivers so they can also encourage their child's participation. You may also reach out to existing school groups with related themes that may want to bring the schoolwide book talk into their domain—for example, a book club, a comic book club, a news team, the National Junior Honor Society, the National Honor Society, a writing club, or a student government. Groups like these have activities rooted in literacy or service, and a schoolwide book talk may make a valuable contribution to their respective missions.

- **Choose a book that will capture a wide audience in the school community:** Facilitate a discussion among the planning team about the values and interests of the school community; those ideas can help the team select a book. Develop criteria with students to guide them in their book-selection process. Use figure 4.1 and the reproducible, "Thinking Routine for Selecting a Schoolwide Book Talk Book" (page 121) to initiate the discussion. Add the identities in your school community and ideas of your students to the checklist.

Potential Book Considerations:	Decision-Making Process Questions:
Represent a value of the school community	☐ What topics are important to our school community? ☐ What values do we want to promote in our school? ☐ What topics or issues do we not want to promote at this reading event?
Represent general interests of students in the school community	☐ What are students interested in? ☐ What are do students in various grade levels have in common?
Appropriate level of text complexity so a wide audience can access	☐ What age level is the book listed for? ☐ What is the text level of the book? ☐ What grades is the book listed for?
Inclusive and represent a diverse population, provide opportunities for school community members to read with the book as a mirror or window (Bishop, 1990)	☐ What are the identities of the characters? ☐ Where does the story take place? ☐ Whose voice does the author amplify in the story?
Provide opportunities for a balance of joyful and reflective conversation	☐ What is joyful about the book? Are the characters interesting? Is there humor? What will attract readers? ☐ What lessons can a reader learn from the book that may come up in conversation?

Source: Adapted from Bishop, 1990.

FIGURE 4.1: Checklist to initiate the book-selection discussion.

This part of the process may take several meetings. Challenges may arise depending on how well versed the students are in titles appropriate for their age group. Give the student planning team the time and space to read or research potential book choices to familiarize themselves with book recommendations; this results in student choice staying at the center of this process. You could initiate the process by asking students to create a book recommendations list based on their own reading and what they see their peers reading. Then, suggest titles for the planning team to research and select the book together.

You may choose to encourage students to use figure 4.2 or the reproducible "Selecting a Book for a Schoolwide Book Talk Chart" (page 122) to capture notes about the potential book choices. Once the student planning team gathers their notes, members then begin the review process. The team, under the guidance of an adult, selects a book just right for the context of the school community.

Selecting a Book for a Schoolwide Book Talk

Book Title Author Number of Pages	What topics or themes are essential to the story? What life lesson does the author highlight?	What interest areas pertain to the characters or general story?	What age level is the book listed for? What grades is the book listed for? What is the text level of the book?	What are the identities of the characters? Whose voice does the author amplify?	What about the book may bring joy to conversations?
Example: *The Fort* by Gordan Korman (2022), 256 pages	Family dynamics (blended family) Divorce Mental health (OCD) Domestic abuse Friendship Bullying Acceptance	History (bomb shelter from the Cold War) Creative ways to earn money Being new to school Friendship groups	Ages nine to twelve Grade levels: 3–7 Lexile: 740	Mostly male cast in grade 8 with older boys who cause conflict Various family structures (divorce, blended, grandparents) Each chapter told from a different character's perspective to amplify many voices	Different personalities of the characters—someone for many different readers to identify with Humor in dialogue between characters Genuine displays of friendship, care, and concern among characters

Source: Korman, 2022.

FIGURE 4.2: Selecting a book for a schoolwide book talk.

Another option is to survey the school community and invite them to vote on a book for the book talk. The student planning team can select three or four books from the review list to share with the school community for a vote. Using a Google Form or another survey tool, the student planning team can create a way for students and staff to vote.

- **Introduce the schoolwide book talk to your school community:** While everyone in the school community may not participate in this event, it is beneficial to launch the invitation through a shared experience. Provide the first chapter of the selected book to teachers and ask them to read it aloud to their class to generate interest among students. In a secondary school, English teachers may read the first chapter to each of their classes or do a read-aloud during one period of the day (for example, for period one, teachers will read the first chapter). This demonstrates a schoolwide commitment to reading to students. At the conclusion of the read-aloud, teachers can invite students to read on and join the book talk.

- **Consider options for book access:** Book access is an important component to this process; the adult working with the student planning team will need to address access. While the student planning team can brainstorm ways to provide access to books to students, an adult will need to facilitate the access to support participation. Here are ways to increase access to the schoolwide book talk book selection.

    - *Communicate with your school librarian*—The school librarian may be able to access print or digital copies of the book. If your school uses a digital platform for reading like Follet (https://follett.com) or Sora (https://soraapp.com/welcome), the librarian can increase the number of copies of a book available with an additional purchase.

    - *Communicate with the public library*—If you have a public library in your school's town, inform the public librarian about your school reading event and ask the librarian to make additional copies of the book available. Advertise to school community members the public library as a place to access the book.

    - *Purchase books through your school budget*—If money is available in your school budget, anticipate purchasing copies of the book talk book. It is not necessary to purchase a book for every student; you can purchase a bulk amount and distribute books to those interested in participating. After the book talk, collect the books back and disperse them into classroom libraries so that the purchase continues to benefit the reading program in your school.

    - *Advertise the book selection to caregivers*—When promoting the event to families, mention the book is available via school access points as well as through an online retailor or bookstore. Some caregivers may want to purchase their own copy of the book for their child.

    - *Host a book fair during the time you launch your schoolwide book talk*—If you plan to host a book fair through a company (see the Build a Book Fair section in chapter 3, page 81), consider requesting a bulk order of your schoolwide book talk book and have copies available for purchase at the book fair. Work with the company to sell the book at a lower price than the original or gain several free copies through book fair sales.

- **Plan the logistic items of the book talk:** There are always logistic items to plan when organizing a school event. Coach students to consider the diversity of the school community and how to reach the largest audience possible when making decisions about planning. Here are logistic items for the student planning team to determine.
    - *Time of day*—This reading culture event is similar to a school concert, sporting event, or production the school hosts before or after school hours. Choose a time of day—during school hours, in the morning, in the afternoon, or in the evening—that will complement your existing calendar and appeal to participants. If you host this event during the school day, consider it an in-school field trip and anticipate the need to excuse participating students from one or two classes. You may also schedule the event near lunch periods. If you host the event before or after school hours, consider providing transportation for students who want to participate or schedule the event at a time when transportation is already available. Note your attendance at the event, and after a few years of hosting your schoolwide book talk, the planning team will be able to make decisions based on past participation rates.
    - *Choose the location*—Engage your student planning team in a conversation about the benefits and challenges of hosting a schoolwide book talk in both physical and virtual spaces. After hosting many large group events during the COVID-19 pandemic, gathering for school events via a videoconferencing tool has become a norm. Make a location decision that will best support your school community.
    - *Prepare an invitation with an RSVP*—The student planning team will be excited to create an invitation to share with the school community. Options for invitations with RSVP tools are Google Forms, smore invitations (https://smore.com), and a document with a QR code participants scan to RSVP. The student planning team will better plan the event knowing how many people will attend.
- **Engage participants in activities leading up to the schoolwide book talk:** There are several weeks between the initial announcement about the schoolwide book talk and the actual event. I recommend four to six weeks of reading time. Participants need time to access the book, read it, and prepare for the discussion. There are ways to keep participants engaged and enthusiastic about the event during the reading time leading up to the discussion. The student planning team can produce and facilitate an activities calendar. The planning team creates and strategically connects activities to themes, topics, or items in the book for the book talk. Here are examples of activities to prepare book talk participants.
    - *Prepare a reading calendar*—Take the number of chapters or pages in the book and divide them among the number of weeks between the launch and the book talk event. Create reading checkpoints on a calendar to keep readers on pace.
    - *Create opportunities for readers to respond along the way*—Set up a Google Classroom (https://classroom.google.com) or another type of shared platform for readers to respond to questions throughout the reading experience. The student planning team can post a question each week, and readers can share a response to engage in written dialogue before the discussion. This will also create content to reference at the culminating event.

Reading Culture in Action
Reflections From Those Who Are Making It Happen

My Long Beach planning team and I selected *Shouting at the Rain* by Lynda Mullaly Hunt (2019) as a potential book for our middle school's schoolwide book talk. We chose this option because the story takes place in Cape Cod, a popular destination beach community, which is similar to the location of our school. Our school is in a beach community with unique entities recognizable to visitors, just like Cape Cod. When brainstorming ideas to keep students engaged during the weeks leading up to the book talk, the planning team developed the idea to invite students to create a photo story to connect their reading to their own community. Students could take pictures of places—the beach, park, town, and so on—that remind them of settings described in *Shouting at the Rain* since the two communities are so similar. They would then post their pictures with written responses on the Google Classroom created to share information about the schoolwide book talk. This was a way for students to capture descriptions from the book they were reading in relation to their own community. It was also a fun way to keep readers connected throughout the reading experience before getting together to discuss the story.

- *Get local businesses involved*—Connect with local businesses—an ice cream shop, a coffee shop, a pizza restaurant—to solicit their support of the reading event. Inquire to see if managers would be willing to provide a discount or a small item at no charge (a small hot chocolate or a slice of pizza) to students if they visit the business during the weeks leading up to the book talk and mention they are participating in the event. The student planning team may even generate questions about the book to provide to staff members at the local business so they can talk to students about the book.

- **Get ready for the event!** The student planning team can create and organize a structure for the event to ensure participants have opportunities to share their thoughts and reactions and listen to those of others. The invitation RSVP responses will help the student planning team decide which structure they would like to use. Consider either of the following structures.

  - *Participants arrive and then divide into small groups for discussion*—Assign participants each a number as they arrive, which will eventually be their table number. In this model, the student planning team will need to create a discussion leader group. Each member of the student planning team can be a discussion leader. If there aren't enough members on the planning team, students can recruit peers or adults to be discussion leaders. Be sure that each discussion leader has a copy of the prepared discussion questions (see the next bullet point).

  - *Participants arrive and stay in one large group for discussion*—This structure works well when there is a smaller number of participants in the book talk (ten to twelve people). Expect to proceed with caution as there may or may not be many participants in this event. There are many factors that impact attendance—availability, interest, location (digital versus physical spaces), age of students, level of promotion and advertisement, and enthusiasm from staff when sharing with students. But keep planning! Reading culture takes time to develop, and each year brings a new context to plan in. One year may yield something very different from the next.

In addition to deciding the event structure, the student planning team should develop book discussion questions. Each book discussion leader should have a copy of the questions and also be prepared to let the conversation take shape based on participants' responses. While most of the questions may be specific to the story, the following are general questions my students chose or generated.

- Which scene can you not stop thinking about?
- If you could ask the author anything, what would it be?
- If you had to trade places with one character, who would it be?
- Which character did you sympathize or empathize with?
- What surprised you the most in the book?
- Do you agree with the author's decision on how to end the book?
- What did you not like about this book?

- **Host your schoolwide book talk event:** Put your student planning team front and center as they welcome participants and run the show. Students may need coaching on how to address a group in a brief welcome speech and then how to organize groups for discussion. Make this part of the planning so during the course of the event, students lead with confidence. Capture this joyous school event with pictures and share them with staff, on school social media platforms, and on the school website. Remember, what people see is a signal of what the school values in the culture. Student literacy leaders rallying people together behind reading exemplifies the social and participatory nature of building reading culture. This promotes joy and collaboration in schools.

Reading Culture in Action
Reflections From Those Who Are Making It Happen

The typical day of the high school principal is far from typical. On a daily basis, the high school principal attends to matters regarding school improvement, scheduling, caregiver support, student needs, teacher evaluations, and state and federal mandates while working to create and maintain a healthy environment for all members of the school community. It can be challenging to focus on curriculum and instruction to bring about systemic change and academic improvements. Among all the responsibilities, it is important for the principal to prioritize supporting a culture where students have a choice in their reading.

Fostering a love of learning and cultivating student leadership is a priority for me as a leader. Being part of a student-led book talk was a chance to connect with students and build community as we spoke honestly about the critical issues we discovered in the text we all read. Educators and leaders look for ways to inspire innovation and empower students to be passionate about their learning. All the students, faculty, and administrators who participated in the student-led book conversation benefited from the students who created and designed the learning environment. The magical power of this activity was that it not only showed what could happen when students lead the learning but also that adults can successfully provide students with choices and build a safe learning community in the midst of the day-to-day challenges. (J. Myers, high school principal, personal communication, June 16, 2022)

Host Student-Led Book Talks in the Classroom

You can offer similar leadership opportunities in the classroom in addition to a schoolwide approach or instead of it. If you are a teacher, consider hosting book talks in your classroom as reading culture events, or revise your curriculum to include student-led discussions about books. Regular book talks in the classroom encourage student-led conversation and have the potential to expose students to new titles they may not have read without the collaborative experience.

- **Host a book talk to boost reading morale in the classroom:** Work with the students in your class to choose a book they will all read independently to prepare for a class book talk. You may consider doing this once per quarter or semester. Consider the availability of books in your classroom or school and the potential to order new books for this event. Set up a book tasting (see chapter 2, page 27) for students to sample different books. You will need multiple copies of different titles so all students can sample the same books. Then, survey the students to choose their top three selections from the book tasting and pick the book that has the most votes. Invite all students to read the book and schedule a date to have a book talk in class. Students can volunteer to lead the discussion among the whole class or in small groups. Use the resources in the previous sections for the student leadership team to aid in selecting a book, planning items, and developing questions.

  Not all students will read the book independently, even though there was a vote among the class. This is one of those moments that has potential for disappointment and frustration. It's OK. Embrace the students who read the book and are eager to participate in conversation. For those students who don't read the book, they can listen to their peers discuss the text and possibly contribute to the discussion about issues that arise in conversation about the book.

- **Integrate book club units of study into the curriculum:** Book club units of study afford students choice, agency, and independence in their reading lives. Book club units of study are typically designed within a specific genre or format like dystopian book clubs, series book clubs, social issue book clubs, historical fiction book clubs, graphic novel book clubs, literary nonfiction book clubs, and so on. Within the genre, students are given a choice of which book they want to read. A book tasting (see chapter 2, page 27) is an efficient way expose students to the books they will choose from. After sampling the books, collect students' top three choices from the book tasting selection and create book club groups to give students their first or second choice for reading. Book club members work together to create a calendar for reading, plans for discussion questions, and responsibilities to prepare for club meetings. Instead of a book talk being a culminating event, book talks are a regular part of classroom practices as students read, analyze, and respond to the book they are reading in their club.

Launch a Readers as Leaders Program

Over the past several years during the month of June, many social media posts from administrators and teachers showed video clips of high school seniors walking the hallways of their elementary schools in their graduation caps and gowns. The elementary students and teachers lined the hallways and cheered the graduates on as *Pomp and Circumstance* played in the background. While this ceremony can be reminiscent for the graduates as they again walk the hallways that once felt gigantic, it is a celebration of learning and achievement that younger students get to be a part of. Younger students get to look into the future and see what they are working toward during their time in school. Seeing the end point when at the beginning of a journey can be impactful; it's what students can look forward to.

A Readers as Leaders program shares the intention of the graduation ceremony in elementary school hallways. The purpose of the program is to unite older and younger students through reading. Students read together and connect through text. Older students serve as model readers and thinkers for younger students. Cultivate all reading identities through the literacy leadership of older students and the literacy learning of younger students.

You can cultivate literacy leadership in additional ways. Older students can serve as writing partners to younger students and provide feedback while conferring about their writing pieces. This provides an opportunity for younger students to gain writing advice from someone other than their teachers. Older students can publish for younger students. They can write and draw picture books for a younger audience. Older students can also design a coloring book for younger students. An English teacher in my department hosted a coloring book project as a community service opportunity for high school students. Students made a beach-themed coloring book they printed and bound for all kindergarten students. High school students can also visit elementary classes to distribute their work. Think about the creative ways a Readers as Leaders program can enhance the literacy work and student service opportunities in your school or class community.

- **Define how a Readers as Leaders program can work in your school:** Decide if you will run the program in one school or across multiple schools. If the program runs in one school, perhaps the oldest students in the school can be Readers as Leaders for the youngest students in the school. If the program runs across multiple schools, perhaps students in middle or high school can be Readers as Leaders for students in elementary schools. It is important to collaborate with the teachers of the classes that participate to schedule time and space for a reading event.

- **Decide when Readers as Leaders can take place:** This program can take place during the school day as an enhancement to instructional time.
    - *Elementary Readers as Leaders*—Work with grade-level teachers to schedule time for the classes of older and younger students to meet. You may look at a master schedule and pair grade levels that support the infrastructure of the building. If you are a teacher looking to generate this experience, consider approaching colleagues to launch a Readers as Leaders initiative among your classes.
    - *Secondary Readers as Leaders*—This program may complement other clubs or programs that require service hours for older students (see the next bullet point) and can run on a volunteer basis under the supervision of an adult. Middle or high school students who participate can visit elementary students as a field trip from their secondary school day.

- **Make the Readers as Leaders program a complement to other programs in the school:** Similar to forming a reading ambassadors team, integrate Readers as Leaders as a way to support existing group structures in your school. You may consider building service options into the Readers as Leaders program. Older students often strive to become members or already hold memberships in organizations with service requirements like a religious group, a community group, an honor society, or a college application process group. Participating in Readers as Leaders can be a way for students to earn service hours toward larger projects or commitments.

- **Choose reading events to gather students behind:** The program may consist of a book buddy structure or whole-class read-aloud. If pairing elementary classes, a book buddy structure will give all the older students each a chance to be a model reader for their younger book buddy. If smaller groups of middle or high school students visit an elementary school, a whole-class read-aloud works well. Each older student can visit a classroom to conduct a read-aloud and discuss the importance of reading.

A Readers as Leaders program requires collaboration among adults to schedule time for students to meet and plan the time they will spend reading together. Both administrators and teachers can initiate this program. It is another way for adults to demonstrate to students that reading is important. Educators often look to older students to be role models and represent the values and demonstrate the behaviors and skills they learned throughout their earlier years in school. Reading is one of the first encounters students have when they enter school; to circle back to the school's youngest readers and be role models is a great way to bring purpose to learning how to read and to get younger students excited about reading.

A Readers as Leaders program contributes to the sustainability of reading culture within and across schools because students from multiple grade levels participate in reading events together. There is a natural balance in promoting reading for various grade levels across a school or district with students of several ages.

Summary

Establishing a student literacy leadership team in your school or class community promotes authenticity and agency in learning. Use the infrastructure of your school or class to incorporate a student reading ambassadors team or a Readers as Leaders program. Making the decision to prioritize a student group dedicated to reading or literacy work illuminates the value reading has in your school community. Students learn and practice skills like event planning, organizing, decision making, collaborating, and communicating through their work in a leadership group and through planning events like a schoolwide book talk or book talks in the classroom. This is not something that will appeal to every student and that is OK. You create a space for those students who are interested in school leadership opportunities, whether they love to read or not, and for those who feel comforted and inspired by belonging to reading community to thrive in school.

In this chapter, the resources outline ways for students to engage in phases of planning for various reading or literacy events. Adding an author visit to a schoolwide event elevates a reading or writing experience. In the next chapter, I explore ways to incorporate author visits into your school or class's literacy program to authenticate literacy learning.

Reflection Questions

On your own or with a collaborative team, answer the following questions.

1. Does our master schedule allow for student literacy leadership opportunities?
2. What do we have in place that we can add to or change to include a reading ambassador team in our school?
3. What structures do we have in place that we can add to or change to include a Readers as Leaders program in our school?

4. What is the availability of and support for adults who want to supervise a student literacy leadership group?

5. Do we have resources or methods of communication in place to inform the school or class community about the student literacy leadership work and events?

6. How can adults in the school community help elevate the work of the student literacy leadership group? What platforms are available to showcase the work?

School Resources Tool Kit

Ways to Build Excitement About Your Reading Culture	
Reading Culture–Building Strategies	**Our Planning: Make a Connection to Your School**
Transform your school environment so fellow students see evidence of the importance of reading. Examples of this work include putting books on display, making posters for the hallways, and making bookmarks for school and classroom libraries.	
Share a book of the day during morning or afternoon announcements. Survey students about which books they love and plan to share those books each day.	
Bring your love of reading and books into your classes. Share about your reading culture leadership position with your teachers and ask if you can make a connection between the reading culture work and class projects. For example, create a drawing or painting of a book cover in art class and hang the painting in your school.	
Host a schoolwide read-aloud	
Host a schoolwide book talk	

School Reading Event Planning Page
Consult with the adult your leadership team is working with as you plan each step listed.

Planning List		Who Is Responsible?	To-Do List
Planning Item	**Recording Space**		
Choose an event to host. *Tip: Think about which students in your school would be most interested in participating.*			

Decide on the materials needed for the event and create a plan to access materials. *Tip: Collaborate with people in your school for resources you may need. If you need copies of books, consult the school librarian and other adults to discuss book access.*			
Pick a date for the event. *Tip: Look at your school calendar to make sure the reading event is not scheduled the same time or day as another event.*			
Pick a time for the event. *Tip: Choose a time when most school community members are available. If you are planning for a specific group or grade level, check the school calendar and schedule.*			
Advertise the event. *Tip: Use systems already in place in your school (email, morning or afternoon announcements, news team reports, school website, social media, fliers in the hallway, and so on).*			
Plan the details of the event. *Tip: Work as a team to plan the schedule and main activities ahead of time so you can enjoy your event.*			
Make a plan to solicit feedback from participants. *Tip: Leaders gather feedback about and engage in conversation about culture building work so they are responsive to the school community. Decide how you will gather feedback from your participants so you can use it to plan future events.*			

Advertise Your Reading Event!

Here are ways to share about upcoming reading culture events (with permission from a teacher or school administrator).

- ☐ Write an email to school community members about the event and ask a school administrator to send it out.
- ☐ Write an informational paragraph about the event and submit it to read during school announcements or share it on a school news platform. Ask if teachers can post the information on their class learning management system.
- ☐ Create a flier to post on walls in classrooms and hallways. Send the flier home with students as well.
- ☐ Post a digital flier on the class website, school website, or both.
- ☐ Design a formal invitation to the event and ask a school administrator to send it out.
- ☐ Create a video commercial and ask a school administrator to share it.

Book Discussion Questions

- Which scene can you not stop thinking about?
- If you could ask the author anything, what would it be?
- If you had to trade places with one character, who would it be?
- Which character did you sympathize or empathize with?
- What surprised you the most in the book?
- Do you agree with the author's decision on how to end the book? Why?
- What did you not like about this book?
- Does this book remind you of another book or a movie that you have seen? How so?
- What kind of personal connections can you make with this book?
- Which character would you like to be friends with?
- How did the author's style of writing impact your experience while reading the book?
- If you were to cast the characters in a movie or television show adaptation, who would you pick to play the roles?
- Would you recommend this book to other readers? Why or why not?
- If you could give this book a new title, what would it be?
- What is something you would change about the characters or plotlines?
- Would you want to live in the world the character lives in? Why or why not?
- Is this book a mirror, window, or sliding glass door for you (Bishop, 1990)?
- What lessons can we learn from this book?
- What might we learn from this book to bring back to our school community?

Source: Adapted from Bishop, R. S. (1990). Mirrors, windows, and sliding glass doors. Perspectives, 6(3), ix–xi.

Thinking Routine for Selecting a Schoolwide Book Talk Book

Book Selection Considerations Potential books should:	Questions to Help the Decision-Making Process:
Represent a value of the school community	• What topics are important to our school community? • What values do we want to promote in our school? • What topics or issues do we not want to promote in this reading event?
Represent general interests of students in the school community	• What are students interested in? • What are some things students in various grade levels have in common?
Written at an appropriate level of text complexity so a wide audience has access	• What age level is the book listed for? • What is the text level of the book? • What grades is the book listed for?
Inclusive and represent a diverse population to provide opportunities for school community members to read with the book as a mirror or window (Bishop, 1990)	• What are the characters' identities? • Where does the story take place? • Whose voice does the author amplify in the story?
Provide opportunity for a balance of joyful and reflective conversation	• What is joyful about the book? Are the characters interesting? Is there humor? • What will attract readers? • What lessons can a reader learn from the book that may come up in conversation?
	• •
	• •
	• •

Source: Adapted from Bishop, R.S. (1990). Mirrors, windows, and sliding glass doors. Perspectives, *6(3), ix–xi.*

Selecting a Book for a Schoolwide Book Talk Chart

Book Title Author Number of Pages	What topics or themes are essential to the story? What life lessons does the author highlight?	What interest areas are part of the characters or general story?	What age level is the book listed for? What grades is the book listed for? What is the text level of the book?	What are the identities of the characters? Whose voice does the author amplify?	What about the book may bring joy to conversations?
Example: *The Fort* by Gordan Korman (2022) 256 pages	Family dynamics (blended family) Divorce Mental health (OCD) Domestic Abuse Friendship Bullying Acceptance	History (bomb shelter from the Cold War) Creative ways to earn money Being new to school Friendship groups	Ages: nine–twelve Grade Levels: 3–7 Lexile: 740	Mostly male cast in grade 8 with two older boys who cause conflict Various family structures (divorce, blended, grandparents) Each chapter told from a different character's perspective to amplify many voices	Different personalities of the characters—someone for many different readers to identify with Humor in dialogue between characters Genuine displays of friendship, care, and concern among characters

Source: Korman, G. (2022). The fort. New York: Scholastic Press.

CHAPTER 5

Positioning Authors as A-List Celebrities

How to Make Author Visits Part of the Reading Culture Experience

This Chapter Features...

Ways to Integrate Author Visits to Build a Celebratory Reading Culture

- ♥ Anticipate a planning process (page 125).
- ♥ Rally students to prepare for the author visit (page 127).
- ♥ Develop connections between the curriculum and the author's work (page 130).
- ♥ Expand an author's impact to several stakeholder groups (page 134).

Think about successful icons who have become part of the definition of the culture that they have impacted (for example, Elvis Presley in music, Steve Jobs in technology, Tom Brady in football, Leonardo da Vinci in art). They made their marks in their respective fields in successful ways that stand the test of time. The excitement, enthusiasm, and, in some cases, disbelief these figures spark in their audience have influenced what it means to be a *fan*. Authors can change the course of reading engagement and transform the culture of your class or school in similar ways. While it won't be exactly the same as Elvis shaking his hips for the first time or Tom Brady winning his seventh Super Bowl championship, authors visiting your class or school can certainly bring a high level of excitement and anticipation among students and adults—and change the landscape of what it means to be a reader and a writer. Author visits create new spaces for fandom, as authors take on celebrity status in the reading community.

In addition to excitement, author visits provide valuable learning opportunities for students and can complement curriculum work. The following are some of the benefits of bringing authors into the learning space of your class or school.

- **Students interact with text in new spaces through conversations with the author:** While they may read a text, write about a text, and discuss a text with their teacher and peers, experiencing it with the author brings a new dimension to the reading experience. Students can ask questions about the author's choices in writing and learn background information about how and why the author wrote a text, which can enhance the students' overall meaning-making process.

- **Students get an in-depth look at the writing process:** Authors often discuss their process as a writer as part of their presentation to students or will do so on request. They may discuss their process for generating ideas, where traits for characters come from, the impact of their personal life on their writing, and how they schedule time for writing. Visiting authors may also show students snapshots from a writer's notebook, drafts of original writing with revision notes, and different versions of book cover art from when a book was in production. In some cases, there may be opportunities for the authors to conduct a writing workshop session with students. The idea of a process can be abstract for young writers, so to see the author unfold it can solidify the importance of learning and working on a writing project over time.

- **Students learn about perseverance from authors:** Authors often share about how they wrote a lot and publishers rejected their work several times before publishing their first book. Lessons about overcoming challenges, welcoming and applying feedback, and working hard toward something you love are valuable for students.

- **Students may consider authorship as a possible career path:** Students have access to people in different career paths through life experience or media, but authors may not as visible as others students may look up to or strive to be like one day. Making authors visible creates new possibilities for student interests and plans for the future.

The Roots of This Work

Author visits support the notion that people acquire literacy skills through social practices and participating in certain spaces dictates the literacies and discourse a student will develop (Gee, 1999; Street, 2016). When students and teachers gather with their class or a larger community to meet and learn from an author, they are participating in a space where literacies will develop in response to the conversation and culture in that space. Conversations about the writing process, text selections, and appreciation for books and reading all contribute to how students and adults conceptualize being readers and writers. Learning to read and write is skill based, with standardized ways of teaching students how to read and write (Street, 2016). Literacy learning, however, happens in a variety of sociocultural contexts, and discoveries from those contexts contribute to how students and adults develop their literacy skills and competencies.

Literacy is not defined by one skill set. Often, learning spaces are informal and allow students and adults to make their own meaning from the context they are participating in (Rogers, 2014). While a team may schedule an author visit with a formal plan for the session, the learning during the event can be more informal since there is not a structured learning objective. It is not a skill-based lesson. Students and adults are immersed in a literacy experience.

How to Make It Happen

Author visits can shift the trajectory of how students experience developing as readers and writers at all ages. Author visits expose elementary and secondary students to the creators of content written specifically for people their age. While these events will shine bright during the year, there is a crucial planning process. Anticipate this process will take time and layers of organization. You may consider working with a team to plan the author visit to make it more manageable with shared leadership. The following section outlines the steps I suggest for planning an author visit to your class or school.

Anticipate a Planning Process

The author or the author's representative may have a scheduling process or outline already in place. There may also be a class or school planning process to embrace. When planning my first author visit, there was so much I didn't know or realize. During this planning, I not only learned about the logistics of the planning process but also how to make an author visit a celebration that perpetuates reading culture. I learned from students and teachers about how to best welcome authors to the school and roll out the red carpet—metaphorically or literally!—for the celebrity appearance in class and school reading communities. Embrace the first author visit as a learning experience to help you make plans for future events.

You may have other class or school events scheduled during the school year; consider starting with one author visit during your first year of reading culture–building. Learn the landscape of how to best support this event in your class or school community, and then you may decide to host multiple author visits throughout the school year in the future. The following is a planning process to consider.

- **Determine the purpose for the author visit:** Whether wanting to plan an author visit for one class or a larger group of students, think about the intention of the visit. The intention will help you determine which author (or group of authors) you might want to visit. Throughout the previous chapters, I mention pairing an author visit with other reading culture–building events as part of the reading campaign in your class or school. Consider these questions when determining the intention of an author visit.
    - Will the author visit help motivate and engage students in reading?
    - Does the author visit support a curriculum unit of study?
    - Will the author visit help launch your class or school reading campaign? (See chapter 1, page 9.)
    - Might the author visit contribute to and enhance a teacher book club experience? (See chapter 2, page 27.)
    - Is the author visit a culminating event to a read-aloud event or series? (See chapter 3, page 81.)
    - Is the author visit part of your celebratory book month? (See chapter 3, page 81.)
    - Is the author visit part of a class or school book fair celebration where the author's book is featured at the fair? (See chapter 3, page 81.)
    - Is the author visit part of a class or schoolwide book talk? (See chapter 4, page 103.)
    - Is this author visit part of the work of a committee? (See chapter 4, page 103.)
- **Decide how you will initiate contact with an author:** The type of contact to begin scheduling your visit will be dependent on which author you want to host in your class or school. Levels of popularity and accomplishment play important roles in how available some authors are for communication and scheduling. I suggest being open to many authors if the visit does not tie with a specific curriculum project or author study. The broader your search, the more options you will have in terms of accessibility, payment, and scheduling. Decide what kind of author will work best for your intention and consider these options for sharing an inquiry.

- *Investigate an author's website*—If an author has a website, contact information will most likely be included. There may be a direct link to the publisher or author's representative, or an email address that may be a direct line to the author. You may also learn about the program the author offers for a visit on the website.

- *Share a message on social media*—Many authors are active on social media and interact with readers via streams or private messaging. Look at authors' social media pages and see if they accept direct messages or appear to be in contact with readers and fans via streams. You may share an inquiry via a message and get directed to the author's representative or receive a reply directly from the author.

- *Look to your local or neighboring communities for authorship*—You never know if there is a rising author in your school community or neighboring communities who would be willing to do a visit. Authors who are in the early stages of establishing their work may be looking for opportunities to promote their writing to schools and reading communities. Share with friends and families that you are looking for an author to visit with students in your class or school.

- *Reach out to staff members*—Staff members may know an author or may "know someone who knows someone" who has a relationship with an author. This may be a way to share an inquiry or set up initial contact with an author and might allow for a customized experience for your class or school community.

- **Name the details of your event:** If you work with a publishing company representative or an author's representative, the person will most likely outline the details of the event for you, or you may have a menu of options to choose from. If you're working with an independent author, you may have the ability to customize the experience to fit the exact needs of your class or school structure and schedule. Either way, here are common details to anticipate.

  - *Is there a budget for this event?* You may be able to host an author for a fee. Many authors offer a choice of a virtual visit (via a videoconferencing platform) or an in-person visit. Virtual visits are typically lower cost because travel fees are not included in the price. In-person visits have a higher cost because of travel fees and the greater amount of time the author must allot for the event. If you do not have access to any budget for an author visit, consider a local author who may be willing to volunteer to contribute to your school reading culture, or reach out to staff to see if anyone has a personal relationship with an author who is willing to visit your school for no fee or a small fee. You may offer to promote the author's work in your school and professional organizations as well as on social media in return for the visit. While this may not be acceptable to all authors, it is worth looking into.

  - *Who is the audience for the visit?* Decide who will participate in the author visit. Will the author visit with one class, multiple classes, one grade level, or multiple grade levels? The audience should tie to the intention of the visit.

  - *What format will you use for the event?* Compare and contrast hosting the author visit in-person and virtually. Each format has benefits and challenges. In-person visits offer realism to authorship for students but can be costly and require more organization of space in the school building. Virtual visits still offer students an opportunity to connect with an author and ask questions verbally or via a chat feature. The virtual visits often are more cost-effective, and people in the school building can still gather in a central location with access to technology to experience the visit together, even if multiple groups are participating. There is a distance factor in virtual visits; they aren't as intimate. In deciding the format, plan the desired amount of time for the visit. Younger students may require short, interactive experiences. Older students may desire informative sessions with workshop options to work with an author on a piece of writing.

- *What content will be included in the presentation?* Whether communicating with the author directly or with a representative, be sure to choose or know the content of the presentation prior to the visit. You may be able to work with the author to design content, the author or representative may ask you to choose from a menu of presentation topics, or the author may have a predetermined presentation. If you can, talk to the author or representative about the reading identities of your students, books you may want them to highlight, topics that may be relevant to your school community, and the importance of learning about an author's writing process. You may also share topics you prefer the author not discuss during the presentation. You may request the author share a copy of the presentation or an outline of what the author will share with students so you can approve it and avoid any conflicts in your class or school.

- *If hosting an in-person event, will books be available for sale, signing, or both?* Decide if you will sell the author's books at the event. I typically don't have this option because not all students are able to purchase a book at the time of the event. Instead, I provide four or five copies of books for each classroom for the students who participate in the author visit. Students have the chance to read a book by the author, or the teacher will conduct a read-aloud with the book (or part of the book) to prepare for the visit. Authors may also offer to have a book signing portion to the event. Decide if to include one; if so, students can bring copies of the books from the classrooms and have the author sign the books for the classroom so all benefit from the visit.

Figure 5.1 (page 128) is a chart for taking notes on each of these items as you plan your author visit. Also see the reproducible "Author Visit Planning Page" (page 140).

Rally Students to Prepare for the Author Visit

Once you schedule the author visit, it is time for students to bask in the excitement and anticipation while preparing to welcome the author icon into their class or school. This is another instance when students can contribute to building reading culture in authentic ways. Welcoming students to make choices about how to prepare for an author visit creates space for them to act with agency in their class or school community (Vaughn et al., 2000). Students become designers of a culture that celebrates reading. This is a moment to step back and learn from students. Even when stepping back as a literacy leader, it's helpful to have a tool kit with ideas and resources available to offer students and colleagues, if needed, as you work together to celebrate reading. Here are items and suggestions for your ideas and resources tool kit.

Purpose of the Author Visit:	
Budget Amount	
Audience	☐ Class ☐ Grade level (Grade: _____) ☐ Multiple grades (Grades: _____) ☐ Schoolwide
Format **Space to Use**	
Time of Day **Duration**	
Student Interests to Communicate to Author	
Presentation Content	Include: Do not include:
For an In-Person Format: Book Availability and Book Signing Plan	
Notes:	

FIGURE 5.1: Author visit planning page.

- **Read the author's work:** Find ways to integrate the author's book or books into the classroom or school. If preparing your classroom, you can do a class read-aloud with one of the author's books. If the author has more than one book, you can read multiple books in book clubs, or let students choose a book of interest and read it with a group of peers. Students can also integrate the author's works into their own independent reading. If preparing for multiple grade levels to participate in the visit in a school, perhaps you can use a book by the author for a schoolwide read-aloud or book talk (see chapter 3, page 81, and chapter 4, page 103). Exposing students to the author's writing will contextualize the visit and make for rich conversation about a shared text.

- **Generate questions for the author:** Questioning the text and analyzing an author's craft are important skills for readers and writers to practice. It's not often readers get to know exactly why an author made a certain choice in a text; an author visit is a time when students can share their questions, discuss their own analyses, and learn about an author's thinking behind craft moves that students may bring into their meaning-making, as well as their own writing process. Encourage students to generate questions to ask the author and to share their wonderings if they have a chance to engage in conversation. It broadens their literacy skills, which students are practicing when they think about text and meaning-making as a whole from a reading, writing, and analysis perspective. Figure 5.2 provides a way for students to organize their questions. Teachers can use this form as an informal assessment of student thinking about reading or awareness of the writer's craft and purpose. See the reproducible "Generating Questions for an Author Visit" (page 141).

Questions About What Happens in the Text	Questions About the Author's Craft and Techniques	Questions About the Author's Writing Life and Writing Process

My Top Three Questions:

1.

2.

3.

FIGURE 5.2: Author questions organizer.

- Common questions that students of various ages have shared include:
    - Why did you make the character _____?
    - Why did you choose this ending?
    - Why did you decide to put (event) in that part of the story?
    - Why did you choose to write in this format (prose, graphic novel, and so on)?
    - Where did you get the idea for the character? Is the character based on someone you know?
    - Where do you get ideas for stories?
    - How many books did you write before one was published?
    - What is the most difficult part of being an author? What is the most rewarding part of being an author?
    - How do you handle rejection about something that you love and worked hard on?
    - Did you always want to be an author? How did you decide on your career path?
- **Prepare fan material:** When fans visit a concert or sporting event, they may make signs and banners, wear special T-shirts, or bring items to the event to show their fandom. Students can prepare in similar ways when getting ready for an author visit. Take out the markers, poster board, and large paper and invite students to get creative in how they want to celebrate the author who is visiting. Be sure to include artifacts that represent a thriving reading culture. If the author visit is held in the classroom or school building, hang up the signs and posters in the areas where the visit will be held. If the author visits virtually, have students decorate the space behind them to generate excitement. Perhaps you can show the author the fandom through the camera feature on the computer. Students can also set up a welcome area filled with signs and copies of the author's books. Visit www.lorrainemradice.com/blog for examples of student-created fan material for author visits.

    Students may display their fandom through creating a T-shirt to wear on the day of the author visit. For example, one of my students drew the cover of *Happy Dreamer* by Peter H. Reynolds on a T-shirt and proudly showed it off on that day. Author visits are not only about the author's visit but also about spreading enthusiasm for reading. This contributes to the reading culture in the class or school.
- **Plan a student welcome address:** Plan for a group of students to introduce the author prior to the start of the presentation. Consider soliciting a group of student leaders to do this work: student council members, students from a Readers as Leaders group (see chapter 4, page 103), students from a book talk or author visit planning committee (see chapter 4, page 103), or ultimate fans of the author. Students can work together to write an introductory speech that includes author background information, a list of author accomplishments, a list of the author's books, and why the class or school is excited to welcome the author into the reading community (see the reproducible "Author Visit Welcome Address Planning Page," page 142).

Develop Connections Between Curriculum and the Author's Work

An author visit can stand on its own as you build reading culture. Or you may tie an author visit to a project or a unit of study in the designated curriculum for a class or grade level. In the latter case, the author visit enhances the content of and learning from the unit, and you may use the visit as a culminating celebration for the students' work. If you are planning an author visit for one class, audit your curriculum to see where it may be best to incorporate a visit to elevate student learning. If you are planning an author visit for a grade level or multiple groups, collaborate with other teachers and staff members to engage in shared decision making about how you can use an author visit to maximize the potential of a project or unit of study. The following are ideas about how to integrate author visits into curriculum areas.

- **Promote the author's books:** Introduce a book by the author as a recommendation for independent reading and display books in the classroom or school library for students to read. The books may relate to a topic, theme, or genre of a curriculum area.

- **Read an excerpt:** Spark interest for students by reading the first chapter of the author's book for a First Chapter Friday reading (see chapter 3, page 81). The book may relate to a topic, theme, or genre of a curriculum area.

- **Use selections from the author's work as a mentor text for writing lessons:** Capture passages that exemplify craft moves and techniques like dialogue, imagery, use of multiple character perspectives, and foreshadowing that you plan to teach students to incorporate into their own writing. Using the author's work as a mentor text for writing is a way to weave the text into a unit or process you already plan for.

- **Use the author's work for a read-aloud or shared reading experience:** If you have scheduled a read-aloud or shared reading work in elementary and secondary classrooms, teachers can choose a book or several works by the author to use during these experiences. Consider the themes and content of the book and how the reading experience may help shape other areas of learning. For example, you may select the author's book to share a value of the school community (for example, empathy, perseverance, or kindness). Or you may select the author's book to support ideas in content-area curricula (immigration, culture, or historical events). The author visit can be a culmination to this type of reading experience.

- **Invite the author to be part of an author study:** An author study invites students to learn about an author and the author's work as a way to become avid readers and intentional writers. Students learn about the author's personal history and journey to authorship. As they study the author's writing, students develop an appreciation for character choices, the way the author developed the plots, and the themes that transcend the author's multiple works. Students also explore the author's craft, technique, and style to learn how to navigate text and, in some cases, emulate those choices in their own writing.

An author visit can be a motivating factor to add to a project or unit of study in the curriculum. Grade-level teams may already have dedicated texts by an author in the curriculum and may be looking to elevate the experience. Conduct author studies at all levels in students' education experience; they hold value to elementary and secondary literacy experiences. Early childhood classes may study a series of picture books by one author, upper-elementary classes may study a series of chapter books by one author, and secondary classes may study one author with one or multiple works in depth. Table 5.1 (page 132) contains suggestions of author study structures.

TABLE 5.1: Author Study Structures

	An Author Study in Early Childhood	**An Author Study in Grades 3–5**	**An Author Study in Middle School**	**An Author Study in High School**
Introduction	• Introduce the author to students by showing pictures or a video of the author.	• Introduce the author to students by showing pictures or a video of the author.	• Introduce the author to students by showing media (images, video, social media postings) about the author; set up time for students to read about the author independently.	• Choose an author to study through multiple mediums—novels, short stories, poetry, and so on. • Introduce the author to students by showing media (images, video, social media postings) about the author; set up time for students to research the author independently.
Read-alouds	• Read a picture book during read-aloud time.	• Read a chapter book aloud during read-aloud time. Consider reading more than one chapter book by the author across the school year. • Use the read-aloud book as a demonstration text during reading lessons to model aspects of reading.	• Read a chapter book as a read-aloud and model aspects of reading you want to encourage students to incorporate into their independent reading (questioning the text, connecting to a character, tracking a theme that develops, and so on). • Read a chapter book or excerpts from a chapter book as a read-aloud while students in book clubs are using various works by the author. This allows the reading community to discuss and celebrate several of the author's books.	• Read selections from the author's work as a read-aloud to demonstrate analysis of text while students in book clubs are using various works by the author to practice analysis skills and collaborative thinking. This allows the reading community to discuss and celebrate several of the author's works.

Positioning Authors as A-List Celebrities 133

Shared reading			• Read a chapter book as a shared reading experience.	• Read the author's work as a shared reading experience. Use the shared reading experience to practice text analysis, cross-text synthesis, or connections to other content material.
Displays	• Display picture books in the classroom library and the classroom. • Create a bulletin board of the picture book covers that you read, along with student work (drawings, responses), and questions they may have for the author.	• Add additional works by the author to classroom and school libraries.		
Writing		• Incorporate the read-aloud text into writing lessons. Encourage students to use the craft and technique of the author in their own writing.	• Incorporate the author's work into writing lessons. Encourage students to use the craft and technique of the author in their own writing.	• Have students read works in various mediums about the author and do a cross-text synthesis. • Incorporate the author's work into writing lessons. Encourage students to use the craft and technique of the author in their own writing.
Family extensions	• Invite families to learn along with you by sending home information about the author you are studying.	• Invite families to learn along with you by sending home or posting on your online learning management system information about the author you are studying.	• Invite families to learn along with you by sending home or posting on your online learning management system information about the author you are studying.	• Invite families to learn with you by sending home or posting on your online learning management system information about the author you are studying.

Expand an Author's Impact to Several Stakeholder Groups

An author may visit with stakeholder groups like teachers and caregivers to influence their reading lives and engage in conversation about the chosen topic the visit will highlight. Literacy leaders strive to advocate for all adults to impact the reading lives of students (see chapter 2, page 27) and an author visit is a way to cultivate engagement in reading culture among adults. Here are ways to expand the potential of an author visit to adult groups in a school community.

- **Host an author visit event for caregivers:** Caregivers are essential to a school's reading community; they are the adults who support students and their reading lives at home. Research shows better outcomes in student achievement when schools purposely build positive relationships with parents and families (Ishimaru, 2003; Jeynes, 2018). Immersing caregivers in an author visit experience can contribute to relationship building. Caregivers, teachers, and administrators can engage in conversations about why reading is important to how children develop socially, emotionally, and academically. Educators can use the author visit as an opportunity to invite caregivers to share their family and community literacy experiences. The following are options on how to invite caregivers to an author visit celebration.

    - *Invite the author who is speaking to students to meet with caregivers at a separate event—* When communicating with the author or the author's representative about visiting with students, inquire about the author also speaking to caregivers at a separate time, either during the school day or in the evening (in person or virtually). You may be able to plan this as part of the time allotted in the author's contract. The author can speak to caregivers about the books students are interested in and the messages in those books. For example, if an author writes books with topics or themes like empathy, mental health, or family history, perhaps the visit can include strategies for reading and talking about those topics with students at home. Plan to support caregivers who speak a language other than English with interpreters, a translation device, or both during the author visit.

    - *Host an informational session for caregivers about a topic specific to an author's work—* You may use an author's book as a tool to plan an event for caregivers to learn about ways to support their children's reading at home. For example, caregivers of students in middle school may learn from Phyllis L. Fagell (2019), author of *Middle School Matters: The Ten Key Skills Kids Need to Thrive in Middle School and Beyond—and How Parents Can Help*. The event can be a book study. Invite caregivers to read the book in preparation or after the author visit (see chapter 6, page 143) or simply mention the book during the author's presentation as a suggestion for future reading. Plan to support caregivers who speak a language other than English with interpreters, a translation device, or both during the author visit.

- **Integrate an author visit into professional learning for teachers and staff:** There are often topics or themes the adults in a school community rally behind as focus points for a school year or several years (see chapter 7, page 165). There are school values to cultivate and new learning becomes available. Consider inviting an author to speak to adults in the school at a faculty or department meeting, or during a day dedicated to staff development. The author may write books for young people, but that same author can share similar information to what was shared with students, but in a way that supports teachers and instruction.

The author may also be a writer of professional books, and you can use the visit as a way to move instructional or culture work forward. The faculty may engage in a book study or book club reading the author's work (see chapter 2, page 27). Or the author may visit to share ideas from the author's work related to school priorities. This results in an opportunity for the author to promote the book as educators read it.

While reading culture continues to be a priority in school communities, leaders often other initiatives (see chapter 7, page 165). Exploring those initiatives through a book study or an author who writes about ideas that connect to the initiatives is a way to integrate your commitment to reading culture into other avenues in the learning community.

- **Expand an author's presence across multiple schools in a district:** Technology affords pathways to connectivity and can create opportunities for reading experiences to transcend across learning spaces in multiple schools. There are authors who write books across multiple age groups to allow for several grades to celebrate the author together via a virtual visit. For example, if an elementary school class and a middle school class each read a book by the same author, both classes could join together for the author visit. Or if a middle school class and a high school class each read a book by the same author, they could join together for the author visit. Also, each class would read a different book but still experience the author visit together. This option requires more planning since it involves multiple schools and grade levels; scheduling can be a challenge when trying to find a time in the school day that aligns in more than one master schedule. It also requires a more in-depth research process to find an author who writes for multiple audiences.

Table 5.2 (page 136) features an example of how you can organize the work of authors who write for multiple age groups and in different formats. There are sample titles for the categories; however, each author has several books to consider when deciding what best fits your school community. Also, while I categorized books in this chart, don't limit exploration of books based on the ages they are marketed for. This is especially true for older students reading books that appear to be only appropriate for younger audiences. The content can be meaningful in several contexts for students of all ages depending on the purpose of the exploration.

Another way to consider joining several groups of students together for an author visit is to capitalize on the power of a picture book. Picture books create a space for authors to raise attention to important topics in an accessible way to a broad audience. While authors write some picture books to support emergent and early readers, not all picture books are juvenile. Often authors share deep, insightful messages about culture, identity, historical events, relationships, and humanity through their words and the illustrations in a picture book. These messages land differently on young children, teenagers, and adults. Picture books have a place in all classrooms in a school district and in the hands of all readers, no matter their age.

Support the opportunity to learn from picture books by planning an author visit for readers of multiple ages. You may do this as part of a Readers as Leaders program (see chapter 4, page 103) so young readers can partner with older readers to celebrate their reading. This is another example of how reading culture gains a natural sustainability through uniting students of all ages through reading; young readers collaborate with

TABLE 5.2: Authors Who Write for Multiple Age Groups and in Several Formats

Author	Illustrated Book (Early Readers)	Chapter Book (Middle Grades)	Chapter Book (High School)
Elizabeth Acevedo		*The Poet X*	*Clap When You Land*
Kwame Alexander	*How To Read A Book*	*Crossover* series	*Solo* (with Mary Rand Hess)
Chelsea Clinton and Alexandra Boiger	*She Persisted* collection: *She Persisted: Thirteen American Women Who Changed the World; She Persisted in Science; She Persisted in Sports; She Persisted Around the World*	*She Persisted* chapter book series written by various authors to follow up Clinton and Boiger's collection: *Ruby Bridges Maya Lin Virginia Apgar Sonia Sotomayor Temple Grandin Sally Ride Harriet Tubman Nellie Bly Helen Keller Patsy Mink*	
Kate DiCamillo	*Mercy Watson* series	*The Beatryce Prophecy*	
Matt de la Peña	*Love*		*Mexican White Boy*
Gene Luen Yang		*American Born Chinese*	*Dragon Hoops*
Grace Lin	*A Big Mooncake for Little Star*	*Where the Mountain Meets the Moon*	
Jason Reynolds	*Stuntboy, in the Meantime*	*Track* series	*For Every One*
R. J. Palacio	*We're All Wonders*	*White Bird*	
Renée Watson	*Ways to Share Joy*	*Some Places More Than Others*	
Jacqueline Woodson	*The Day You Begin*	*Harbor Me*	
Kelly Yang	*Yes, We Will: Asian Americans Who Shaped This Country*	*Front Desk*	*Parachutes*

older readers to learn from the same author and internalize how reading grows with you as a learner and individual. Table 5.3 is a list of books and topics that may match school values or ideas that both younger and older readers may connect to curriculum areas and explore in conversation. The availability of these authors may shift; if a visit from the author is not accessible, you might still consider having younger and older students join together for conversation.

TABLE 5.3: Books for Younger and Older Readers to Explore Together

Book Title and Author	Topics for Exploration
All Are Welcome by Alexandra Penfold	Community building Diversity as a strength Celebrating culture
I Am Human: A Book of Empathy by Susan Verde	Empathy Caring for others Considering the perspectives of others Compassion
I Am One: A Book of Action by Susan Verde	Activism Collaboration One action can lead to collective change
Islandborn by Junot Díaz	Multigenerational and narrative storytelling Discovering family history and culture Identity
Love by Matt de la Peña	Expressions of love, kindness, and joy
Mango, Abuela, and Me by Meg Medina	Intergenerational connection and conflict Language barriers and opportunities Family dynamics Culture Identity
My Papi Has a Motorcycle by Isabel Quintero	Gentrification Community connections Identity
Say Something! by Peter H. Reynolds	Find your voice Make the world a better place Responsible use of words and actions Empowerment Self-esteem
The Good Egg by Jory John and Pete Oswald	Stress management Anxiety Self-reflection Self-care Prioritizing actions and work plans
The Invisible Web: An Invisible String Story Celebrating Love and Universal Connection by Patrice Karst	Connectivity Human responsibility Friendship
The Proudest Blue: A Story of Hijab and Family by Ibtihaj Muhammad	Bullying Cultural pride Prejudice and racism Family relationships Identity
The Whatifs... by Emily Kilgore	Worry and anxiety Instilling hopeful thoughts
The Year We Learned to Fly by Jacqueline Woodson	Perseverance Resilience Intergenerational storytelling Power of imagination for problem solving

There are many possibilities for how to integrate author visits into your class or school community, and the ways these visits can impact reading culture are vast. Don't feel you need to do everything at once. Since an author visit requires planning with someone outside your school, it may seem challenging, especially if you are launching other new initiatives to build your reading culture. An author visit may be something you plan for once your reading campaign and culture are underway. Or it may be the culture-building event you want to plan first as a way to generate new buzz about reading in your class or school. If you are an administrator, connecting with teachers in the planning process is essential, as they will help develop the intention and contextualize the visit; many intentions tie to what students are doing in the classrooms. Shared leadership elevates the impact of an author visit. Prioritize what fits well in your context and then how to enhance it along the journey.

Reading Culture in Action
Reflections From Those Who Are Making It Happen

Shared summer reads, schoolwide read-alouds, and teacher book clubs were an important and cherished part of our #booklove culture in Long Beach. While selecting the right book to appeal to a wide audience was always a challenge, we also prioritized titles that would afford us the opportunity to meet the author. Having a shared experience with a text is already powerful, but when readers navigate that text knowing they will be able to dialogue with the story's creator about the parts they loved, the parts they could do without, or simply the parts they wondered about, it is transformative.

One visit, following a schoolwide read-aloud of an author's debut novel, culminated with the students helping to determine the title of the author's second book, which eventually went on to win a Newbery Medal. The author thanked our middle school students on the book's dedication page. The visit was truly beneficial to all!

Of the many efforts that foster an authentic reading community in our district, the shared reads tied to the author visits certainly generated some of the most lively discussions about books, made reading more interactive and engaging, and helped our students see themselves as writers. While hosting shared reads and author visits in isolation are valuable, the partnership between the two is one of the most effective ways to build #booklove. (B. Zirogiannis, former director of English language arts, personal communication, June 18, 2023)

Summary

An author visit can be a unifying event for your school or class community, something all share and anticipate together. Bringing authors to your school authenticates literacy practices by showcasing the writing process required to publish a text. Anticipate the layers of planning and consider working with a team through the stages of this process. Students can plan how to welcome and introduce the author, as well as prepare questions to help the presentation flow.

Author visits can also be part of your school or class strategic action plan to share information about an important message or initiative. Authors can support district work by speaking to various stakeholders, using literacy as a frame for the many areas schools commit.

Author visits are not always easy to host in your school or class. There are budgetary constraints and rules about who is permitted to enter schools and when. If an author visit is not feasible at a certain time, consider bringing authors to schools and classrooms in other ways. Authors sometimes have free streaming events via social media platforms during the school year, like World Read-Aloud Day or Read Across America Week. Authors may also host events on social media during the time they are promoting a new book. You may also embrace an author study; celebrate an author through reading many of the author's works, as well as by bringing several grade levels of students together to have conversations about reading. Educators each teach and work in different contexts; plan for what your reading culture needs.

In the next chapter, I explore additional ways to partner with caregivers and families to build a reading culture that lasts.

Reflection Questions

On your own or with a collaborative team, answer the following questions.

1. Will an author visit be a general reading culture–building event or will it connect to a specific curriculum unit or project?
2. Why is an author visit important for our school community? Will it help build engagement in reading? Will it help bring the writing process to life? What does our literacy culture need?
3. Are there or will there be funds available for an author visit?
4. Are there opportunities to involve multiple stakeholders in an author visit?
5. How can an author visit inspire and complement the reading work happening in the classroom or library?

Author Visit Planning Page

Purpose of the Author Visit:	
Budget Amount	
Audience	☐ Class ☐ Grade level (Grade: _____) ☐ Multiple grades (Grades: _____) ☐ Schoolwide
Format **Space to Use**	
Time of Day **Duration**	
Student Interests and Reading Experiences to Communicate to Author	
Presentation Content	Include: Do not include:
For an In-Person Format: Book Availability and Book Signing Plan	
Notes:	

Generating Questions for an Author Visit

Questions About What Happens in the Text	Questions About the Author's Craft and Techniques	Questions About the Author's Writing Life and Writing Process

My Top Three Questions:

1.

2.

3.

Author Visit Welcome Address Planning Page

Background information about the author to share with the audience:	Author accomplishments and career highlights:	Published books the author wrote:	Why our class or school is excited to welcome the author to our reading community:

Write your welcome address here:

CHAPTER 6

Partnering With Home and School
How to Engage Families and Caregivers in Building Reading Culture

This Chapter Features...	• Launch a learning academy for caregivers (page 146).
Ways on How to Involve Families and Caregivers in Reading Culture Events	• Host a book study for caregivers (page 153).
	• Invite caregivers and students to participate together (page 157).

Common among the strategies and events I present in this book is they are all grounded in honoring literacy as a sociocultural practice in school communities to build culture on a commitment to reading and literacy learning. An essential component to school or class culture is designing experiences that acknowledge and honor the social and cultural experiences students each have prior to entering school and continuing at home while they go through school. A student's family and home environment matter to the ways educators choose to invite caregivers to participate in developing reading culture together.

This chapter focuses on the essentiality of caregivers in the reading culture experience in your class or school community, and how caregivers can create their own reading culture in the home in ways that support family routines and cultural practices. There may be annual events, like Back-to-School Night, parent-teacher conferences, or typical performance-related events the school invites caregivers to participate in. Coauthors Monique Sénéchal and Laura Young (2008) call these events "home-school conferencing involvement," and the purpose for the connection is to share in evaluation of student progress (p. 881). The events I share in this chapter are explicitly to contribute to reading culture–building, and your reading campaign sponsors all of them (see chapter 1, page 9). These events are exclusive to reading and literacy development, and their presence on the school calendar is an indication of the school's commitment to students' reading lives and building connections with families.

The Roots of This Work

Literacy learning begins at infancy, years before a child enters the school doors for the first time. Children acquire language and print skills through the social and cultural experiences in their family or community groups (Heath, 2010; Street, 2003, 2016; Taylor, 1997; Taylor & Dorsey-Gaines, 1988). Ken Goodman (1996), a professor emeritus in language, reading, and culture in the College of Education at the University of Arizona, explains that school instructional programs must build on students' early experiences because life before school may already be rich in literacy activities, and they may have already learned to make sense of print. On the contrary, the experiences students have prior to starting school may not be rich in literacy activities similar to those they will encounter in school, and their print experiences may be limited. It's important not to judge prior school experiences, but to use these experiences as pathways for learning in school. It would behoove literacy leaders to honor and celebrate the literacy experiences students have with their social and cultural groups; these experiences influence students' understanding of and growth in instructional work. All children have a place in school, and it's the important work of literacy leaders to build on the various experiences children come to school with.

Classrooms should be rich, literate environments that extend and strengthen the literacy development that began for students before school explorations (Goodman, 1996). Making caregivers aware of this commitment is one step in partnering with families to build a culture committed to encouraging students to read often and across many genres. If educators have curricula and school spaces that create pathways to a student's home life, it signals that home culture and home literacy are important to the culture and literacies the student develops in school. Honor who students are and where they come from as you invite families to collaborate in developing a school reading community.

In their review of the research, assistant professors Osly J. Flores and Eric Kyere (2021) explain that positive relationships between the school and students' parents and families yield positive influences for students in achievement (Fan & Chen, 2001; Jeynes, 2018), decrease chronic absenteeism (Epstein & Sheldon, 2002), and improve psychoeducational and health outcomes (CDC, 2012). Sénéchal and Young (2008) conducted a meta-analysis of the effects of family literacy interventions on students' acquisition of reading from kindergarten to grade 3 and find that parental involvement has a positive effect (equal to a ten-point gain on a standardized test) on students' reading acquisition. This contrasts with San Diego State University researchers Doreen J. Mattingly, Radmila Prislin, Thomas L. McKenzie, James L. Rodriguez, and Brenda Kayzar's (2002) reporting that there is little empirical evidence supporting the notion that parent involvement can help student academic achievement. The difference is in Sénéchal and Young's (2008) study, there was a focused approach on how parents can support reading acquisition. A wide range of skills and grades were covered in Mattingly and colleagues' (2002) study of the relationship between parent involvement and student achievement. While the type of parental involvement can vary, the ideas I share in this chapter support the two types of involvement Sénéchal and Young (2008) define in their analysis: (1) school-based involvement and (2) home-based involvement.

School-based involvement refers to parents participating in activities that occur in the classroom or school environment. *Home-based involvement* refers to parents actively encouraging children to engage in learning and providing learning opportunities in the home. The reading culture events I share in this chapter are school-based events that encourage home-based involvement and invite caregivers to learn about topics that relate to students' academic, social, and emotional growth. From their review, Sénéchal and Young (2008) share a variety of ways parents can influence their child's literacy learning: access to materials, educational aspirations (Dandy & Nettelbeck, 2002), and the quality of their mother's language (Yont, Snow, & Vernon-Feagans, 2003). I considered these ideas when developing the reading culture events I share in this chapter.

Extensive research over several decades document a broad range of academic and social-emotional benefits associated with caregiver involvement in the school experience (Emerson, Fear, Fox, & Sanders, 2012; Wilder, 2014). While family lives differ among a school community, these benefits are evident regardless of family social and economic background (Wilder, 2014). Students of all ages can benefit from social and academic caregiver support when schools provide equitable opportunities for family involvement in reading culture events.

Students need to engage in reading at home and school to maintain motivation, discover reading identities, and see gains in achievement (Allington & McGill-Franzen, 2021).

Literacy development encompasses students' experiences as a whole, not just the time spent in school. Educators are always striving for students to transfer learning between home and school and school and home, and reading engagement is no different. To become avid, lifelong readers, young people need encouragement from multiple reading role models or "cheerleaders" at school *and* at home (Scholastic, 2019). Hosting specific events for caregivers that tie to reading culture–building can help them develop as the reading role models or cheerleaders young people need to grow as readers.

How to Make It Happen

Planning events for caregivers is about being responsive to the needs of students as they develop across the years. As you watch and observe students' reading lives—how they are thriving and what they need support with—reflect on ways to partner with caregivers. You should encourage time for reading through dialogue as you learn about the home routines of students' families.

While time for reading is important for all students—it is one of the most important factors that influences learning and achievement—the access to time for reading may differ across families. Educators often need reminders of this, as days in a classroom and school sometimes feel like all hustle and bustle. Caregivers may also benefit from reminders of the importance time for reading at home for students. Just as students need support with cultivating their reading lives and identities, caregivers may need support in helping their children do so. In *How to Raise a Reader*, coauthors and *New York Times Book Review* magazine editors Pamela Paul and Maria Russo (2019) write, "It's stressful to be a parent. It's stressful to be a *person*" (p. x). But Paul and Russo (2019) go on to explain that even in the most difficult and tiring moments, reaching for a book to share with children can change people's perspective of the world *in that moment*. This is a sentiment parents of adolescent children can pass on to their older readers; while parents of tweens and teens may not sit next to and read with their child in the same way a parent with a five-year-old would, older readers can find peace and new perspective when turning to a book in their own moments of stress, worry, anxiety, boredom, curiosity, and confusion. Paul and Russo (2019) suggest parents of older readers get to know their child's passions and preferences and "the landscape of books that are out there to help her, tempt her, console her, and inspire her" (p. 120).

The following are event types with different structures to consider when initiating a reading partnership with caregivers. You can host all the events I describe in your school building, and most via a videoconferencing platform. Consider what forum would best support families and provide both in-person and virtual events throughout the year. Use your reading campaign (see chapter 1, page 9) to promote these events; your reading logo will be a visual indication to caregivers of the type of event you are inviting them to. As with all the ideas in this book, every context is unique. As you read through these events, think about what would work best for your class or school community and what you can rally others behind and get excited about. You may start with one reading-inspired event during the year, as there are layers of planning when welcoming families. Once you establish your own routines for planning these types of events, consider increasing the number of events in the future.

Launch a Learning Academy for Caregivers

Schools can be a place for caregivers to learn alongside their children. Host a learning academy event for caregivers to learn about a specific topic relative to literacy development at your school. Caregivers leave the learning academy event with new information and strategies to support their child at home.

I often receive inquiries from caregivers asking how they can help their child at home, how they can support their reluctant reader, and what to consider when choosing books to read. In response to these inquires, I began to host themed events about the most frequently asked questions. The following are considerations for planning.

Create a Name for the Learning Event

Use a name that signals the event is for adult learning and follow up with a specific focus so the content is responsive to student needs in your school and (possibly) caregivers inquiries. I use the term *learning event* to refer to an adult learning event throughout this chapter. For example, the event name in my school community is *Parent Academy*. Some other names for these types of events include: *Parent University, Literacy Academy, Parent Learning Institute,* or *Caregivers Coaching Institute*. The learning event, while always focused on some aspect of literacy development, usually has a theme you give to caregivers. In May, the theme may support readers over the summer to prevent summer slide, as in Ways to Make Time for Reading This Summer. In October, the theme may be about ways to coach readers at home to set up a new school year, as in Coaching Our Kids.

Decide on the Target Audience

Learning events can target a wide audience; you can present general information with specific strategies for students of certain ages. You may also consider having learning events for caregivers of students at specific grade levels so the information can be relevant to the target audience. For example, I started a Parent Academy: Junior Edition event dedicated to caregivers of students in preK, kindergarten, and grades 1 and 2, the information and strategies geared toward emergent and early literacy development. In August, before our school year begins, I host a Parent Academy: Junior Edition for parents of students entering preK and kindergarten dedicated toward supporting caregivers with building readiness for school at home. In October, I expand the audience and host the event for caregivers of preK, kindergarten, and grades 1 and 2 students and provide information and strategies for supporting young readers and writers. I inform caregivers about what children in their emergent and early literacy phases look like and how to cultivate their reading and writing lives at home.

You can hold similar events for caregivers of students in middle and high school, as the reading lives of these students will shift as they enter their secondary school years—book options change, lifestyles shift, and new habits develop. It's important to support caregivers along the continuum of how students develop as readers.

Schedule Events Based on Where Students Are in Their Reading Development

School calendars often fill up quickly! There are essential events that reserve space during school year; as a literacy leader who is establishing reading culture, it is important to prioritize one or more events dedicated toward partnering with caregivers relative to reading. Doing this reinforces the school's commitment to supporting students' reading lives. Literacy development doesn't happen in isolation in a classroom; caregivers are essential to their child's development. In some ways, what is on your school calendar is an indication of what you prioritize as a leader. The calendar can also be a tool for planning themed events to anticipate how to support caregivers. Table 6.1 (page 148) is a list of potential learning event themes with specified student grade-level groups based on how readers typically develop across a school year. The content would differ across grades, but the topic remains relevant.

Decide on a Structure for the Event

There are factors that may influence the structure you choose for your event—the grade-level span of the audience, how many people attend, the purpose for the event, and the space available. Consider these two structures.

- **One group, one informational session:** In this structure, all caregivers stay in one space and administrators or teachers share information in a formal presentation style.

- **Start in one group, then break off into smaller workshop sessions:** In this structure, all caregivers gather in one space at the beginning of the event for a brief introductory presentation of information related to the event theme. Caregivers then choose workshops to attend that are specific to the interest or age of their child (see figure 6.1, page 150) or all caregivers carousel through a series of short workshops that target areas related to the event theme. If hosting in your school building, hold workshops in different classrooms or school spaces. If hosting virtually, consider using breakout rooms for workshops (see figure 6.2, page 150) or separate virtual meeting links (see figure 6.3, page 151) for each workshop. With this event structure, you will need participation from colleagues to host workshops (see figure 6.4, page 151, for a sample email). Consider hosting planning meetings as you lead up to the event so your team can participate in shared decision making about event items and you are aware of the content colleagues will share in their workshop sessions.

Advertise and Promote the Event Frequently

Advertise and promote the event to caregivers in various ways leading up to the event to ensure all are aware of the event and have an opportunity to participate. Following are ways to advertise and promote your event.

- If possible, put the Parent Academy event on the class or school calendar at the start of the school year so caregivers are aware of the event in advance. If you decide to host the event after the calendar is produced, you may skip this step.

- Send a Save the Date flier home (on paper and via email) at least three weeks before your event to raise awareness.

- Send a letter (on paper) home with students that includes details about the event. Suggestion: Send a letter two weeks prior to the event.

TABLE 6.1: Potential Caregiver Learning Event Themes by Grade-Level Group

Time of Year	Learning Academy Theme	Caregiver Audience	Possible Content
Anytime in a class, grade level, or school Suggestions: **To start the school year**—August, September, or October **A midyear refresher**—February or March	Rebuilding Reading Readiness: Establishing Routines for Reading at Home	Grades preK–12	**PreK–2**—Encourage adults to read with their children at home for enjoyment and provide mild coaching for development in phonological awareness, phonemic awareness, phonics, and comprehension. **Grades 3–8**—Teach caregivers how to encourage student independence at home and talk to children about their reading to foster enjoyment and comprehension. **Grades 9–10**—Coach adults to help students manage their workload, extracurricular activities, and employment while making time to read at home for enjoyment and learning. **Grades 11–12**—Teach their children how to foster reading routines at home for enjoyment and prepare for college and career.
October or November	Work in Their Shoes: Experience What It's Like to Be a Reader or Writer at Your Child's Age	Grades preK–12	Simulate a school environment where caregivers take on the role of students and engage in reading and writing work in the classroom. An administrator or teacher can teach a reading lesson and writing lesson that caregivers participate in as if they were readers and writers of that age.
October or November	Artificial Intelligence and Its Place in Your Child's Reading and Writing Life	Grades 6–12	Inform caregivers of literacy-based artificial intelligence (AI) platforms and model how to use them. Discuss how AI platforms can influence a student's reading and writing life in and out of school.
November or December	Books Look Different These Days: Preparing for Your Adolescent Reader	Grades 5–8	Inform caregivers about how books change from picture books to early readers to middle grades novels to young adult novels. Inform about book formats (highly illustrated, graphic novel, verse, prose, and so on). Teach adults how to encourage their child's growing independence as a reader. Demonstrate how to navigate conversations about mature topics in middle grades and young adult novels.

Partnering With Home and School 149

January	Your Child is Reading: Ways to Support Your Developing Reader at Home	Kindergarten, Grade 1	Teach adults to read at home with children for enjoyment. Practice ideas for building phonological awareness, phonemic awareness, concepts of print, phonics, and comprehension. Review different types of books young readers read and their purpose (decodables, leveled texts, trade books, emergent storybooks, and so on).
April, May, or June	Surf, Not Slide: Keeping Your Child Engaged in Reading This Summer	Grades K–12	Inform caregivers about summer slide and supporting research. Offer strategies for encouraging reluctant readers. Provide ways to integrate reading into play and routines that tie to extracurricular activities. Share access points for books and reading material.
Anytime in a class, grade level, or school	Ways to Make Reading Real: Embracing Multimodal Reading to Encourage Your Teen	Grades 9–12	Inform caregivers about multimodal approaches to reading and the expanding definition of *text*. Share data about teens and media use (visit https://www.commonsensemedia.org/search/teens%20and%20media%20use for information). Provide ways to connect student interests in media to reading experiences. Provide caregivers with digital access points for students to blogs, news publications, ebook platforms, and so on, so they can spend time reading with their children and talk to them about their reading.
Anytime needed for families of students who are learning English as a new language in a class, grade level, or school	Celebrate Your Native Language in Literacy Development: The Benefit of Reading in Multiple Languages	Grades K–12	Inform caregivers about how proficiency in a native language can support the learning of a new language. Introduce bilingual books as a tool to support reading development. Model the use of translation tools to support students and families in navigating English in school. Share access points for books and other reading materials. Celebrate how different languages enhance a school community.

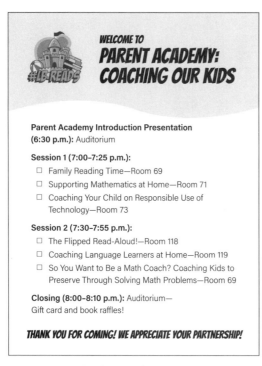

FIGURE 6.1: Sample schedules of Parent Academy events in a school building.

Workshop Title: Participants will attend two workshops (twenty minutes each)	Room
Writing in PreK: Learn about ways to develop and support your child's emergent writing using oral language, colors, and shapes. **Target Grade Level:** PreK, Kindergarten	1
Easy Ways to Build Phonological and Phonemic Awareness at Home: Learn about fun activities to practice early language skills using household items with minimal preparation. **Target Grade Level:** PreK, Kindergarten, Grade 1	2
How to Help Your Child Choose a Just Right Book: Learn about how to motivate your child to read and keep reading alive at home.	3
Tips and Tricks for Finding Moments of literacy in Everyday Life: Learn about how to integrate singing, talking, reading, writing, and playing into everyday moments (the host will teach this workshop in English and Spanish). **Consejos y trucos para encontrar momentos de alfabetización en la vida cotidiana:** Aprende a integrar el canto, la conversación, la lectura, la escritura el juego en los momentos cotidianos (este taller se impartirá en inglés y español).	4
Sound Boxes for Phonemic Awareness: Learn about how to use an easy tool to help your child decode and spell words.	5
Digital Resources at Home: Learn about the digital reading tools students use in school that you can also use at home.	6
All About RAZ-Kids: Learn about how to navigate RAZ-Kids, an interactive reading tool that students use in school (the host will teach this workshop in English and Spanish). **Todo sobre RAZ-Kids:** Aprenda a navegar por esta herramienta de lectura interactiva que los aluminos utilizan en la escuela (este taller se impartirá en inglés y español).	7
How to Talk to Your Child About Reading: Learn about different questioning techniques to help deepen your child's understanding of reading.	8

FIGURE 6.2: Sample schedule of a Parent Academy event held in digital space using breakout rooms.

Partnering With Home and School   151

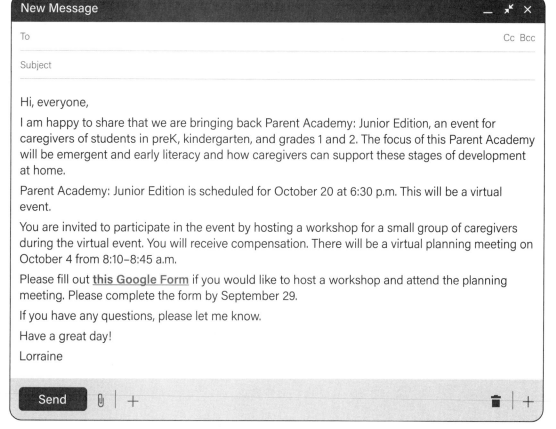

Presenter	Meeting Link	Link to resources you want to share with caregivers (please check the link to make sure it's accessible to people outside our network)
Presenter A	Join Zoom meeting Meeting ID: Passcode:	Emergent writing resources
Presenter B	Join Zoom meeting Meeting ID: Passcode:	Activities for developing phonological awareness at home

FIGURE 6.3: Part of a resource for caregivers to access meeting links that pairs with the schedule in figure 6.2.

New Message

To   Cc Bcc

Subject

Hi, everyone,

I am happy to share that we are bringing back Parent Academy: Junior Edition, an event for caregivers of students in preK, kindergarten, and grades 1 and 2. The focus of this Parent Academy will be emergent and early literacy and how caregivers can support these stages of development at home.

Parent Academy: Junior Edition is scheduled for October 20 at 6:30 p.m. This will be a virtual event.

You are invited to participate in the event by hosting a workshop for a small group of caregivers during the virtual event. You will receive compensation. There will be a virtual planning meeting on October 4 from 8:10–8:45 a.m.

Please fill out **this Google Form** if you would like to host a workshop and attend the planning meeting. Please complete the form by September 29.

If you have any questions, please let me know.

Have a great day!

Lorraine

Send

FIGURE 6.4: An email to solicit participation from colleagues in a Parent Academy.

- Send an email to caregivers. Suggestion: Send emails two weeks prior to the event, a week prior to the event, and then a reminder three days prior to the event.
- Make a video about the event similar to a commercial advertisement. Share a link to the video in an email to caregivers, post the video on a class or school website, or both. (Scan the QR code to see an example of how I advertised a Parent Academy event through a video.)
- Post information on a parent portal.
- Post information on a class, school, or district website.
- Post information on class or school social media sites.
- Contact caregiver groups like the PTA and ask members to promote the event within their group and on their social media pages.
- Encourage registration (via paper or a digital form) to help with planning. Send home a (paper) registration form students can give to their teacher once their caregivers complete it. QR codes and links to digital forms are helpful tools for online registrations. Options for registration may be helpful to families.
- Share advertising material in the languages students represent in your class or school community.

Incorporate Additional Attractions to the Event

Consider the following options.

- **Ask local businesses to donate a gift card or coupon to include in a raffle:** You may also ask the PTA for donations of books, games, or both. Staff members may also donate raffle prizes. For example, one staff member in my school has a spouse who works for a professional baseball team and donated two tickets to a game. Pair a book list with each raffle prize matching the theme of each book. Appendix A (page 181) provides sample book lists by theme for raffle prizes, including books about food, sports, clothing, and community. For example, match baseball tickets with a baseball book list and match ice cream with an ice cream book list.
- **Work with parent leaders to host a book fair in conjunction with the Parent Academy event:** You could also host a book drive; participants bring gently used books to the event and are welcome to take books others bring free. This is another form of a book swap. Students eventually *age out* (or become too mature) of books they want to read independently, so caregivers who attend usually bring books for other age groups.
- **Attach the Parent Academy event to another event in your school:** Schedule a Parent Academy when there is another event happening caregivers may be interested in attending. Is there a student artwork display or art show in the school you can advertise while inviting caregivers to Parent Academy? Is there a school board meeting or another type of meeting event your Parent Academy can partner with? Get creative with how to position Parent Academy as a must-attend event!

Use Parent Academy to Promote Other Forms of School Reading Culture

While the purpose of the event is to inform caregivers about aspects of reading development, you may also use it as an opportunity to promote other reading events happening during the school day to share your reading culture. Share about author visits (see chapter 5, page 123), schoolwide book talks or read-alouds (see chapter 4, page 103), summer reading initiatives (see chapter 1, page 9), book fairs (see chapter 3, page 81), and work happening in classrooms. This demonstrate the school's commitment to reading. Student engagement in reading during the school day is important for caregivers to witness.

Send Home a Resource Kit

It's helpful for caregivers to leave the Parent Academy event with resources to refer back to and utilize at home. Resource options follow.

- A list of websites and links to articles caregivers can refer to for more information about the topic of the Parent Academy event
- A list of book titles that refer to the topic of the Parent Academy event
- A list of book titles to share with their child at home (See appendix B, page 187 for sample book lists to share with caregivers of readers at various ages; list high-interest books so students can read for enjoyment, which may lead to conversations about reading at home. Fiction and nonfiction books should be on the list.)
- A copy of the presentations shared during the event
- Prompts and questions caregivers can use to talk to their child about the Parent Academy event topic (See the reproducible "Tips for Caregivers," page 164, for sample prompts and questions to support caregivers when talking to their child about their reading and tips for supporting reading engagement at home.)
- Activities presented during the Parent Academy workshops (If caregivers participate in a workshop that features a game or activity they can do at home, send home a set of materials so they can implement the strategies at home right away.)

Ask for Feedback

Share a brief survey with participants to gather their feedback about the Parent Academy event. Their feedback will help you plan future events.

Host a Book Study for Caregivers

Students may participate in book clubs using the text in curriculum units of study and schoolwide book talks (see chapter 4, page 103), and teachers and staff may have the opportunity to participate in book clubs (see chapter 2, page 27). Extend this form of reading culture–building to caregivers by inviting them to participate in a book study. You may choose an informative book on a particular topic related to social, emotional, or academic development, or you may choose a book for students to support caregivers with strategies on how to talk about what their child is reading.

Engaging caregivers in the acts of reading and talking about reading encourages their reading identities and connects those at home with those in school to collectively cultivate the reading lives of students. During these conversations, prioritize learning about caregivers' relationships with reading, and how they feel you can best support their child. You may collect information about the families in your class or school to represent family identities you then integrate into reading events at school. For example, what are some family traditions? What are popular hobbies or sports families enjoy?

What ethnicities do families represent? What are family cultural practices? What staples in the community can families identify with? What is important to the community culture outside of school? Here are considerations to explore if you choose to host a book study for caregivers.

- **Choose a book or topic, whichever is more accessible based on your goal:** Think about the conversations that interest caregivers based on other interactions you may have had and what you observe in students at school. Consider how a book study can support those conversations. Should you devote conversations to developing students' reading lives, understanding how students develop socially, or improving student mental health and emotional well-being? Whatever the topic, a book study can open and guide the conversation. Table 6.2 features titles and topics to consider based on the needs in your context.

TABLE 6.2: Sample Books for a Caregiver Book Study

Book Title	Topic
How to Raise a Reader by Pamela Paul and Maria Russo	Reading development (birth to young adult) Reading engagement (birth to young adult) Book suggestions (birth to young adult)
Life Skills for Teens by Karen Harris	Teenage parenting
Middle School Matters: The Ten Key Skills Kids Need to Thrive in Middle School and Beyond—and How Parents Can Help by Phyllis L. Fagell	Transition from childhood to adolescence Skills for thriving in middle school and beyond
Raising an Entrepreneur: How to Help Your Children Achieve Their Dreams—99 Stories From Families Who Did by Margot Machol Bisnow	Cultivating confidence, creativity, and resilience in young people
Reader, Come Home: The Reading Brain in a Digital World by Maryanne Wolf	Impact of technology on reading and brain functioning (early childhood, adolescence, and young adult)
Reading Magic: Why Reading Aloud to Our Children Will Change Their Lives Forever by Mem Fox	Reading to and with children (early childhood)

- **Share an invitation with caregivers and advertise your event:** You may use strategies similar to those you use to advertise and promote a Parent Academy event (see page 146). You may choose to have one book study meeting to discuss the content in the book or host a few meetings, depending on the structure and content of the book. Paul and Russo (2019) structured their book *How to Raise a Reader* by the age of the reader. I chose to host two separate book study meetings—one for caregivers of elementary school students and one for caregivers of middle and high school students (see figure 6.5). Unique to a book study is addressing caregivers' access to the book. Here are options for caregivers to access the book for the book study.
  - Provide books to those interested in participating in the book study. This may be an option if your school or district has budgeted the money to buy a bulk set of the chosen book. You may ask caregivers to return their book after the book study to reuse them in the future.

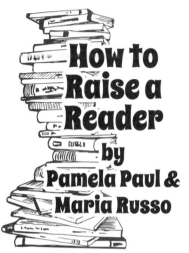

FIGURE 6.5: An invitation and reading schedule for a book study on *How to Raise a Reader*.

- Contact your public library and request the book be available in print and digitally. Public librarians may be willing to partner with you to have print copies available.
- Offer the option for caregivers to purchase the book online or at a local bookstore.

Provide copies of excerpts from the book for all who participate but may not want or access the book. Use a translation service or tool for excerpts in multiple languages, if needed.

Host the event and stress that caregivers don't need to read the book to attend. Participation in the conversation about ideas the book addresses is a valuable experience. I often struggle with this as a literacy leader—if I don't provide books to everyone interested in participating, how can I ensure all caregivers have access to the content? This is something I continue to work on in my own practices. Make reading the book an option, but not a requirement to participate.

- **Start your event with acknowledgments about the diversity in peoples' lifestyles and home routines:** Lead with sensitivity when bringing families together and avoid generalizations. Part of a book study is to engage in conversation. To invite conversation, name how everyone experiences reading, learning, and life routines differently. I begin the conversation with the following agreement statements.
  - Everyone's home life is different.
  - Every adult has a different relationship with reading.
  - Every child has a different relationship with reading.
  - "It's stressful to be a parent. It's stressful to be a *person*" (Paul & Russo, 2019, p. x).
  - There isn't one "right" way to raise a reader.
  - We're so happy you're here. This is a safe space. We can learn from one another.

Prepare questions to generate conversation about the reading and topic. Some caregivers will read the book prior to participating in the book study. Other caregivers may not have been able to read the book, but came to learn. Anticipate both scenarios so you include everyone. Table 6.3 lists questions to help participants enter the discussion.

TABLE 6.3: Discussion Questions for Caregiver Book Study

Questions for Discussion About a Text	Questions for Discussion About a Topic
What did you affirm while reading? What did you learn that may influence how you approach reading or learning with your child? What did you find interesting and want to discuss with others? What were you wondering about while reading? Do you have any experiences or advice to share related to the book content that have been successful in your home?	Why are you interested in learning about this topic? What has been mentioned about this topic that you want to talk more about? What are you wondering about the topic that we can explore through conversation? Do you have any experiences or advice to share related to the topic that have been successful in your home? How has listening to others influenced your own learning?

- **Consider incorporating an author visit (see chapter 5, page 123) with the author of the book in the book study:** Host an author visit with a children's books or young adult author and engage in a book study of books young people are reading.
- **Use the book study as an opportunity to create ongoing future dialogue about the topic:** This one event can lead to a stronger relationship among administrators, teachers, staff, and caregivers. While the book study will end, the relationships can remain and encourage ongoing partnerships.

Reading Culture in Action
Reflections From Those Who Are Making It Happen

The *How to Raise a Reader* (Paul & Russo, 2019) book study provided an opportunity for caregivers to come together to discuss strategies for supporting readers at home while managing many other responsibilities. Teachers and administrators also joined this event. A parent who attended the book study shared the following email after the event.

> *Happy Saturday! I just had to share this picture. We are celebrating my son's birthday and I am giving away books. I got the idea from the* How to Raise a Reader *book! Thank you.* (L. Voege, parent, personal communication, April 24, 2021)

The parent included a picture of the baskets of books she prepared for the birthday party. This illustrates how reading and learning together through a reading culture event can influence a caregiver's practices and decisions outside of school to support the importance of reading.

Invite Caregivers and Students to Participate Together

Caregivers can learn how their child is immersed in reading in the school and partner with their child for a reading culture event. Teachers and administrators also have an opportunity to learn more about the families in their class or school community to prioritize inclusivity and collaboration. Parent engagement should not only be about educators telling families what they should do but also about establishing two-way communication so families and educators coconstruct school culture (Auerbach, 2010). Design events (see the following sections) so caregivers have the opportunity to share their thoughts, ideas, and responses to literature and reveal their perspectives. Also welcome caregivers to make choices with their child about books to read as they participate in activities like the school library tour or a book tasting. These events are opportunities for literacy leaders to receive feedback from caregivers and engage them in dialogue about what is important when it comes to a thriving reading culture for their child. Partnering with caregivers shifts leadership authority from one central voice to that of various stakeholder groups, who bring unique perspectives and contribute to shared decision making (Daniel, 2017).

You may use many of the strategies I mention in previous chapters when planning an event for caregivers and students to share. It's unnecessary to create entirely new experiences for caregivers; caregivers should feel welcome to contribute to the reading culture so all school community members share in a common vision and experience. Decide when you will host an event for caregivers and students, and use the advertising suggestions I outlined in previous sections to promote the event (see page 147). Invite caregivers of younger readers to join during the school day to participate in a reading event in their child's class. Schedule a separate event after school or in the evening for caregivers of readers of all ages (elementary and secondary). Consider providing opportunities at different times during the year, as caregivers' work schedules vary. If you choose to host an event during the school day in your classroom, plan ahead to ensure students whose caregivers can't attend have another adult to celebrate reading with (a teacher, teaching assistant, administrator, family friend, and so on). Here are the types of reading events caregivers and their child can celebrate together.

Host a Book Tasting

A book tasting is an interactive experience caregivers and their child can participate in together to learn about the different types of books available for readers at the child's age and create a list of books to read in the future. See chapter 2 (page 27) for a full description of how to host a book tasting event, along with the materials to use. See also www.lorrainemradice.com/blog for additional materials relating to book tastings.

The facilitator (a teacher or administrator) can lead with instruction on how to preview books to help decide which book to read next. Caregivers and students practice these strategies together while engaged in the book tasting. The facilitator can encourage caregivers to reinforce the strategies when helping their child to find new books to read. The facilitator may also inform caregivers about the different types of books they will preview in the book tasting. Options (depending on the child's age) include board books, picture books, illustrated books, graphic novels, comics, novels in verse, novels in prose, and series sets.

Use books from the classroom, school library, or both to put out on display. Consider diversity in format, genre, identities of families, character and author representation, or theme when making decisions about which books to incorporate into the tasting: It's important for families to engage with books that represent parts of their identities, as well as the identities of others. Books should be mirrors and windows (Bishop, 1990). During this event, caregivers learn more about the books for readers of their child's age, and students preview books to take out from their classroom, school library, or both. If using books from the school library, consider partnering with your school librarian and allowing families to check out a book from the book tasting (often the highest rated on the "menu"), so each family leaves the event with a new book for their child to read. Ask caregivers to share their reactions and thoughts on the books available during the event. Discuss the diversity in book selection and if the caregivers believe the school represents their family and cultural identities. Are there adequate offerings of books as mirrors and windows (Bishop, 1990)?

This type of event is both informative and celebratory. Students may have experienced a book tasting in their class during the school day and now get to experience it with an adult. This second tasting experience reinforces instruction about choosing a book or types of books, while providing the excitement of previewing new book selections that could be a next great read! Consider planning a book tasting during your celebratory book love month (see chapter 3, page 81) or at a time of year when you want to encourage (even more) student independence in committing to reading—before an extended break from school or the summer months begin. Partner with teachers to strategize when caregivers and students can benefit most from a book tasting experience.

Conduct an Interactive Read-Aloud

An *interactive read-aloud* is a "systematic approach to reading aloud where the teacher models vocabulary development, reading fluency, and comprehension strategies, and requires the students to interact and participate in their own learning" (Johnston, 2016, p. 40). Inviting caregivers and their child to participate in an interactive read-aloud offers opportunities for them to think and talk about reading together during a shared experience. The benefits for caregivers are twofold: first, they can learn strategies for using read-aloud as a tool to support readers at home; the Commission on Reading notes, the most important activity for building the knowledge required for eventual success in reading is reading aloud to children (as cited in Fisher et al., 2004). Second, read-alouds expose caregivers to the thinking and responses their child engages in when participating in a reading event an adult in the school facilitates. Caregivers get a peek at their child as a learner in school.

Conduct read-alouds with the goal of students listening for enjoyment and sharing in reading (see chapter 3, page 81); you can also plan read-alouds so students participate in the reading experience and actively engage in thinking to cultivate new learning and meaning-making. Literacy instruction in general is stronger when you include read-alouds as a method to see how students engage with reading (Stoetzel & Shedrow, 2021).

- Students benefit from learning new words in context, not in isolation (Calderón & Solo, 2017).
- Read-alouds increase opportunities for students to make in-text connections with depth (Roessingh, 2020).
- Students engage in sustained shared thinking through turn-and-talks or in conversations with reading partners, which helps them elevate their comprehension and meaning-making and make gains in vocabulary learning, especially English learners (Roessingh, 2020).

These skills are not reserved for young readers; an interactive read-aloud is a worthwhile practice for students of all ages. Research supports the idea that adults should read to K–12 students daily (Layne, 2015). Literacy leaders can design an interactive read-aloud event for caregivers and students of any age to encourage shared thinking and conversation about age-appropriate texts and topics.

When planning your event, consider the space you will use in your school and the types of books you will use for various age groups. If multiple grade levels are participating, consider hosting several read-alouds; teachers or administrators can facilitate additional read-alouds in separate spaces using books appropriate for the age of the group. For example, for caregivers of kindergarten students, use an emergent storybook for the read-aloud. For caregivers of grade 4 students, use a more complex picture book or a chapter in a middle grades novel. For caregivers of grade 9 students, use a picture book featuring a mature issue, a short story, or a chapter from a young adult book. Adults involved in hosting this event should reflect on what they know about the families in their class or school community and select texts based on that information.

Prior to the event, plan for the interactive read-aloud and be intentional about how caregivers and their children share in conversation. Coauthors Lana Edwards Santoro, David J. Chard, Lisa Howard, and Scott K. Baker (2008) assert that before teachers enter into a text with their students, they should engage in conscious planning to benefit students' comprehension. Design this added layer of caregiver participation carefully as well. Students' comprehension is not the sole purpose of this experience; welcoming caregivers to converse with their child about reading and building reading community are also priorities. The following are tips for planning your interactive read-aloud.

- Read several texts popular in your class or among students in the same grade level to generate ideas for text-selection options. Also consider the identities of families in your class or school when selecting choices for an inclusive read-aloud experience. See appendix B (page 187) for book lists to help select a text and a picture books list to use to select an interactive read-aloud that encourages participation and imagination from young readers.

If you are planning read-aloud work for older students (either with caregivers or in the classroom), consider using a picture book, short story, or concise nonfiction work. Here are three contemporary short story anthologies to consider.

- *Flying Lessons and Other Stories* edited by Ellen Oh (middle grades or high school)
- *The Hero Next Door* edited by Olugbemisola Rhuday-Perkovich (middle grades or high school)
- *The Moth Presents All These Wonders: True Stories About Facing the Unknown,* edited by Catherine Burns (high school)

- Choose a text that is age and grade-level appropriate for the participating students with their caregivers.

- Reread the text several times with a different focus each time: how characters develop, how the author develops the theme, how conflict impacts character and plot development, which craft moves the author uses, powerful language choices the author makes, new vocabulary to explore, implicit and explicit ideas the author suggests to the reader, opportunities for personal or family connections, opportunities to share personal reactions, or opportunities to pose questions or wonderings. Using a different focus when rereading will help you generate prompts and questions for caregivers and their child to discuss.

- Decide where in the text caregivers and their child will turn and talk to discuss your prompts and questions. Write the prompts and questions on sticky notes and put them on the pages where you will stop the participants' reading for discussion. You may also want to decide when the conversation will be solely between the caregiver and their child and when to open the conversation to the entire group. Caregivers and their child can be partners in offering prompts and questions for others to consider.

- Have a list of general prompts and questions to distribute so caregivers can reference it when reading or talking about reading with their child (see the reproducible "Tips for Caregivers," page 164).

After the read-aloud, engage families in dialogue about the experience. Gather their input about the book selection and their conversations. Survey if and how families felt represented and given opportunities to share their perspectives. You may also discuss the types of books students can access in their classrooms, and if students feel their identities are represented to honor a shared responsibility and decision-making process in the types of books available for students (DeMatthews, 2018).

Explore the School Library

Collaborate with your school librarian to host an event where caregivers and their child are invited to visit the school library together. Participants tour the library to learn how it is organized, the type of support a library space and librarian offer, the books available to students, and how to best utilize the space as a place to cultivate reading identities and reading engagement. Consider having several school representatives join families on the library tour to learn more about their reading identities. Also, discuss ways to ensure student feel represented in the text selections in the school library and so books serve as mirrors and windows for students (Bishop, 1990).

Students may have a similar experience during the school day if they visit the library as part of an instructional program; librarians typically conduct a library tour to explain how students can utilize the space as readers and writers. Inviting caregivers and their child together during a separate event can support conversations about how to choose appropriate and interesting books and reinforce students' access to develop their reading lives in the school library space. Work with your school librarian to decide if families can check out a book during this event so caregivers and their child can experience what the library has to offer together and bring this aspect of reading life into their home.

Host a Schoolwide Book Talk

In chapter 4 (page 103), I explain how to plan a schoolwide book talk. Refer to the Host a Student-Led Schoolwide Book Talk section (page 107) and consider inviting caregivers to participate in the event with their child. Inform caregivers about the book talk using the advertising methods I outline in this chapter (page 147). On the day of the event, include caregivers in their child's discussion group. When you invite caregivers, a schoolwide book talk transforms into an opportunity for a reading experience that represents all stakeholder groups. If you choose to invite caregivers, consider the time and space of the book talk; when and where matter to access the event. You may survey families to gather their preferences for time of day and location (in person or virtual) for attending school events.

Hold a Curriculum Celebration

At the end of reading and writing units, students should celebrate their progress. Examples of reading celebrations are students talking about a book they read and loved during the unit, sharing new learning from informational text with reading partners, and reflecting on progress and setting goals for future reading. Examples of writing celebrations are students sharing their writing with writing partners or with an entire class, or sharing writing with adults connected to the topics students wrote about. If students write argument essays about school-related topics, the principal could join the class to listen to students share their arguments through writing. Other examples are adding students' writing to classroom or school library collections for other students to read, and reflecting on progress and setting goals for future writing pieces. Consider inviting caregivers to participate in these celebrations to highlight curriculum work and students' progress as readers and writers.

Collaborate with teachers to choose one reading and one writing celebration throughout the year dedicated to sharing with caregivers during the school day. Videoconferencing platforms like Zoom (https://zoom.us) and Google Meet (https://apps.google.com/meet) have access for caregivers to join class celebrations. Caregivers can join a class meeting and listen to students share about their reading and writing while at work or performing other daily obligations that may prevent them from attending an event during the school day.

The Importance of Access and the Need for Ongoing Reflection

From a social justice and equity standpoint, a plethora of research shows parent engagement approaches are often Eurocentric, middle class based, and contingent on resources such as time, and financial, cultural, and social capital, which may be limited for minoritized and low-income parents (Auerbach, 2010; Baquedano-López, Alexander, & Hernandez, 2013; Lee & Bowen, 2006). I must admit, when planning events for caregivers, I feel challenged to make sure all caregivers feel welcome and have access to participate, whether it be access to time, resources, language, or transportation. I worry my invitation for involvement is inappropriate for my entire school community. Diversity exists in school communities and takes on different meaning depending on the context; communities are diverse in socioeconomic status, culture, ethnicity, family structure, occupation of caregivers and the work schedules they manage, and languages spoken. Through my involvement in my district's equity committee and my partnerships with teachers and school leaders, I work with teams to develop opportunities to welcome caregivers to the school reading community and ensure strengths of diverse parents are not ignored (Auerbach, 2010).

In response to the needs and feedback from my school community, I work with teams to provide supports to welcome all families to the reading community and invite them to participate in literacy opportunities, which develops a two-way directional practice in school and family relationships (Chavkin & Williams, 1987; DeMatthews, Edwards, & Rincones, 2016; Lopez, Scribner, & Mahitivanichcha, 2001). The following are supports to consider having in place, depending on the needs of your community.

- Use traditional and digital communication methods. Send information on paper home with students and email the same information. You can also post information on the school website and share it on students' digital learning platforms (if available).
- Share written and oral communication in multiple languages using translation tools and support from multilingual staff members.
- Conduct presentations in languages other than English. Alternate languages while delivering the presentation so families who speak a language other than English can listen to an interpreter via a transmitter during the presentation.
- Have language interpreters available at events.
- Share recorded versions of presentations via email and on the school website for families who could not attend presentations live or online.
- Provide a balance of events you host in the school building and virtually to give options for live participation.
- Vary the locations of live and in-person events. For example, I use different schools in my district for event locations throughout the year and also hold school events in the public library, which is centrally located in the community.
- When hosting literacy events live and in-person, consider providing transportation if your school district has a transportation system. Notify families of pick-up and drop-off locations in town.
- When hosting events live and in-person, and your target audience is adults (for example, a Parent Academy event), consider providing childcare. Welcome caregivers to bring their children and hire staff to provide activities for children while their caregivers participate in the event. Also provide games, crafts, drawing, and books as options for the children. You can use the school library, a cafeteria, or a classroom for this purpose.

Summary

This portion of the reading culture–building work can be simultaneously rewarding and challenging. It often feels difficult to make connections with every family in the school community, despite the efforts of teachers and community members. However, it is encouraging when you solidify school and family partnerships. Go back to one of the ideas in the introduction (page 1) for when you want there to be a stronger or different type of connection between your school and families, and keep going. Share the school's literacy values with caregivers by inviting them to learn with you through academy events. Use a book study as a way to build a social experience about reading with caregivers and discuss topics relevant to the ages of the students in your class or school. Finally, embrace invitations to have caregivers and students participate in reading and literacy events together. By varying the ways in which you partner with families and creating space for caregivers to participate in reading culture development out of altruism (not obligation), you are providing several pathways to make connections.

Reflection Questions

On your own or with a collaborative team, answer the following questions.

1. What are the identities of our families? How can we design literacy events that celebrate the identities of families and promote shared partnerships?

2. What do we want to inform caregivers about relative to literacy development? What information will be helpful to caregivers in building awareness and understanding of what educators teach in school?

3. What supports do we need to put in place to increase caregiver access to participating in school reading culture events?

4. What are we noticing in our students' reading development—engagement or identities—that may need support outside of school? What is the most accessible way to have conversations with caregivers about this topic?

5. What are students excited about celebrating in school relative to their reading and writing? How can we position caregivers to join in that excitement?

Tips for Caregivers

Support Reading Engagement at Home

- Encourage a variety of reading. Read print books, ebooks, labels, signs, packages, game directions, websites, apps, blogs, recipes, and so on.
- Create a routine with your family to read to or with your child as much as possible (depending on the child's age). Reading in the same space as your child helps the child position you as a model reader.
- Think about times of the day when your child can read and handle a book or digital text—after school, in the car, bus, or train while traveling somewhere, while waiting for an appointment, in the morning, and so on.
- Support your child by providing a preferred place to read (inside or outside the home).
- Visit the public library to read new books and spend time in a print-rich environment.

Prompts and Questions to Engage in Conversation With Your Child About Reading

- Tell me about what you just read.
- What is your favorite part?
- What are you learning or did you learn from your reading?
- Tell me about what you found (or are finding) interesting about your reading.
- Tell me about your favorite character.
- Does what you are reading remind you of any movie or television show?
- Tell me about why you chose to read this text.
- Would you recommend the text you're reading or just read to someone else? Why or why not?
- Is there anything you find challenging? What strategies have you learned to help you understand the text or word solve?
- What are some of your reading goals?
- Which genres do you enjoy? Which genres do you not enjoy?
- Do you like reading print or digital text? Is there a difference for you?
- Have you seen any books advertised on social media you're interested in reading? (For older readers)

CHAPTER 7

Elevating Reading When Other Endeavors Come Into Focus
How to Continue to Prioritize Reading and Reading Culture

This Chapter Features...
Ways to Use Your Reading Culture to Elevate the Work in Content-Focus Areas

- Support a new focus area through read-alouds and book additions (page 167).
- Share a Spotlight Book of the Month celebration (page 170).
- Generate book lists for school events (page 172).
- Team up with other departments (page 173).

School leaders have good intentions when introducing new focus areas or projects. New endeavors are usually in response to new learning and ideas that present new opportunities for students relevant to the world around them. It may feel, though, as if previous areas of work are vulnerable and seem less important. As a teacher or administrator, you have been working hard at developing curriculum, projects, and culture in one area and now feel the pressure to support new content. As a new school leader, I remember worrying about the state of reading culture as my school district began to integrate other areas of focus. One year, district emphasis was on innovation as we introduced Makerspaces (https://makerspaces.com) in our schools. The next year, there was a new STEM program to focus on the importance of science, technology, engineering, and mathematics collectively. There was also a focus on internships and work experiences for high school students related to their potential fields of study. These are all extraordinary opportunities for students, which I never forgot. I feared, though, that the enthusiasm about reading among stakeholders and the developing reading culture would begin to wane because of the new initiatives. Maintaining a commitment to fostering students' reading engagement should parallel all the other exciting work happening in schools because reading is foundational. Reading is important!

The Roots of This Work

Schools should be spaces that reflect the times in which people live. Education helps to prepare young people to participate in larger communities outside their school experiences. It is only natural that as the world evolves—and as business models develop, technology advances, and science research grows—schools transform to parallel the changes. A report by the World Economic

Forum (2016) notes that 65 percent of the children who entered primary school in 2017 will have jobs that do not exist yet. Education must adapt to what is seemingly unknown. It is the responsibility as educators to continuously reflect and adjust to provide relevant learning opportunities for students so they are prepared to make informed decisions and can understand and think critically about the information and experiences they have access to. Because advanced thinking and innovations can lead to new pathways for students to explore in school, there are often new goals and initiatives in schools to help organizations grow to be relevant spaces for students. Areas of focus change over time in response to new information and new learning. Instructional practices, areas of study, and offerings for students can't stay the same—just as schools can't stay the same.

Reading filters into places like Makerspaces and is part of programs like STEM. Strong experiences with reading will better position students as they explore career paths through internships and new work experiences. Reading and identifying as readers are implicit supports for students in many other areas of learning and creating. In teacher, author, speaker, and coach Kelly Gallagher's (2022) presentation at the New York State English Council conference, he shared his research to exemplify the amount and depth of reading colleges will ask young people to pursue by gathering college invitations that show potential students what to read, think, and write about. Gallagher (2022) presented these writing prompts from three colleges:

> *Identify an idea or challenge in the world (e.g., mass incarceration) and contribute your thinking to readings which will be discussed in class. Respond to the author(s) as you shape your thinking.*
>
> *Analyze a movie trailer of choice. (6–8 page essay).*
>
> *Describe how you would stage one scene from a play we read, and explain how your staging supports what the author is trying to accomplish.*

Each of these prompts to think, write, and create are derived from reading. While not all students will choose to attend college, reading will ultimately be a foundation or enhancement to what students choose to do outside of school and after high school.

Coauthors and educators Kylene Beers and Robert E. Probst (2013) argue that while some aspects of reading have changed in response to increased use of technology and social media, some have not:

> *We still decode symbols to make sense of the text; we still must interact with the text, bringing our own experiences to the words; we still must question what was written, must infer what wasn't written, and must make connections between the text and ourselves and others and the world around us. We must decide when we agree with the author and when we reject his ideas or her attitudes. And we still get swept away by the words, forgetting for a moment that we are in Houston or in Marathon, and believe for that moment that we are in Narnia or Oz or on a space battleship with a boy named Ender. (p. 15)*

Because parts of reading transcend change, the commitment to reading culture must remain and become part of the other areas of focus in the classroom, school, or district.

I learned to reframe my thinking when I worried about the state of reading culture. I started chapter 3 (page 81) by emphasizing reading culture is not a trend. It's about tradition, something that lives in your class, school, or district no matter what else is happening. Just as literacy experiences are present in all facets of life, reading culture can be among the threads of the fabric that represent the vision for your class, school, or district. While you may initially begin to develop your culture with a hyperfocus on books, authors, and the reading itself, the work can evolve into promoting other areas of focus through your already established reading culture. After years of supporting new endeavors in my organization, I learned how the reading culture needs space to grow and transform as well. The commitment to reading remains, and with new projects, new staff, and a changing world (for example, a global pandemic), the reading culture takes different shapes depending on what your class, school, or district needs at that time. The established reading culture helps to perpetuate the new ideas and projects come into focus. Reading and books are immersed in other students' work, which is ultimately what literacy leaders hope for. Reading is performed not in isolation; reading is a part of it all. The ability to read well and the motivation to want to read positions young people to participate in a plethora of learning experiences in other disciplines and content areas.

All the roles in a school district play an important part in introducing new ideas and initiatives to the culture and students. Examples of endeavors, projects, or ideas educators often explore, which may be new to some schools, are a growth mindset (Dweck, 2006), equitable practices, technology tools and innovation, hybrid learning, blended learning, mindfulness, STEM or STEAM programs, approaches to social-emotional learning, attention to and concern for students' mental health, developing a profile of each graduate, exploring new national or state curricula standards, new curricula adaptation, and so on. Leadership and teaching involve juggling many priorities. New projects require time and attention, which may leave you exhausted as you think about prioritizing reading culture as well. This chapter shares ideas about how you can elevate your reading culture through supporting new endeavors and integrate reading into new student work. These ideas may make that juggling more manageable.

How to Make It Happen

The following ideas are ways to merge reading and literacy work into the new projects or endeavors in your school or district. While reading may not be front and center (like when you first launch a reading campaign), reading does become part of the energy that fuels the academic or creative programs you offer students.

Support a New Focus Area Through Read-Alouds and Book Additions

Students will begin to think about new content by participating in read-alouds. Student immersion in books can spark ideas and wonderings about content. Merging reading with other experiential activities in a specific content area provides multiple entry points to learning and student conversations. When my district first introduced Makerspaces (https://makerspaces.com) in the elementary schools, I partnered with the director of instructional technology to meet with all elementary grade-level teams in their new Makerspaces. My colleague introduced the purpose of Makerspaces and its new tools available for exploration. I followed up with a read-aloud paired with an activity to invite teachers to be designers and creators using the tools in Makerspaces. I read *What to Do With a Box* by Jane Yolen (2016), and teachers collaborated to create something original with a box, an activity designed for students. We discussed how books can be entry points into innovative thinking in Makerspaces. As Makerspaces became a part of a new STEM program, picture books and informational books began to fill the shelves, along with robots, building blocks, and computers. Through the read-aloud, teachers began to make connections to Makerspaces and carried through those connections to students.

While scouring sources for new books to share with students is exciting work, it can be time-consuming to find titles matching the new endeavor. Here are ways to support the process of growing new projects through read-alouds and book access.

- **Form a committee or partner with your reading ambassadors team (see chapter 3, page 81) to identify books related to new work:** Committees bring various perspectives to a topic and their contributions provide diverse representation. Working with a team to pair books with new endeavors allows more voices to contribute to the efficient productivity of the work. When meeting, have access to devices so your committee members can essentially go book shopping to search for and read about titles that connect to the content area of the project. Form subgroups to divide the work by grade level or topic. For example, when my committee began to diversify the reading experiences for students in my school district, members set a goal to integrate books that represent students' identities in the schools *and* the global population. The committee wanted to amplify voices in often marginalized stories. *Inclusivity* is a pillar of how educators can frame literacy experiences. After an inventory of read-aloud collections currently in my schools, a committee of staff members—teachers, administrators, and social workers—came together to develop collections of picture books to purchase and add to the read-aloud collections in all kindergarten through grade 5 classrooms.

  This large project benefited from the participation of twenty-five people. Small groups within the committee worked on grade-level book lists and then each grade-level group shared the book list they developed with the entire committee to value the collective opinions and ideas of the group. During this process, small groups may conduct research using bookstore websites, book organizations, and other online resources to find titles that connect to focus-area topics. Small groups may also consult with librarians (see the next bullet point) to partner with for this work. The small group members may not read all the books in their entirety, depending on availability prior to purchasing. When the books are in hand, lead your committee in reading all books that will go into classrooms prior to distribution; this is done to verify the books are appropriate and relevant to the grade level they were selected for. Your school may have a committee structure you can integrate this work into. Committee participation can be voluntary before or after school, or a paid opportunity.

- **Partner with a librarian:** Work with your school or public librarian to curate books. Libraries have a wealth of resources that can support any new endeavor; a librarian can provide a list of books about a topic to consider. A librarian may also provide copies of books to share with your students. Consider working with your school librarian to create a book display in your school library about the new endeavor, so students see visual reminders of the connection between reading, books, and new learning.

- **Integrate read-alouds into new student content work:** New focus areas in a school or district transpire in each classroom in different ways. In some cases, classroom teachers are responsible for introducing new initiatives. Specialists or counselors may also be involved in new curricular work. Encourage those involved in this work with students to make read-alouds a part of how students explore new material. Read-alouds inspire conversation about topics and can provide a space for students to approach topics through inquiry as they formulate questions and wonderings while immersed in the reading experience (see chapter 6, page 143). Table 7.1 provides examples of pairings between potential school themes and initiatives with picture book titles for read-alouds for various age levels. See appendix B (page 187) for a list of more picture books.

- **Invite staff to participate in a book club:** Engaging adults in book clubs helps cultivate the adults' own reading identities (see chapter 2, page 27) and creates a space for conversation and generating ideas about new focus areas in the school. You may choose to read a reference book for educators, an informational book, or books for young people about the topic. See chapter 2 (page 27) for more about how adult book clubs can make an impact on the work you do with students.

TABLE 7.1: Examples of Picture Books to Explore Topics With Various Age Levels

Book Title and Author	Topic	Elementary Talking Points	Secondary Talking Points
Change Sings by Amanda Gorman	Agency and action	What does it mean to make a difference? How can individuals help make positive change that will impact a community?	What is *a call to action*? Identify social issues you can contribute to making positive change through organizations and community outreach. Use the picture book as a foundation for reading more of Amanda Gorman's poetry and speeches.
Love by Matt de la Peña	Community and connectedness	How do you demonstrate love for someone or something? Select an image from the book and share how it demonstrates love.	Explore how love manifests in relationships with yourself, others, and in a community. Choose an image in the book to analyze and explain how it illustrates the concept of love in yourself or a group. Why does the author include this image?
The Undefeated by Kwame Alexander	Perseverance and determination	What does it mean to be *undefeated*? Pay attention to the meaning of *undefeated* represented in this text. What is the author trying to tell us throughout this poem?	Consider the role of oppression in groups of people and the historical and contemporary implications. Analyze the features of this text like blank pages and different font types. How do the features convey meaning in the poem?

Share a Spotlight Book of the Month Celebration

Support new endeavors and share new book titles through a Spotlight Book of the Month. As you prepare for the school year during the summer months with new work ahead, select a book to highlight and reveal during each month of the school year that relates to district or school projects. Showcasing a new book each month is a way to inform the class or school community about books related to topics of study. If you are sharing this book with teachers to engage students, provide a lesson or activity related to the book that teachers can use with their students. A Spotlight Book of the Month is also a way to unite a class or school community through one book that all are sharing and celebrating. Here are some considerations for selecting the books.

- **Select books related to the new endeavor:** Find book titles supportive of the new goal or initiative by connecting with colleagues for ideas, visiting the library and a bookstore, and using the internet to research. You may also use the book lists I provide in this book. It is helpful to have all the books selected prior to the start of the school year or when the school year begins. Each month of the school year is busy! If you select the books in advance, culture building will be more manageable. While planning in advance may help with management, you should also consider anticipating new books (which may publish after the school year begins) or new events in your school or community (which may occur during the school year).

- **Choose a way to share the Spotlight Book of the Month with your class or school community:** The following are ways to share and highlight the Spotlight Book of the Month.
    - Create a space in your school or classroom to display the book throughout the month.
    - Decorate a bulletin board in a hallway or in your classroom that includes the book cover and any related student work. (Change the board each month to reflect the current Spotlight Book of the Month.)
    - Create a short video to advertise the book. Include the book cover and information about the author. You may also read a few pages from the book to generate student interest and excitement. Consider using iMovie (https://apple.com/imovie) or the recording feature on Zoom to create your video to share with the school or class community.
    - Include information about or excerpts from the Spotlight Book of the Month in the classes or school announcements.
    - Post about the Spotlight Book of the Month on your class or school website, as well as any school social media sites.
    - Include information about the Spotlight Book of the Month in communication with families. Use this featured event as an opportunity to inform caregivers about the content students are learning and emphasize the role books play in your reading culture.

- **Engage students in an activity related to the Spotlight Book of the Month:** When sharing the Spotlight Book of the Month, create an activity for students to engage in related to the book. For example, when *What to Do With a String* by Jane Yolen (2019) was the Spotlight Book of the Month during the year of the Makerspaces introduction, educators invited students come up with innovative and creative uses for a string. Their creations included an attachment for a surfboard to hook on the back of a boat and a ribbon for twirling when dancing. When *If I Built a School* by Chris Van Dusen (2019) was in the spotlight, some classes designed their own contemporary school, along with justifications for why their school looked different from traditional schools.

The discussion during and after the read-aloud was about how reading can help spark new ideas for creativity. If you are a school administrator, consider using this as an opportunity to visit classrooms and read to students, which not only builds relationships with staff and students but also promotes the importance of reading (through your involvement).

- **Designate a platform to store your Spotlight Book of the Month collection, and ensure class or school community members have access:** As you introduce a new book each month, reserve an area where others can still see and access previous books. You may have a space in your classroom, the school library, the main office, or another common area where people frequently gather. You may also post the books on a digital learning management system or a school website so class or school community members can access them throughout the year.

- **Prepare for your Spotlight Book of the Month to evolve, just as the goals and culture of your class or school evolve:** During the first year of this reading culture event, I used the name Spotlight Book of the Month to feature books related to innovation and creativity. Another year, when the process of diversifying reading and learning experiences began, the monthly book celebration title changed to *One Book, Many Stories* (see figure 7.1). The district designed One Book, Many Stories to share diverse stories and so that all members of our school community felt valued and represented. This celebration served as a model to reflect on the types of books and stories we should have in our school and classroom libraries, as well as in other curricular areas. The school invited students and staff to write their own stories each month in response to the shared books. The district posted these stories on a website for the school community to read. Some teachers also shared their students' work on their own social media profiles or class websites.

One Book, Many Stories
#LBReads 2020

Books help us discover ourselves and learn about the lives of others. Through this process, we gain perspective and develop empathy. Each month during the 2020–2021 school year, #LBReads will feature a picture book for students and teachers of all grade levels to share. Through one book a month, we share many stories.

FIGURE 7.1: The One Book, Many Stories website title page, which shares the purpose of the monthly book celebration.

Reading Culture in Action
Reflections From Those Who Are Making It Happen

I was particularly motivated to participate in the districtwide reading initiative One Book, Many Stories because of the freedom to be creative and develop an engaging learning activity appropriate for the unique learners in my classroom. As an elementary special education teacher of students with significant disabilities, I have always tried to balance exposing students to general education curriculum or activities with developing basic fundamental skills in an age-appropriate way.

For this particular activity, I read aloud the Spotlight Book of the Month, *Just Ask: Be Different, Be Brave, Be You* by Sonia Sotomayor. With support, we began applying the concept of being unique to our own lives. We rolled out bulletin board paper, traced the outline of students' bodies (with their permission), and had students write simple words they used to describe themselves on the paper. To this day, I still remember how genuinely happy my students were while participating in this activity! They loved the idea of tracing their bodies on life-sized paper to represent themselves. Inviting them to write simple words to describe themselves was within their skill set and enabled them to feel confident.

As an advocate for people with disabilities, knowing my students were able to make meaningful connections and contributions to this shared text was important to me. Recognizing that there was not one "right" message or activity to take away from this common text enabled us to explore and make sense of our own learning on our own terms. Ultimately, participating in One Book, Many Stories served as an excellent reminder that my students' learning is valued even if it may look different from conventional outcomes, and that *all* students are important members of the greater reading community. (L. Miller, special education teacher, personal communication, June 19, 2023)

Generate Book Lists for School Events

There is a book for just about anything you could explored in school. As you integrate new ideas into your class or school community or explore new curricula, consider creating book lists by topic (see appendix A, page 181) to share with students and families, or a book display with book lists for families to take during a family mathematics night. You don't need to purchase all the book titles you share; a book list serves as an artifact to further the learning about a particular area.

- **Form a committee or partner with your reading ambassadors team (see chapter 3, page 81) . . . again!** Consider making book lists a team project in your class or school. If you are a teacher of upper-elementary or secondary students, invite students to create book lists by topics that are also focus areas in the school. If you are an administrator, plan for a committee subgroup to work on generating book lists to share during school events.
- **Create a system to keep track of new book release dates:** It can be challenging to maintain book lists because new books are constantly published! It may be the responsibility of committee members to pay attention to new book releases in libraries, bookstores, or both. You may also sign up to receive emails from publishing companies so you can record

new releases. Keep your book lists current and representative of school community members and new learning.

- **Become a part of a community invested in books and reading:** Sign up membership in literacy and learning organizations like First Book Marketplace, the International Literacy Association, Literacies and Languages for All, National Center for Families Learning, National Council of Teachers of English, and ASCD. Participate in professional learning opportunities. You may also use social media as a tool to follow thinkers and practitioners in the field of literacy and gather resources for reading and sharing. Being part of a community dedicated to providing students with high-quality, relevant texts will support you in building your own reading identity and the reading culture in your class or school. Committing to ongoing learning will strengthen your ability to position others to be supporters of reading culture.

Team Up With Other Departments

Schools typically provide a range of opportunities for students to explore their passions and interests through different areas of study. Capitalize on the work that departments (art, music, athletics, theater, science, history, and so on) in your school or organization are doing and partner with their work by infusing books and reading to perpetuate reading culture–building. There may be new work that departments plan to explore, and the reading culture may be a vehicle to showcase the success in those areas.

Each school is unique and departments in a school have an array of focus areas and new work students may be exploring and learning. For this How to Make It Happen section, I share examples of how the work in content-area and performance departments can support reading culture–building through capitalizing on the students' strengths and talents that emerge in various types of coursework. You may choose to integrate one of these ideas into your work with your class or school, or you may modify the ideas to fit your context.

Each of the following ideas come to fruition through collaboration between the adults who lead young readers and specific departments in a school. Success in schools is a result of how all the parts work together. If you are part of a leadership team for a district, consider building partnerships with your department-head colleagues to elevate their work through department literacy work. If you are a teacher working with a class of students, consider reaching out to a colleague who teaches a different subject area or different discipline to collaborate on a project together or offer a reading culture idea to integrate into their work.

- **Instructional technology department:** My high school offered a media and broadcasting course and while students enrolled in the class learn how to use the tools and technology in the news studio, there are also opportunities to produce for authentic creations and content for the school community. The realism of this class experience elevates the technology program in the school and gives students opportunities to explore film and production as a possible career path. When the #LBReads reading campaign was launched (see chapter 1, page 9), there was collaboration with the instructional technology department to produce an informational video about the reading campaign. The students enrolled in the news studio class exercised their skills in filming, editing, and producing to make a video the class then shared with the community. The production of the video not only advertised the creativity and abilities of the students in the course but also promoted the #LBReads campaign.

There was also a live streaming component to the news studio and during the high school book fair (see chapter 3, page 81). The student news anchors visited the book fair to interview readers about their experience. All students and staff in the building experienced the live broadcast each morning through a streaming component.

- **Music department:** Collaborate with the music department to invite student musicians to play music during reading culture events to welcome the author (see chapter 5, page 123), and caregivers (see chapter 6, page 143) at a book fair (see chapter 3, page 81). Partnering with the music department invites students to share the talents they craft in their music classes for an authentic experience in school in front of a large audience. For example, on the day of the high school book fair, student musicians play as students enter school to generate excitement and bring merriment to the event. While musicians help to nurture the reading culture, the music department work is simultaneously showcased.

- **Business department:** Consider involving future business majors in the launch of your reading campaign (see chapter 1, page 9) by tasking them to brand *reading* in your school or district. Future entrepreneurs and designers can practice their marketing, advertising, and branding skills for the reading campaign. Exercise your leadership by providing leadership opportunities for others. After four years, my team and I decided to redesign the #LBReads logo. Instead of a graphic designer doing the work (like in the original plan), we invited students to submit original designs for the new #LBReads logo. Our offer was open to all K–12 students; the department also used this invitation as a curriculum project in business classes, as logos and branding are part of the content students learn. Students had an opportunity to use digital tools to redesign the #LBReads logo in their business class.

- **Clubs and service projects:** Some clubs and organizations require students to complete service hours or projects for participation credit. Support the work of clubs or service projects by sharing reading culture ideas to involve students. Perhaps students can get involved by promoting the school book fair (see chapter 3, page 81), organizing a schoolwide book talk (see chapter 4, page 103), or participating in a Readers as Leaders group (see chapter 4, page 103) for service hours or as projects for clubs and organizations. See chapter 4 (page 103) for more information about student leadership and reading culture.

- **Physical education and play:** Incorporate movement breaks through reading. Students can participate in reading relay races outside (on a field or track) to preview new book pages—instead of passing a baton, they pass new titles to one another to promote interest in a next great read. You may also post excerpts or images from the book text in sequence around the field or track, and students incorporate reading or discussing the passages as they run or walk in *fartleks* (intervals of fast- and slow-paced running or walking). Use this activity as a preview of a new unit of study or new content students will explore.

- **Mathematics department:** Mathematics class can be a place where literacy skills develop and reading culture thrives. Students often exercise academic literacy skills in mathematics class (for example, by developing numeracy as a literacy, reading and annotating word problems, writing explanations for problem solving, or engaging in word studies of new vocabulary). However, here are some additional ways mathematics teachers can contribute to reading and literacy culture.

- Incorporate a read-aloud (with students of all ages) to introduce or reinforce mathematics concepts.
- Assess through student mathematics journals. Invite students to keep a mathematics journal of how they solve problems or when and how they engage with mathematics or utilize mathematics concepts in their lives outside of school.
- Design a book-making project. Students create a book to demonstrate their understanding of a mathematics concept or components related to what they are studying. Types of books that connect well to mathematics work are how-to books, informational books, and alphabet books (students create a page for each letter of the alphabet and then link the alphabet letters to mathematics related content).

- **Art department:** Consider beautifying your school by lining the hallways or walls in the classroom with illustrations or paintings of book covers. Students use mathematics to sketch book covers to scale (similar to a mosaic format) and work in an art class to bring color to their sketches. The skills in mathematics relative to drawing and painting techniques (for example, ratios and proportions), are at the center of what will eventually make classrooms and schools inviting places that celebrate and promote books and reading. Art teachers can also inventory the content and skills they teach at various grade levels and decide if they can include any reading culture work in the project choices they share with students.

- **Any curricular area that promotes choice:** I describe specific ways adults can plan student work in content areas that can influence reading culture. If there is choice and autonomy laced into the learning opportunities students encounter throughout their school experience, students may be the ones to integrate reading culture into their choices for projects. A mark of the culture's strength is if students are so immersed in reading and books that they are the ones to make connections with reading, books, and their learning and exploration in new topic areas. At the beginning of a speech and debate unit, which was a part of a new curricular area for elementary students, students chose their own topics to begin to formulate a debate. While popular issues were *Should students wear uniforms to school?* and *Is Fortnite (https://fortnite.com) harmful for children?* one student chose to integrate his experience with and interest in different types of books and explore the question: *Which is better? Chapter books or picture books?*

The organic integration of reading culture into curricular areas may transpire when teachers receive choices on how to plan and promote the work of their department. This, too, can be a mark of how your school reading culture reaches all teachers in the school community. For example, a world languages teacher integrates a read-aloud into her curriculum with a middle grades novel by a Latinx author. Also, for Hispanic Heritage Month, the middle school world languages department creates a book display featuring book covers and quotes from Hispanic authors. This book display lines a main hallway in the school.

Educators who may not always have the opportunity to share in building a reading culture can help elevate it through collaboration. In the process of engaging in discourse about the content-area or performance skills in classes, a dialogue about books and reading identities may emerge. Partnerships among departments create spaces for authentic work; the partnerships involve students in developing the reading culture while they are learning new skills, techniques, and information.

Summary

This chapter serves to help you bring several dimensions to reading culture and broaden what it means to participate in a literacy community. Integrating books into any new project or endeavor offers opportunities for new learning and also creates access to literature and reading experiences in ways different from what teachers typically expose students to. Broadening reading culture to all departments and disciplines in a school provides students access to more adults who can influence their reading lives. Perhaps a student may connect to book making in mathematics class because the student loves mathematics more than writing a story in English class.

Prioritizing reading in other content areas in your school also creates spaces for you to continue to grow and learn as a literacy leader. When you step outside your familiar spaces and explore possibilities in other aspects of your school, you can gain new perspectives and new ideas.

Reflection Questions

On your own or with a collaborative team, answer the following questions.

1. What new initiatives has our school introduced that we can support with book connections or reading experiences?

2. How can the school library contribute to elevating reading experiences about new initiatives?

3. What are the themes can amplify the school or district vision through books?

4. What work in department or content areas can the reading culture support?

5. Is there time and space for departments and colleagues to collaborate to make connections among content, projects, and the reading culture? If not, how can colleagues work together to advocate for collaboration time?

6. How can a book list support events or informational sessions for families? How might a book list be a helpful resource for understanding topics we frequently discuss in our class or school?

EPILOGUE

Embracing *Some*

During periods of reflection, a fellow champion of reading asked me, "If you don't do this important work, who will?" This question resonates. It's a reminder that building reading culture is important work and needs to prevail among other initiatives. It's an affirmation that communities need literacy leaders to consistently rally people behind the importance of reading. A strong culture creates pathways for new ideas to emerge and opens doors for new curricula work. Culture breaths energy into your learning community!

This book is about creating school community conditions that encourage and motivate all members to believe in the importance of reading as a lifelong practice. The reading culture events I describe in each chapter provide ways to instill this value into students as they grow as learners and individuals.

As you do this work for students, keep in mind that reading manifests differently for people. Part of leading through literacy work in your school or classroom is embracing that people are different and because of that fact, students will engage differently in the reading culture work. I am not suggesting doing this work will result in you no longer hearing students say, "I hate reading" or "I can't find a book to read." And I'm not suggesting you will no longer have students choose to play video games at night instead of read. Rather, I encourage you think reflect on all the ways reading can effect students and how the culture in your learning community can encourage, guide, and affirm readers. Embrace *some*.

- Some readers love the escape while reading fiction.
- Some readers appreciate the opportunities to learn in nonfiction.
- Some readers need time to find something of interest to read.
- Some readers thrive by listening to audio versions of written text.
- Some readers prefer to read and scroll in short bursts throughout the day.
- Some readers like to read numbers.
- Some readers like to read words.
- Some readers like to read images.
- Some readers need time to process.
- Some readers have eyes that move rapidly across text.
- Some readers read to help make decisions.

- Some readers read across many languages.
- Some readers flip pages.
- Some readers press buttons.
- Some readers prefer silence when reading.
- Some readers need a little bit of noise when reading.
- Some readers have access to an abundance of reading material.
- Some readers need help in gaining access to reading material.
- Some readers visit the library.
- Some readers visit the bookstore.
- Some readers swap books with friends.
- Some readers evolve in their taste.
- Some readers stay true to their favorite genres and formats.
- Some readers see a lot of adults reading in their lives outside of school.
- Some readers don't see many adults reading in their lives outside of school.
- Some readers make time for reading.
- Some readers have to find time for reading.
- Some readers think reading is easy.
- Some readers think reading is difficult.
- Some readers need a partner to help in making meaning.
- Some readers want to be writers.
- Some readers discover who they are through reading about others.
- All readers read because it's necessary.

Students' relationship with reading will develop over time as they continue to grow in your school and class. Their reading identities will change as they participate in reading culture experiences and gain access to adults who help cultivate their reading lives. Identities will also transform as they age as learners and individuals. This is part of how young people mature in their academic, social, and emotional areas of development. Keep in mind the following about student reading development.

- Some students will fluctuate in their relationship with reading throughout their lives.
- Some students may have an instant love for reading and maintain that love.
- Some students may connect with reading sporadically throughout their school years, loving it at times and not connecting with it at other times.
- Some students' reading lives at school and home may differ.
- Some students may enjoy reading but have commitments outside of school that limit their time for reading.
- Some students may initially read to be compliant during their school years, but may also develop a more altruistic relationship with reading later in their lives.

- Some students may never like reading during their school years because they think it's boring or nerdy, can't find a book they like, or would rather watch YouTube. (Don't be discouraged . . . embrace the honesty!)
- Some students may avoid reading because it's challenging for them.
- Some students need the a school community to be the foundation of their reading lives.

Part of being a champion of reading is to navigate the variety of readers in your learning community. While you should include everyone in reading culture events, some will form niches, some will orbit, and some will observe. Be patient! Not every student will connect with every reading culture experience you share. That's OK because you never know when or which event will impact an individual, or which teacher, experience, or book may ignite a spark for reading.

Design reading culture events to be responsive to your school community. As you plan events, observe the reactions of people and their levels of enthusiasm and participation. You may decide to sustain some events throughout the school year or make an event an annual celebration. There are also events that will only be necessary or relevant at certain times in your culture-building trajectory. An event like a book swap may be a way to rally people behind reading as part of how you build the reading culture foundation. However, you may find a book swap is not an event to host multiple times or even annually during a school year.

You also introduce initiatives or events that do not come together in the classroom, library, or school community. Gather feedback from stakeholders to revise these plans, or consider abandoning some ideas if the plans simply don't fit or can't sustain in your school community. It's OK to take risks and adjust plans. It's OK to fail forward.

If you need to emphasize inspiration or students' courage to give reading a book a try, consider more reading in one of the following picture books to get started.

- *Because* by Mo Willems
- *I Will Make Miracles* by Susie Morgenstern
- *Life* by Cynthia Rylant
- *Maybe* by Kobi Yamada
- *My Heart* by Corinna Luyken
- *When You Are Brave* by Pat Zietlow Miller

You are ready! Your learning community needs you to do this work. If you don't do this important work, who will?

APPENDIX A

Recommended Book Lists

These books represent a wide range of topics that address different focus areas in schools and classrooms. The books may not appeal to every community member since literacy work is vast and varied. Choose books based on the goals and values in your learning community.

Diverse Identities and Communities Book List

- *A Different Pond* by Bao Phi
- *Alma and How She Got Her Name* by Juana Martinez-Neal
- *Along Came Coco: A Story About Coco Chanel* by Eva Byrne
- *Eyes That Kiss in the Corners* by Joanna Ho
- *Fry Bread* by Kevin Noble Maillard
- *I Am Perfectly Designed* by Karamo Brown
- *I Dream of Popo* by Livia Blackburne
- *Islandborn* by Junot Díaz
- *Last Stop on Market Street* by Matt de la Peña
- *Mango, Abuela, and Me* by Meg Medina
- *My Footprints* by Boa Phi
- *My Papi Has a Motorcycle/Mi Papi Tiene Una Moto* by Isabel Quintero
- *Patchwork* by Matt de la Peña
- *Same, Same but Different* by Jenny Sue Kostecki-Shaw
- *Saturday* by Oge Mora
- *Thank You, Omu!* by Oge Mora
- *The Name Jar* by Yangsook Choi
- *The Invisible Boy* by Trudy Ludwig
- *The Proudest Blue* by Ibtihaj Muhammad and S.K. Ali
- *Watercress* by Andrea Wang
- *Where Are You From?* by Yamile Saied Méndez
- *Your Name Is a Song* by Jamilah Thompkins-Bigelow

School Values Book Lists

Agency and Action

- *Be You!* by Peter H. Reynolds
- *Change Sings: A Children's Anthem* by Amanda Gorman
- *I Am Courage: A Book of Resilience* by Susan Verde
- *I Am Enough* by Grace Byers
- *I Am Me: A Book of Authenticity* by Susan Verde
- *I Am Peace: A Book of Mindfulness* by Susan Verde
- *Malala's Magic Pencil* by Malala Yousafzai
- *Little Libraries Big Heroes* by Miranda Paul
- *Maybe* by Kobi Yamada
- *Mister Tiger Goes Wild* by Peter Brown
- *More Than a Peach* by Bellen Woodard
- *Say Something!* by Peter H. Reynolds
- *The Cool Bean* by Jori John and Pete Oswald
- *The Floating Field: How a Group of Thai Boys Built Their Own Soccer Field* by Scott Riley
- *What's In Your Pocket: Collecting Nature's Treasures* by Heather L. Montgomery
- *When You Are Brave* by Pat Zietlow Miller

Community and Connectedness

- *All Are Welcome* by Alexandra Penfold
- *All Are Neighbors* by Alexandra Penfold
- *Dreamers* by Yuyi Morales
- *Extra Yarn* by Mac Barnett
- *Home Is in Between* by Mitali Perkins
- *The Invisible String* by Patrice Karst
- *The Invisible Web: An Invisible String Story Celebrating Love and Universal Connection* by Patrice Karst
- *Love* by Matt de la Peña
- *Meanwhile Back on Earth: Finding Our Place Through Time and Space* by Oliver Jeffers
- *Our Table* by Peter H. Reynolds
- *The Day You Begin* by Jacqueline Woodson
- *This Is a School* by John Schu

Feelings and Emotions

- *Big Feelings* by Alexandra Penfold
- *My Heart* by Corinna Luyken
- *The Day the Crayons Quit* by Drew Daywalt
- *The Girl Who Never Made Mistakes* by Mark Prett and Gary Rubinstein
- *The Good Egg* by Jory John and Pete Oswald
- *The Smart Cookie* by Jory John and Pete Oswald
- *The Sour Grape* by Jory John and Pete Oswald
- *The Whatifs* by Emily Kilgore
- *When Sadness Is at Your Door* by Eva Eland

Imagination and Creative Thinking

- *Boxitects* by Kim Smith
- *Going Places* by Peter H. Reynolds and Paul A. Reynolds
- *If I Built a Car* by Chris Van Dusen
- *If I Built a House* by Chris Van Dusen
- *If I Built a School* by Chris Van Dusen
- *I Have an Idea!* by Henré Tullet
- *ish* by Peter H. Reynolds
- *I Wonder* by Kari Anne Holt
- *Imagine That* by Jonathon D. Voss
- *Not a Box* by Antoinette Portis
- *The Superpower Sisterhood* by Jenna Bush Hager and Barbara Pierce Bush
- *What Do You Do With an Idea?* by Kobi Yamada
- *What Do You Do With a Problem?* by Kobi Yamada
- *What to Do With a Box* by Jane Yolen
- *What to Do With a String* by Jane Yolen

Kindness and Consideration

- *Each Kindness* by Jacqueline Woodson
- *Evelyn Del Rey Is Moving Away* by Meg Medina
- *Just Ask! Be Different, Be Brave, Be You* by Sonia Sotomayor
- *Oddbird* by Derek Desierto
- *Strictly No Elephants* by Lisa Mantchev
- *The Iheards* by Emily Kilgore
- *The Kindest Red: A Story of Hijab and Friendship* by Ibtihaj Muhammad and S. K. Ali
- *Those Shoes* by Maribeth Boelts

Perseverance and Determination

- *Jabari Tries* by Gaia Cornwall
- *Knight Owl* by Christopher Denise
- *I Promise* by LeBron James
- *Life* by Cynthia Rylant
- *The Oldest Student: How Mary Walker Learned to Read* by Rita Lorraine Hubbard
- *The Undefeated* by Kwame Alexander
- *We Are Water Protectors* by Carole Lindstrom
- *The Magical Yet* by Angela DiTerlizzi
- *Questioneers* collection by Andrea Beaty

Books About Food

- *Cloudy With a Chance of Meatballs* by Judi Barrett
- *Dragons Love Tacos* by Adam Rubin
- *Eating the Alphabet* by Lois Ehlert
- *If You Give a Mouse a Cookie* by Laura Numeroff
- *The Candymakers* by Wendy Mass
- *The Popcorn Book* by Tomie dePaola

Books About Pizza

- *Curious George and the Pizza Party* by Margret and H. A. Rey
- *Fiesta con pizza/Pizza Party* by Juan Carlos Gonzalez Espitia and Lawrence Schinel
- *Mr. Tony is Full of Baloney* by Dan Gutman
- *Pizza Day: A Picture Book* by Melissa Iwai
- *Secret Pizza Party* by Adam Rubin

Books About Sports

- *Clifford's Sports Day* by Norman Bridwell
- *Football Genius* by Tim Green
- *Players in Pigtails* by Shana Cory
- *Salt in His Shoes: Michael Jordan in Pursuit of a Dreams* by Deloris Jordan and Roslyn Jordan
- *Travel Team* by Mike Lupica

Books About Clothing

- *Caps for Sale: A Tale of a Peddler, Some Monkeys, and Their Monkey Business* by Esphyr Slobodkina
- *Captain Underpants* series by Dav Pilkey
- *Corduroy* by Don Freeman
- *Fancy Nancy* by Jane O'Connor
- *The Hundred Dresses* by Eleanor Estes
- *The Mitten* by Jan Brett

Books About Community

- *All Are Neighbors* by Alexandra Penfold
- *Home* by Carson Ellis
- *Other Words for Home* by Jasmine Warga
- *This Is How We Do It: One Day in the Lives of Seven Kids From Around the World* by Matt Lamothe
- *Same, Same but Different* by Jenny Sue Kostecki-Shaw
- *Some Places More Than Others* by Renée Watson

Interactive Read-Aloud Books for Younger Audiences

- *Jumanji* by Chris Van Allsburg
- *If Kids Ruled the World* by Linda Bailey
- *Interrupting Chicken* by David Ezra Stein
- *Perfect* by Max Amato
- *The Book Hog* by Greg Pizzoli
- *The Day the Crayons Quit* by Drew Daywalt
- *The Little Old Lady Who Was Not Afraid of Anything* by Linda Williams
- *The Remarkable Farkle McBride* by John Lithgow
- *We Don't Eat Our Classmates* by Ryan T. Higgins

APPENDIX B

High-Interest Book Lists to Share With Caregivers

Picture Books

- *Are Your Stars Like My Stars?* by Leslie Helakoski
- *Hair Love* by Matthew A. Cherry
- *Koala Lou* by Mem Fox
- *Love* by Stacy McAnulty
- *Pete the Cat and His Four Groovy Buttons* by Eric Litwin
- *Soup Day* by Melissa Iwai
- *Today I Will Fly!* by Mo Willems
- *The Napping House* by Audrey Wood
- *The Pigeon Will Ride the Roller Coaster!* by Mo Williams
- *What Should Danny Do?* by Ganit Levy and Adir Levy

Early Chapter Books (Grades 1–3)

- *Dog Man* by Dav Pilkey
- *Don't Worry, Bee Happy* by Ross Burach
- *Jada Jones Rock Star* by Kelly Starling Lyons
- *Meet Yasmin!* by Saadia Faruqi
- *Peanut Butter and Jelly* by Ben Clanton
- *National Geographic Readers* by National Geographic Kids
- *Mercy Watson to the Rescue* by Kate DiCamillo
- *Ordinary People Change the World* collection by Brad Meltzer
- *Owl Diaries* series by Rebecca Elliot
- *Super Interesting Facts for Smart Kids: 1272 Fun Facts About Science, Animals, Earth and Everything in Between* by Jordan Moore

Chapter Books (Upper-Elementary Aged Readers, Transition to Middle School)

- *From an Idea to Disney: How Imagination Built a World of Magic* by Lowey Bundy Sichol
- *From an Idea to LEGO: The Building Bricks Behind the World Largest Toy Company* by Lowey Bundy Sichol
- *My Life* collection by Janet Tashjian
- *Out of My Mind* by Sharon M. Draper
- *Red: The (Fairly) True Tale of Red Riding Hood* by Liesl Shurtliff
- *Stargazing* by Jen Wang
- *The Contract* series by Derek Jeter and Paul Mantell
- *The Last Kids on Earth* series by Max Brailler
- *The Magic Treehouse* series by Mary Pope Osborne
- *Who Was?* series by various authors

Middle Grades Books

- *A Rover's Story* by Jasmine Warga
- *Artists, Writers, Thinkers, Dreamers: Portraits of Fifty Famous Folks and All Their Weird Stuff* by James Gulliver Hancock
- *From an Idea to Google: How Innovation at Google Changed the World* by Lowey Bundy Sichol
- *Look Both Ways: A Tale Told in Ten Blocks* by Jason Reynolds
- *Pashmina* by Nidhi Chanani
- *The Fort* by Gordon Korman
- *The Midnight Children* by Dan Gemeinhart
- *Those Kids From Fawn Creek* by Erin Entrada Kelly
- *Restart* by Gordan Korman
- *When Stars Are Scattered* by Victoria Jamieson and Omar Mohamed
- *Ground Zero* by Alan Gratz

Young Adult

- *A First Time for Everything* by Dan Santat
- *Dragon Hoops* by Gene Luen Yang
- *Clap When You Land* by Elizabeth Acevedo
- *Hey, Kiddo* by Jarrett J. Krosoczka
- *One of Us Is Lying* by Karen M. McManus
- *Poisoned* by Jennifer Donnelly

- *Arc of a Scythe* series by Neal Shusterman
- *The 57 Bus: The Story of Two Teenagers and the Crime That Changed Their Lives* by Dashka Slater
- *Patron Saints of Nothing* by Randy Ribay
- *The Way Things Work* by David MacAulay
- *This Mortal Coil* by Emily Suvada

Adult and Those Approaching High School Graduation

- *Anxious People* by Fredrik Backman
- *Atomic Habits: An Easy and Proven Way to Build Good Habits and Break Bad Ones* by James Clear
- *Educated* by Tara Westover
- *Hidden Pictures* by Jason Rekulak
- *Outliers: The Story of Success* by Malcolm Gladwell
- *Quiet: The Power of Introverts in a World That Can't Stop Talking* by Susan Cain
- *Remarkably Bright Creatures* by Shelby Van Pelt
- *The Four Agreements: A Practical Guide to Personal Freedom* by Don Miguel Ruiz
- *The Midnight Library* by Matt Haig
- *The Vanishing Half* by Brit Bennett

REFERENCES & RESOURCES

Alhabash, S., & Ma, M. (2017). A tale of four platforms: Motivations and uses of Facebook, Twitter, Instagram, and Snapchat among college students? *Social Media+ Society, 3*(1).

Allington, R. L., & Gabriel, R. (2012). "Every child, every day." *Educational Leadership, 69*(6), 10–15.

Allington, R. L., & McGill-Franzen, A. M. (2021). Reading volume and reading achievement: A review of recent research. *Reading Research Quarterly, 56*(S1), S231–S238.

Anderson, M., & Jiang, J. (2018, May 31). *Teens, social media and technology 2018.* Accessed at https://pewresearch.org/internet/2018/05/31/teens-social-media-technology-2018 on March 30, 2023.

Atwell, N. (2015). *In the middle: A lifetime of learning about writing, reading, and adolescents* (3rd ed.). Portsmouth, NH: Heinemann.

Auerbach, S. (2010). Beyond coffee with the principal: Toward leadership for authentic school-family partnerships. *Journal of School Leadership, 20*(6), 728–757.

Baker, E. A. (2010). *The new literacies: multiple perspectives on research and practice.* New York: The Guilford Press.

Baquedano-López, P., Alexander, R. A., & Hernandez, S. J. (2013). Equity issues in parental and community involvement in schools: What teacher educators need to know. *Review of Research in Education, 37*(1), 149–182.

Bartlett, C. E. (2020). *The winter duke.* New York: Little, Brown.

Beers, K., & Probst, R. E. (2013). *Notice and note: Strategies for close reading.* Portsmouth, NH: Heinemann.

Bennis, W. (2009). *On becoming a leader* (Rev. and updated ed.). New York: Basic Books.

Bilton, H. (2010). *Outdoor learning in the early years: Management and innovation* (3rd ed.). New York: Routledge.

Bishop. R. S. (1990). Mirrors, windows, and sliding glass doors. *Perspectives, 6*(3), ix–xi.

Bottoms, H. (2018, June 17). *How to host a completely awesome book swap.* Accessed at https://bookriot.com/how-to-host-a-book-swap on March 30, 2023.

Brooks, M., & Grennon Brooks, J. (2021). *Schools reimagined: Unifying the science of learning with the art of teaching.* Teachers College Press.

Brown, B. (2018). *Dare to lead: Brave work. Tough conversations. Whole hearts.* New York: Random House.

Bunting, E. (1991). *Fly away home.* New York: Clarion Books.

Burnett, C., & Merchant, G. (2020). Literacy-as-event: Accounting for relationality in literacy research. *Discourse: Studies in the Cultural Politics of Education, 41*(1), 45–56.

Calderón, M., & Solo, I. (2017). *Academic language mastery: Vocabulary in context.* Thousand Oaks, CA: Corwin.

Cambourne, B. (1988). *The whole story: Natural learning and acquisition of literacy in the classroom.* Jefferson City, MO: Scholastic.

Center for Disease Control and Prevention. (2012, November). *Promoting parent engagement: Improving student health and academic achievement.* Accessed at www.cdc.gov/healthyyouth/protective/pdf/parentengagement_teachers.pdf on July 20, 2023.

Chavkin, N. F., & Williams, D. L., Jr. (1987). Enhancing parent involvement: Guidelines for access to an important resource for school administrators. *Education and Urban Society, 19*(2), 164–184. https://doi.org/10.1177/0013124587019002005

Clinton, K., Jenkins, H., & McWilliams, J. (2013). New literacies in an age of participatory culture. In H. Jenkins & W. Kelley (Eds.), *Reading in a participatory culture: Remixing* Moby-Dick *in the English classroom* (pp. 3–24). New York: Teachers College Press.

Common Sense Media. (2020). *2020 annual report*. Accessed at https://commonsensemedia.org/sites/default/files/featured-content/files/2020-annual-report-web-resolution.pdf on March 30, 2023.

Costner, A. (2022). *My life as a potato*. New York: Random House Children's Books.

Couros, G. (2015). *The innovator's mindset: Empower learning, unleash talent, and lead a culture of creativity*. San Diego: Dave Burgess Consulting, Incorporated.

Dandy, J., & Nettelbeck, T. (2002). A cross-cultural study of parents' academic standards and educational aspirations for their children. *Educational Psychology, 22*(5), 621–627. https://doi.org/10.1080/0144341022000023662

Daniel, J. (2017, August 31). *Strong collaborative relationships for strong community schools*. Accessed at https://nepc.colorado.edu/publication/leadership on March 30, 2023.

Deedy, C. A. (2020). *Rita and Ralph's rotten day*. New York: Scholastic.

Degman, L. (2019). *Just read!* New York: Sterling Children's Books.

de León, C. (2020, January 27). Graphic novel wins Newbery Medal for the first time. *The New York Times*. Accessed at https://www.nytimes.com/2020/01/27/books/newbery-new-kid-jerry-craft-caldecott-undefeated-kwame-alexander.html#:~:text=%E2%80%9CNew%20Kid%E2%80%9D%20and%20%E2%80%9CThe,and%20Randolph%20Caldecott%20Medal%2C%20respectively.&text=The%20writer%20and%20illustrator%20Jerry,outstanding%20contribution%20to%20children's%20literature. on July 12, 2023.

DeMatthews, D. E. (2018). Social justice dilemmas: Evidence on the successes and shortcomings of three principals trying to make a difference. *International Journal of Leadership in Education, 21*(5), 545–559.

DeMatthews, D. E., Edwards, D. B., & Rincones, R. (2016). Social justice leadership and family engagement: A successful case from Ciudad Juarez, Mexico. *Educational Administration Quarterly, 52*(5), 1–39.

De Naeghel, J., Van Keer, H., Vansteenkiste, M., & Rosseel, Y. (2012). The relation between elementary students' recreational and academic reading motivation, reading, frequency, engagement, and comprehension: A self-determination theory perspective. *Journal of Educational Psychology, 104*(4), 1006–1021.

Donnelly, J. (2019). *Stepsister*. New York: Scholastic Press.

Dooley, C. M., Ellison, T. L., Welch, M. M., Allen, M., & Bauer, D. (2016). Digital participatory pedagogy: Digital participation as a method for technology integration in curriculum. *Journal of Digital Learning in Teacher Education, 32*(2), 52–62.

DuFour, R., & Marzano, R. J. (2011). *Leaders of learning: How district, school, and classroom leaders improve student achievement*. Bloomington, IN: Solution Tree Press.

Dweck, C. S. (2006). *Mindset: The new psychology of success*. New York: Random House.

Eccles, J., & Gootman, J. A. (Eds.). (2002). *Community programs to promote youth development*. Washington, DC: National Academy Press.

Eeds, M., & Wells, D. (1989). Grand conversations: An exploration of meaning construction in literature study groups. *Research in the Teaching of English, 23*(1), 4–29.

Elder, J. M. (2020). *Hood*. Los Angeles: Hyperion.

Emerson, L., Fear. J., Fox, S., & Sanders, E. (2012). *Parental engagement in learning and schooling: Lessons from research*. Canberra, Australia: Australian Research Alliance for Children and Youth (ARACY) for the Family-School and Community Partnerships Bureau.

Epstein, J. L., & Sheldon, S. B. (2002). Present and accounted for: Improving student attendance through family and community involvement. *The Journal of Educational Research, 95*(5), 308–318. https://doi.org/10.1080/00220670209596604

Fagell, P. L. (2019). *Middle school matters: The ten key skills kids need to thrive in middle school and beyond—and how parents can help*. New York: Hachette.

Fan, X., & Chen, M. (2001). Parental involvement and students' academic achievement: A meta-analysis. *Educational Psychology Review, 13*(1), 1–22.

Ferriter, B. (2014, January 28). *Should we be engaging or empowering learners?* [Blog post]. Accessed at https://blog.williamferriter.com/2014/01/28/should-we-be-engaging-or-empowering-learners on July 17, 2023.

Fisher, D., Flood, J., Lapp, D., & Frey, N. (2004). Interactive read-alouds: Is there a common set of implementation practices? *The Reading Teacher, 58*(1), 8–17. https://doi.org/10.1598/RT.58.1.1

Flores, O. J., & Kyere, E. (2021). Advancing equity-based school leadership: The importance of family-school relationships. *The Urban Review, 53*(1), 127–144. https://doi.org/10.1007/s11256-020-00557-z

Gallagher, K. (2022, October 21). *Engaging adolescent readers* [Conference presentation]. New York State English Council Conference, Albany, NY.

Gardner, J. W. (1993). *On leadership*. New York: The Free Press.

Gates, M. (2015). *Good night yoga: A pose-by-pose bedtime story*. Boulder, CO: Sounds True.

Gee, J. P. (1999). Critical issues: Reading and the new literacy studies: Reframing the National Academy of Sciences report on reading. *Journal of Literacy Research, 31*(3), 355–374. https://doi.org/10.1080/10862969909548052

Gee, J. P. (2010). A situated-sociocultural approach to literacy and technology. In E.A. Baker (Ed.), *The new literacies: Multiple perspectives on research and practice* (pp. 165–193). New York: Guilford Press.

Gemmink, M. M., Fokkens-Bruinsma, M., Pauw, I., & van Veen, K. (2021). How contextual factors influence teachers' pedagogical practices. *Educational Research, 63*(4), 396–415.

Gitomer, D. H., & Bell, C. A. (Eds.). (2016). *Handbook of research on teaching* (5th ed.). Washington, DC: American Educational Research Association.

Goodman, K. (1996). *On reading: A common-sense look at the nature of language and the science of reading*. Portsmouth, NH: Heinemann.

Groff, J. S., & Mouza, C. (2008). A framework for addressing challenges to classroom technology use. *AACE Journal, 16*(1), 21–46.

Hamre, B., Hatfield, B., Pianta, R., & Jamil, F. (2014). Evidence for general and domain-specific elements of teacher-child interactions: Associations with preschool children's development. *Child Development, 85*(3), 1257–1274.

Hattie, J. A. C. (2009). *Visible learning: A synthesis of over 800 meta-analyses relating to achievement*. London: Routledge.

Hattie, J. A. C. (2012). *Visible learning for teachers: Maximizing impact on learning*. London: Routledge.

Heard, G. (2016). *Heart maps: Helping students create and craft authentic writing*. Portsmouth, NH: Heinemann.

Heath, S. B. (1983). *Ways with words: Language, life, and work in communities and classrooms*. Cambridge, England: Cambridge University Press.

Heath, S. B. (2010). Family literacy or community learning? Some critical questions on perspective. In K. Dunsmore and D. Fisher (Eds.), *Bringing literacy home* (pp. 15–41). Newark, DE: International Reading Association.

Heath, S. B., & McLaughlin, M. W. (1994). The best of both worlds: Connecting schools and community youth organizations for all-day, all-year learning. *Educational Administration Quarterly, 30*(3), 278–300.

Hiebert, E. H. (2014). *Frank views on literacy and the Common Core*. Accessed at https://textproject.org/wp-content/uploads/books/Hiebert-2014-Frank-Views-on-Literacy-and-the-Common-Core.pdf on March 30, 2023.

Hirsh-Pasek, K., & Golinkoff, R. M. (2008). *Why play = learning*. Accessed at https://researchgate.net/publication/237108843_Why_Play_Learning on July 14, 2023.

Hunt, L. M. (2019). *Shouting at the rain*. New York: Paulsen Books.

Ishimaru, A. M. (2019). From family engagement to equitable collaboration. *Educational Policy, 33*(2), 350–385.

Jenkins, H. (2009). *Confronting the challenges of participatory culture: Media education for the 21st century*. Cambridge, MA: The MIT Press.

Jenkins, H., & Kelley, W. (Eds.). (2013). *Reading in a participatory culture: Remixing* Moby-Dick *in the English classroom*. New York: Teachers College Press.

Jewell, T. (2020). *This book is anti-racist: Twenty lessons on how to wake up, take action, and do the work*. London: Frances Lincoln Children's Books.

Jeynes, W. H. (2018) A practical model for school leaders to encourage parental involvement and parental engagement. *School Leadership and Management, 38*(2), 147–163.

Jocius, R., & Shealy, S. (2018). Critical book clubs: Reimagining literature reading and response. *Reading Teacher, 71*(6), 691–702.

Johnston, V. (2016). Successful read-alouds in today's classroom. *Kappa Delta Pi Record, 52*(1), 39–42. https://doi.org/10.1080/00228958.2016.1123051

Kalantzis, M., & Cope, B. (2010). The teacher as designer: Pedagogy in the new media age. *E-Learning and Digital Media, 7*(3), 200–222. https://doi.org/10.2304/elea.2010.7.3.200

Kinney, J. (2007). *Diary of a wimpy kid (#1)*. New York: Amulet Books.

Korman, G. (2022). *The fort*. New York: Scholastic Press.

Layne, S. L. (2009). *Igniting a passion for reading: Successful strategies for building lifetime readers*. Portland, ME: Stenhouse.

Layne, S. L. (2015). *In defense of read-aloud: Sustaining best practice*. Portland, ME: Stenhouse.

Lee, J.-S., & Bowen, N. K. (2006). Parent involvement, cultural capital, and the achievement gap among elementary school children. *American Educational Research Journal, 43*(2), 193–218.

Leland, C. H., Lewison, M., & Harste, J. C. (2013). *Teaching children's literature: It's critical!* New York: Routledge.

Lennox, S. (2013). Interactive read-alouds—An avenue for enhancing children's language for thinking and understanding: A review of recent research. *Early Childhood Education Journal, 41*(5), 381–389. https://doi.org/10.1007/s10643-013-0578-5

Levin, B. (2008). *How to change 5000 schools: A practical and positive approach for leading change at every level*. Cambridge, MA: Harvard Education Press.

Lewis, M., & Samuels, S. J. (2005). *Read more—Read better? A meta-analysis of the literature on the relationship between exposure to reading and reading achievement*. Minneapolis: University of Minnesota.

Lopez, G. R., Scribner, J. D., & Mahitivanichcha, K. (2001). Redefining parental involvement: Lessons from high-performing migrant-impacted schools. *American Educational Research Journal, 38*(2), 253–288.

Luffarelli, J., Stamatogiannakis, A., & Yang, H. (2019). The visual asymmetry effect: An interplay of logo design and brand personality on brand equity. *Journal of Marketing Research, 56*(1), 89–103.

Luke, A. (1994). *The social construction of literacy in the primary school*. South Melbourne, Victoria, Australia: Macmillan Education Australia.

Martin, A. M. (2019). *Karen's witch (Baby-Sitters Little Sister #1)*. New York: Graphix.

Massimino, M. (2020). *Spaceman: The true story of a young boy's journey to becoming an astronaut*. New York: Yearling.

Mattingly, D. J., Prislin, R., McKenzie, T. L., Rodriguez, J. L., & Kayzar, B. (2002). Evaluating evaluations: The case of parent involvement programs. *Review of Educational Research, 72*(4), 549–576.

Middaugh, D. (2019). *What we know about 2018 graphic novel sales*. Accessed at https://publishersweekly.com/pw/by-topic/industry-news/comics/article/79818-what-we-know-about-2018-graphic-novel-sales.html on March 30, 2023.

Miller, D. (2009). *The book whisperer: Awakening the inner reader in every child*. San Francisco: Jossey-Bass.

Mol, S. E., & Bus, A. G. (2011). To read or not to read: A meta-analysis of print exposure from infancy to early adulthood. *Psychological Bulletin, 137*(2), 267–296.

National Center for Education Statistics. (2009). *NAEP 2008 trends in academic progress*. Washington, DC: National Center for Education Statistics, Institute of Education Sciences, U.S. Department of Education.

National Endowment for the Arts. (2007). *To read or not to read: A question of national consequence* (Research report # 47). Washington, DC: Author.

Neumann, M. M., Hood, M., Ford, R. M., & Neumann, D. L. (2011). The role of environmental print in emergent literacy. *Journal of Early Childhood Literacy, 12*(3), 231–258.

New York State Education Department. (2017a). Lifelong practices of readers and writers. In *New York State Next Generation English language arts learning standards* (p. 8.) Accessed at www.nysed.gov/common/nysed/files/programs/curriculum-instruction/nys-next-generation-ela-standards.pdf on March 27, 2023.

New York State Education Department. (2017b). *New York State Next Generation English language arts standards* (Rev.). Accessed at www.nysed.gov/curriculum-instruction/new-york-state-next-generation-english-language-arts-learning-standards on March 27, 2023.

Nosrat, S. (2017). *Salt, fat, acid, heat: Mastering the elements of good cooking.* New York: Simon & Schuster.

O'Neill, A. (2002). *The recess queen.* New York: Scholastic.

Orozco, J.-L. (2020). *Sing with me/Canta conmigo: Six classic songs in English and Spanish.* New York: Scholastic Press.

Paul, P., & Russo, M. (2019). *How to raise a reader.* New York: Workman.

Pew Research Center. (2021). *U.S. 9- and 13-year-olds read for fun less often than they used to.* Accessed at https://www.pewresearch.org/short-reads/2021/11/12/among-many-u-s-children-reading-for-fun-has-become-less-common-federal-data-shows/ft_21-11-09_readingforfun_1/ on July 24, 2023.

Pressley, M., Allington, R. L., Wharton-McDonald, R., Block, C. C., & Morrow, L. M. (2001). *Learning to read: Lessons from exemplary first-grade classrooms.* New York: Guilford Press.

Pruzinsky, T. (2014). Read books. Every day. Mostly for pleasure. *The English Journal, 103*(4), 25–30.

Pyle, A., & Bigelow, A. (2015). Play in kindergarten: An interview and observational study in three Canadian classrooms. *Early Childhood Education Journal, 43*(5), 385–393. https://doi.org/10.1007/s10643-014-0666-1

Reynolds, J., & Kendi, I. X. (2021). *Stamped (for kids): Racism, antiracism, and you.* New York: Little, Brown Books for Young Readers.

Richgels, D. J. (1982). Schema theory, linguistic theory, and representations of reading comprehension. *The Journal of Educational Research, 76*(1), 54–62.

Rideout, V., Peebles, A., Mann, S., & Robb, M. B. (2022). *The Common Sense census: Media use by tweens and teens, 2021.* San Francisco: Common Sense. Accessed at https://commonsensemedia.org/sites/default/files/research/report/8-18-census-integrated-report-final-web_0.pdf on July 7, 2023.

Ripp, P. (2018). *Passionate readers: The art of teaching reading and engaging every child.* New York: Routledge.

Rogers, A. (2014). *The base of the iceberg: Informal learning and its impact on formal and non-formal learning.* Opladen, Germany: Budrich.

Roessingh, H. (2020). Read-alouds in the upper elementary classroom: Developing academic vocabulary. *TESOL Journal, 11*(1), e00465.

Rosenblatt, L. M. (1968). *Literature as exploration.* Champaign, IL: National Council of Teachers of English.

Sachar, L. (2000). *Holes.* New York: Yearling.

Santoro, L. E., Chard, D. J., Howard, L., & Baker, S. K. (2008). Making the very most of classroom read-alouds to promote comprehension and vocabulary. *The Reading Teacher, 61*(5), 396–408.

Schaeffer, K. (2021, November 12). *Among many U.S. children, reading for fun has become less common, federal data shows.* Accessed at https://pewresearch.org/fact-tank/2021/11/12/among-many-u-s-children-reading-for-fun-has-become-less-common-federal-data-shows on March 27, 2023.

Scholastic. (2019). *Kids and family reading report* (7th ed.). Accessed at https://www.scholastic.com/readingreport/home.html on March 28, 2023.

Sénéchal, M., & Young, L. (2008). The effect of family literacy interventions on children's acquisition of reading from kindergarten to grade 3: A meta-analytic review. *Review of Educational Research, 78*(4), 880–907. https://doi.org/10.3102/0034654308320319

Serravallo, J. (2015). *The reading strategies book: Your everything guide to developing skilled readers.* Portsmouth, NH: Heinemann.

Snicket, L. (1999). *The bad beginning (A Series of Unfortunate Events #1).* New York: HarperCollins.

Stoetzel, L., & Shedrow, S. (2021). Making the transition to virtual methods in the literacy classroom: Reframing teacher education practices. *Excelsior: Leadership in Teaching and Learning, 13*(2), 127–142. https://doi.org/10.14305/jn.19440413.2021.13.2.04

Street, B. (1984). *Literacy in theory and practice.* Cambridge, England: Cambridge University Press.

Street, B. (1993). The new literacy studies, guest editorial. *Journal of Research in Reading, 16*(2), 81–97.

Street, B. (1995). *Social literacies: Critical approaches to literacy in development, ethnography, and education.* Michigan: Longman.

Street, B. (1997). The implications of the "new literacy studies" for literacy education. *English in Education, 31*(3), 45–59.

Street, B. (2003). What's "new" in new literacy studies? Critical approaches to literacy in theory and practice. *Current Issues in Comparative Education, 5*(2), 77–91.

Street, B. (2016). Learning to read from a social practice view: Ethnography, schooling and adult learning. *Prospects: Comparative Journal of Curriculum, Learning, and Assessment, 46*(3/4), 335–344.

Street, B. (2021). *Literacy in theory and practice.* Cambridge University Press.

Taylor, D. (1997). *Many families, many literacies: An international declaration of principles.* Portsmouth, NH: Heinemann.

Taylor, D., & Dorsey-Gaines, C. (1988). *Growing up literate: Learning from inner-city families.* Portsmouth, NH: Heinemann.

Torppa, M., Niemi, P., Vasalampi, K., Lerkkanen, M.-K., Tolvanen, A., & Poikkeus, A.-M. (2020). Leisure reading (but not any kind) and reading comprehension support each other—A longitudinal study across grades 1 and 9. *Child Development, 91*(3), 876–900.

Unsworth, L. (2008). Multiliteracies, e-literature and English teaching. *Language and Education, 22*(1), 62–75.

van Bergen, E., Vasalampi, K., & Torppa, M. (2021). How are practice and performance related? Development of reading from age 5 to 15. *Reading Research Quarterly, 56*(3), 415–434.

Van Dusen, C. (2019). *If I built a school.* New York: Dial Books for Young Readers.

Van Oers, B., & Duijkers, D. (2013) Teaching in a play-based curriculum: Theory, practice and evidence of developmental education for young children. *Journal of Curriculum Studies, 45*(4), 511–534. https://doi.org/10.1080/00220272.2011.637182

Vaughn, M., Jang, B. G., Sotirovska, V., & Cooper-Novack, G. (2020). Student agency in literacy: A systematic review of the literature. *Reading Psychology, 41*(7), 712–734.

Vygotsky, L. S. (1978). *Mind in society: The development of higher psychological processes.* Cambridge, MA: Harvard University Press.

Vygotsky, L. S. (1986). *Thought and language* (Rev. ed.). Cambridge, MA: The MIT Press.

Weisberg, D. S., Hirsh-Pasek, K., & Golinkoff, R. M. (2013). Embracing complexity: Rethinking the relation between play and learning—Comment on Lillard et al. *Psychological Bulletin, 139*(1), 35–39.

West, C. (2021, June 14). *Hashtag analytics 101: Using the best hashtags for your social strategy.* Accessed at https://sproutsocial.com/insights/hashtag-analytics on March 30, 2023.

Wilder, S. (2014). Effects of parental involvement on academic achievement: A meta-synthesis. *Educational Review, 66*(3), 377–397.

Wilhelm, J. D., & Smith, M. W. (2016). The power of pleasure reading: What we can learn from the secret reading lives of teens. *English Journal, 105*(6), 25–30.

Willems, M. (2019). *The pigeon has to go to school!* New York: Hyperion Books for Children.

World Economic Forum. (2016, January). *The future of jobs: Employment, skills and workforce strategy for the fourth industrial revolution.* Accessed at www3.weforum.org/docs/WEF_Future_of_Jobs.pdf on June 24, 2023.

Yolen, J. (2016). *What to do with a box.* Mankato, MN: Creative Editions.

Yolen, J. (2019). *What to do with a string.* Mankato, MN: Creative Editions.

Yont, K. M., Snow, C. E., & Vernon-Feagans, L. (2003). The role of context in mother-child interactions: An analysis of communicative intents expressed during toy play and book reading with 12-month-olds. *Journal of Pragmatics, 35*(3), 435–454.

INDEX

A

access, 155, 161–162
Acevedo, E., 33, 52, 136, 188
Acho, E., 53
acknowledging diversity, 156
agency, 105
Alexander, K., 33, 52, 169, 184
Ali, S. K., 91, 181, 183
All Are Neighbors (Penfold), 182, 185
All Are Welcome (Penfold), 137, 182
Alexander, K., 136
Allington, R. L., 11
Alma and How She Got Her Name (Martinez-Neal), 181
Almost American Girl (Ha), 45–46, 52
Along Came Coco (Byrne), 91, 181
Amato, M., 185
Amazon, 62
American Born Chinese (Yang), 136
Amulet series (Kibuishi), 47
analysis skills, 4
Anger Is a Gift (Oshiro), 33
Anisansel, J., 38, 138
anticipatory planning, 6, 123, 125
    contacting the author, 125–126
    determining the purpose, 125
    naming the details, 126–127
Anxious People (Backman), 189
Arc of a Scythe series (Shusterman), 189
Are Your Stars Like My Stars? (Helakoski), 187
art department, 175
Artists, Thinkers, Dreamers (Hancock), 188
ASCD, 173
assessment, 2
Atomic Habits (Clear), 189
Atwell, N., 30
author visits, 5, 95, 123–124
    anticipating a planning process, 123, 125–127
    author questions organizer, 129
    author study structures, 132–133
    authors who write for multiple age groups, 136
    books for younger and older readers to explore together, 137

    developing connections between curriculum and the author's work, 123, 130–133
    expanding the impact to stakeholders, 123, 134–138
    generating questions for, 141
    planning page, 128, 140
    rallying students, 123, 127–129
    reflection questions, 139
    reflections from other teachers, 138
    roots of the work, 124
    welcome address planning page, 142

B

Baby-Sitters Little Sister #1 (Martin), 34
Backman, F., 189
The Bad Beginning (Snicket), 34
Bailey, L., 185
Baker, S. K., 159
Baloney and Friends (Pizzoli), 46
BAND app, 90
Barnett, M., 182
Barrett, J., 56, 184
Bartlett, C. E., 34
Be You! (Reynolds), 182
The Beatryce Prophecy (DiCamillo), 52, 136
Beaty, A., 184
Because (Willems), 179
Beers, K., 166
Bennett, B., 189
Best Friends (Hale & Pham), 35
Big Feelings (Penfold), 183
A Big Mooncake for Little Star (Lin), 136
bilingual books, 56
Bishop, R. D., 48–50, 67, 91, 158
Bisnow, M. M., 154
Blackburne, L., 181
Boelts, M., 183
Boiger, A., 136
#BookADay challenge, 85
book categories, 36
book clubs
    clubs within a club, 45–47
    decide your intent, 44
    discussion questions list, 65
    for adults, 27, 43–44

    for staff, 169
    grades 1–3, 46
    grades 3–5, 47
    middle and high school, 46–47
    norms and agreements, 70, 72
    one book, several meetings, 44–45
    presentation slides, 67–68
    sample email, 46
    several books, several meetings, 47
    think about card, 70
book displays, 95
book drives, 3
book fairs, 9, 95, 98–99, 110
    deciding what type, 98–99
    noticing what students choose, 100
    promoting, 99
    sample advertisement, 100
    summer, 3, 99
The Book Hog (Pizzoli), 185
book lists, 5
    adults/those approaching graduation, 189
    chapter books, 188
    clothing, 185
    community and connectedness, 182, 185
    diverse identities and communities, 181
    early chapter books, 187
    feelings and emotions, 183
    food, 184
    for school events, 172–173
    imagination and creative thinking, 183
    interactive read-alouds for younger audiences, 185
    kindness and consideration, 183
    middle grade books, 188
    perseverance and determination, 184
    picture books, 187
    pizza, 184
    school values, 182
    sports, 184
    to share with caregivers, 187–189
    young adult books, 189–190
book recommendation videos
    classroom connection, 55
    collaborating on, 27, 39–42, 54
    create and share, 55
    find technicians, 54

invite adults to participate, 54
book study for caregivers, 143, 153–154
    acknowledging diversity, 156
    choosing a book or topic, 154
    creating ongoing dialogue, 156
    discussion questions, 156
    incorporating an author visit, 156
    inviting and advertising, 154–155
    sample books, 154
    sample invitation and schedule, 155
book swaps, 3, 95
    classroom connection, 29
    get people talking, 35–37
    get ready to swap, 37
    intrigued by the lead book ideas, 34
    lift a line cards, 36, 64
    mark the calendar, 32
    memorialize the event, 38
    plan with students in mind, 32–35
    planning, 27
    read the rainbow displays, 32–33
    sample invitations, 33
    sending an invitation, 32
    sharing a thank-you, 38–39
book talks, 3, 86
    student-led, 103, 107-114
    with families and caregivers, 110
book tastings, 55
    asking for feedback, 58–59
    buying books, 59
    classroom connection, 59–62
    facilitating, 58
    for students and caregivers, 158
    hosting, 27, 55–61
    images, 61
    preparing a space, 55–56
    preparing materials, 56
    presentation slides, 58, 73, 73–80
    recording sheets, 58, 78–79
    sample menus, 57
    sharing the benefits, 58
The Book Whisperer (Miller), 31
book-making projects, 175
books as mirrors, 48–50, 58, 91, 158
    presentation slides, 67–69
    thinking chart, 71
Boxitects (Smith), 183
Brady, T., 123
Brailler, M., 188
#BrandReading. *See* launching a reading campaign
branding, 5
    strategies, 12–13
Brett, J., 185
Bridwell, N., 184
Bring Your Own Book website, 36
Brooks, J. G., 27–28
Brooks, M., 27–28
Brown, B., 6

Brown, K., 181
Bug Boys (Knetzger), 46
Buntin, E., 34
Burach, R., 187
Burger King
    descriptive logo, 14
Burnett, C., 52, 62
Burns, C., 160
Bush, B. P., 183
business department, 174
Byers, G., 182
Byrne, E., 91, 181

C

Cain, E., 53–54
Cain, S., 189
Cambourne, B., 7
The Candymakers (Mass), 184
Canva website, 41, 94
Caps for Sale (Slobodkina), 185
Captain Underpants series (Pilkey), 185
caregivers. *See* families and caregivers
carrying your book, 86
catchy promotions, 39
celebrations, 3, 81–82, 94–96
Chanani, N., 188
Change Sings (Gorman), 169, 182
Chard, D. J., 159
Charlie and the Chocolate Factory (Dahl), 55
Cherry, M. A., 187
Choi, Y., 181
choice making, 105
Chromebooks, 89, 92
Circulo de la Hispanidad, 23
Clanton, B., 46, 187
Clap When You Land (Acevedo), 52, 136, 188
Class Act (Craft), 45, 47
classroom connections
    book clubs, 52
    book recommendation videos, 55
    book swaps, 39
    book tastings, 59–62
    newsletters, 42
Clear, J., 189
Clifford's Sports Day (Bridwell), 184
Clinton, C., 136
Clinton, K., 82
Closer to Nowhere (Hopkins), 52
Cloudy With a Chance of Meatballs (Barrett), 56, 184
clubs and service projects, 174
collaborating on a book recommendation video, 27, 54–55
collaborating with other departments, 173–176
    art, 175
    business, 174
    clubs and service projects, 174
    instructional technology, 173–174
    mathematics, 174–175

    music, 174
    physical education and play, 174
    promoting choice, 175
comment features, 90
The Common Sense Census (Rideout et al), 9
community and connectedness, 1, 9, 20–24
    local business, 112, 152
    recommended books, 182
Community Programs to Promote Youth Development (Eccles & Gootman), 22
community read-alouds, 20–21
    connect with local camps, 23
    contact local restaurants, 23
    engage the multilingual community, 23
    partner with youth programs, 21–22
    partnering with the local library, 23
    sample schedule, 21
    using outdoor spaces, 21
comprehension, 2, 4
connectedness, 104
continuing to prioritize reading, 165
    book lists for school events, 165, 172–173
    collaborating with other departments, 165, 173–176
    examples of picture books to explore topics, 169
    reflection questions, 176
    reflections from other teachers, 172
    roots of the work, 165–167
    spotlight book of the month, 165, 170–172
    supporting a new focus, 165, 167–169
The Contract series (Jeter & Mantell), 188
The Cool Bean (John & Oswald), 182
Cooper-Novack, G., 105
Corduroy (Freeman), 185
Cornett, D., 88
Cornwall, G., 184
Cory, S., 184
Costner, A., 34
courage, 6–7
COVID-19 pandemic, 2–3
    books clubs by videoconferencing, 44
    use of technology and media increased, 9, 20, 62, 87–88
Craft, J., 45, 47
creating a newscast, 99
creating a slogan or hashtag, 9, 13–14
creating writing invitations, 95
creativity, 6
Crossover series (Alexander), 136
cultural experiences, 5
culture
    building, 62–63
    defined, 6
    personalizing, 62
    work, 3
Cupani, D., 42–43
Curious George and the Pizza Party (Rey & Rey), 184

currently reading signs, 83
    examples, 84–85
    sample email, 84
    using for reflection, 85
curriculum celebration, 161

D

da Vinci, L., 123
Dahl, R., 56
The Day the Crayons Quit (Daywalt), 183, 185
The Day You Begin (Woodson), 136, 182
Daywalt, D., 183, 185
de la Peña, M., 136–137, 169, 181–182
Dear Sweet Pea (Murphy), 52
declaring your own celebratory month, 94
    engaging community members, 95–96
    plan ways to celebrate, 94–95
    promote the event, 94
    sample email, 96
    select the month, 94
decoding, 2
Dee, B., 52
Deedy, C. A., 34
Degman, L., 7
Denise, C., 184
dePaola, T., 184
Desierto, D., 183
designing a logo
    collaborate with the art or technology department, 15
    launching your campaign, 9, 13–15
    open submission opportunity, 15
    partnering with an artist, 15
designing bookmarks, 99
developing a vision, 9, 13
developing connections between curriculum and an author's work, 123, 130–131
    inviting the author to be part of an author study, 131
    promoting the author's books, 131
    reading an excerpt, 131
    using selections as a mentor text, 131
developing role models,
    aiming to personalize culture, 62
    book club launch presentation slides, 67–70
    book discussion questions list, 65
    books as mirrors, windows, and sliding glass doors thinking chart, 71
    collaborating on a book recommendation video, 27, 54–55
    designing a newsletter, 27, 39–42
    facilitating book clubs for adults, 27, 43–54
    hosting a book tasting, 27, 55–61
    how to make it happen, 31
    learning from leaders in the field, 30–31
    norms and agreements, 72
    planning a book swap, 27, 32–39
    reading schedule for a book club, 66
    reflection questions, 63
    reflections from other teachers, 35, 38, 42–43, 47–48, 51–54, 60
    roots of this work, 27–28
    why social/cultural experiences influence literacy development, 28–30
    book tasking presentation slides, 73–80
Diary of a Wimpy Kid (Kinney), 34
Diaz, J., 137, 181
DiCamillo, K., 52, 136, 187
A Different Pond (Phi), 181
Discord app, 12
DiTerlizzi, A., 184
diverse identities and communities
    acknowledging, 161–162
    recommended books, 181
Dog Man (Pilkey), 46, 187
Don't Worry, Be Happy (Burach), 187
Donato, J., 43
Donnolly, J., 52, 188
Dorsey-Gaines, C., 20
Dorsey-Gaines, T., 20
Dragon Hoops (Yang), 52, 136, 188
Dragons Love Tacos (Rubin), 184
Draper, S. M., 188
Dreamers (Morales), 182

E

Each Kindness (Woodson), 183
Eating the Alphabet (Ehlert), 184
Educated (Westover), 189
efficacy, 5
Ehlert, L., 184
El Deafo (Bell), 47
Eland, E., 183
Eleanor and Park (Rowell), 52
Elliot, R., 187
Ellis, C., 185
embracing *some*, 177–179
engagement, 103–104
engaging the community, 1, 20–24
    local restaurants, 23
    supporting literacy development, 20
Escape From Mr. Lemoncello's Library (Grabenstein), 88
Espitia, J. C. G., 184
Estes, E., 185
Evelyn Del Rey Is Moving Away (Medina), 183
everyone is important, 1
expanding an author's impact to stakeholders, 123, 134
    expanding an author's presence across multiple schools, 135–138
    hosting a visit for caregivers, 134
    integrating into professional learning, 134–135
exploring the school library, 160–161
exploring your own reading life, 4
Extra Yarn (Barnett), 182
Eyes That Kiss in the Corners (Ho), 181

F

Facebook, 12
Facebook Live, 89
facilitating book clubs for adults, 27, 43–54
Fagell, P. L., 134, 154
families and caregivers, 5
    book study, 143, 153–156
    book talks, 110
    connecting with, 16
    engaging in building reading culture, 143
    how to make it happen, 145–146
    importance of access, 161–162
    inviting caregivers and students to participate together, 143, 157–161
    learning academy for caregivers, 143, 146–153
    need for ongoing reflection, 161–162
    reflection questions, 163
    reflections from other teachers, 157
    roots of the work, 143–145
    tips for caregivers, 164
Fancy Nancy (O'Connor), 185
fartleks, 174
Faruqi, S., 187
feedback
    asking for, 51–52
    booktasting events, 59–60
feelings and emotions
    recommended books, 183
Ferriter, B., 103–104
Fiesta con pizza/Pizza Party (Espitia & Schinel), 184
The 57 Bus (Slater), 189
Finally, Something Dangerous (Cornett), 88
Finally, Something Mysterious (Cornett), 88
first book marketplace, 173
first chapter Fridays, 86, 131
A First Time for Everything (Santat), 188
flexibility, 6–7
Flipgrid website, 90
The Floating Field (Riley), 182
Flores, L. J., 144
fluency, 2
Fly Away Home (Bunting), 34
Flying Lessons and Other Stories (Oh), 160
Fokkens-Bruinsma, M., 28
Football Genius (Green), 184
For Every One (Reynolds), 136
The Fort (Korman), 122, 188
The 47 People You'll Meet in Middle School (Mahoney), 52
The Four Agreements (Ruiz), 189
Fox, M., 154, 187
Free Lunch (Ogle), 52
Freeman, D., 185
From an Idea to Disney (Sichol), 188
From an Idea to Google (Sichol), 188
From an Idea to LEGO (Sichol), 188
Front Desk (Yang), 136
Fry Bread (Maillard), 91, 181

G

Gallagher, J., 10–11
Gallagher, K., 166
Gardner, J. W., 27
Gates, M., 22
Gemeinhart, D., 52, 188
Gemmink, M. M., 28
Genesis Begins Again (Williams), 53
genre jars, 35
Gephart, D., 52
getting people to talk about books, 35–37
    lift a line prompt cards, 36
Gibbs, S., 88
The Girl Who Never Made Mistakes (Prett & Rubinstein), 183
Gizzoli, G., 185
Gladwell, M., 189
Going Places (Reynolds & Reynolds), 183
The Good Egg (John & Oswald), 137, 183
Good Night Yoga (Gates), 22
Goodman, K., 143–144
Goodreads, 9, 62
Google Classroom, 89–90, 111
Google Doc, 41, 50
Google Forms, 31, 45, 60
Google Meet, 88–90, 161
Google Sites, 41
Google Slides, 20, 41, 60
Gorman, A., 169, 182
Grabenstein, C., 88
Graphic novels, 45–47
Gratz, A., 188
Green, T., 184
Ground Zero (Gratz), 188
guest readers, 95
guides on the side, 104
Gutman, D., 184
Guts (Telgemeier), 33

H

Ha, R., 45–46, 52
Haddix, M. P., 88
Hager, J. B., 183
Haig, M., 189
Hair Love (Cherry), 187
Hale, S., 35
Hancock, J. G., 188
Happy Dreamer (Reynolds), 130
Harbor Me (Woodson), 136
Harris, K., 154
hashtags
    creating, 9–10, 13–14
    defined, 12
    samples, 14
Hattie, J. A. C., 28–30
Hauser, C. M., 47–48
Heath, S. B., 20, 22
Helakoski, L., 187

helping students become literacy leaders, 103–104
    readers as leaders program, 103, 114–116
    reflection questions, 116–117
    reflections from other teachers, 104, 112–113
    roots of the work, 104–105
    schoolwide student-led book talks, 103, 107–113
    student reading ambassadors, 103, 105–107
    student-led book talks in the classroom, 103, 114
The Hero Next Door (Rhuday–Perkovich), 160
Hess, M. R., 136
Hey, Kiddo (Krosoczka), 45–46, 188
Hidden Pictures (Rekulak), 189
Higgins, R. T., 185
Hispanic Heritage Month, 175
Ho, J., 181
Holes (Sachar), 34
Holt, K. A., 183
Home (Ellis), 185
Home Is in Between (Perkins), 182
Hood (Moke), 34
Hopkins, E., 52
hosting community events online, 87
    read-aloud chapter books, 88–90
    using picture books to share community values, 90–93
how to make it happen, 5
    author visits, 125–137
    continuing to prioritize reading, 167–176
    developing role models, 31–62
    engaging families and caregivers, 145–161
    helping students become literacy leaders, 105–116
    launching your campaign, 13–17
    sustaining the culture, 83–100
How to Raise a Reader (Paul & Russo), 145, 154–155, 157
How to Read a Book (Alexander), 136
Howard, L., 159
Hubbard, R. L., 184
The Hundred Dresses (Estes), 185
Hunt, L. M., 52, 112

I

I Am Courage (Verde), 182
I Am Enough (Byers), 182
I Am Human (Verde), 137
I Am Me (Verde), 182
I Am One (Verde), 137
I Am Peace (Verde), 182
I Am Perfectly Designed (Brown), 181
I Dream of Popo (Blackburne), 181
I Have an Idea! (Tullet), 183
I Promise (James), 184
I Survived series (Tarshis), 47
I Will Make Miracles (Morgenstern), 179
I Wonder (Holt), 183
If I Built a Car (Van Dusen), 183

If I Built a House (Van Dusen), 183
If I Built a School (Van Dusen), 171, 183
If Kids Ruled the World (Bailey), 185
If You Give a Mouse a Cookie (Numeroff), 184
Igniting a Passion for Reading (Layne), 10
The Iheards (Kilgore), 183
imagination and creative thinking
    recommended books, 183
Imagine That (Voss), 183
immersion, 7
iMovie, 54
importance of shared planning, 100
In the Middle (Atwell), 31
In Your Shoes (Gephart), 52
inclusivity, 168
individual growth targets, 2
innovative thinking, 6
Instagram, 12, 16
Instagram Live, 88–89, 92
instructional technology department, 173–174
intentionality, 105
interactive read-alouds, 158–159
    defined, 158
interactiveness, 105
International Literacy Association, 173
Interrupting Chicken (Stein), 185
Intrigued by the lead, 33
    ideas for, 34
The Invisible Boy (Ludwig), 181
The Invisible String (Karst), 182
The Invisible Web (Karst), 137, 182
inviting caregivers and students to participate together, 157–158
    book tastings, 158
    curriculum celebrations, 161
    exploring the school library, 160–161
    interactive read-alouds, 158–160
    schoolwide book talks, 161
iPads, 89, 92
ish (Reynolds), 183
Islandborn (Diaz), 91, 137, 181
Iwai, M., 184, 187

J

Jabari Tries (Cornwall), 184
Jackson, T. D., 33
Jada Jones Rock Star (Lyons), 187
James, L., 184
Jamieson, V., 45–46, 188
Jang, B. G., 105
Jeffers, O., 182
Jeter, D., 188
Jobs, S., 123
John, J., 137, 182–183
Jordan, D., 184
Jordan, R., 184
journaling, 175
joy in schools is important, 1, 82
Jumanji (Van Allsburg), 185

Just Ask (Sotomayor), 172, 183
Just Read (Degman), 7

K

Karst, P., 137, 182
Kayzar, B., 144
Kelly, E. E., 188
Kendi, I. X., 53
Kids and Family Reading Report (Scholastic), 54, 100
Kiley-Rendon, P., 22
Kilgore, E., 183
kindergarten reading parade, 96–97
    inviting the community, 97–98
    props and garb, 97
    scheduling, 97
The Kindest Red (Muhammad & Ali), 183
kindness and consideration
    recommended books, 183
Kinney, J., 34
Knetzger, L., 46
Knight Owl (Denise), 184
Koala Lou (Fox), 187
Korman, G., 122, 188
Kostecki-Shaw, J. S., 181, 185
Krosoczka, J. J., 45–46, 188
Kubuishi, K., 33
Kyere, E., 144

L

Lamothe, M., 185
Last Kids on Earth series (Brailler), 188
Last Stop on Market Street (de la Peña), 181
launching a reading campaign, 4, 9
    at-home learning, 18
    children are reading less, 11
    engaging the community, 20–24
    how to make it happen, 13–17
    reflection questions, 24–25
    reflections from other teachers, 10–11, 22
    roots of this work, 11–13
    sample emails, 17, 19
    sample promotional material, 19
    sample schedule of community read-alouds, 21
    sample social media post, 16
    sample visions, 14
    sustaining the momentum, 17–20
    what does it help promote? 16
Layne, S. L., 10
leadership skills, 5
leading with passion, 6
learning academy for caregivers, 146
    advertising and promoting, 147–152
    asking for feedback, 153
    creating a name, 146
    deciding on a structure, 147
    incorporating additional attractions, 152
    potential themes by grade level, 148–149
    resource kit, 153
    sample email, 151
    sample schedules, 150–151
    scheduling events, 147
    target audience, 146
    using to promote reading culture, 152–153
learning engagements rooted in student identities, 3
learning from literacy leaders, 30–31
learning management systems, 90
Levy, A., 187
Levy, G., 187
libraries, 110
Life (Rylant), 179, 184
Life Skills for Teens (Harris), 154
Lin, G., 136
The List of Things That Will Not Change (Stead), 52
Lit Chat, 36
literacy
    as a set of communicative practices, 87
    as social practice, 29, 82
    learning, 124
literacy-as-event, 52, 62
literary canons, 31
Lithgow, J., 185
Little Libraries Big Heroes (Paul), 182
The Little Old Lady Who Was Not Afraid of Anything (Williams), 185
Litwin, E., 187
live chats, 90
livestreaming, 89
logos, 12
    descriptive vs. nondescriptive, 14
    designing, 13–15
    sample, 18
Look Both Ways (Reynolds, J.), 188
lorrainemradice.com/blog, 17, 20, 59–60, 85, 99, 130, 152, 158
Love (de la Peña), 136–137, 169, 182
Love (McAnulty), 187
Ludwig, T., 181
Luffarelli, J., 14
Lupica, M., 184
Luyken, C., 179, 183
Lyons, K. S., 187

M

MacAulay, D., 189
Magic Treehouse series (Osborne), 188
The Magical Yet (DiTerlizzi), 184
Mahoney, K., 52
Maillard, K. N., 91, 181
Makerspaces, 165–168
making books part of your routines, 86–87
making reading culture visible, 81
    currently reading signs, 83–85
    making books part of your routines, 86–87
    sample email, 84
Malala's Magic Pencil (Yousafzai), 182
Mango, Abuela, and Me (Medina), 137, 181
Mann, S., 9
Mantchev, L., 183
Mantell, P., 188
Marks, J., 52
Martin, A. M., 34
Martinez-Neal, J., 181
Mass, W., 184
Massamino, M., 34
mathematics department, 174–175
Mattingly, D. J., 144
Maybe (Yamada), 179, 182
Maybe He Just Likes You (Dee), 52
McAnulty, S., 187
McDonalds
    nondescriptive logo, 14
McGill-Franzen, A. M., 11
McKenzie, T. L., 144
McLaughlin, M. W., 20, 22
McManus, K. M., 52, 188
Meanwhile Back on Earth (Jeffers), 182
Medina, M., 137, 181, 183
Meet Yasmin! (Faruqi), 187
Meltzer, B., 187
Méndez, Y. S., 181
Merchant, G., 52, 62
Mercy Watson series (DiCamillo), 136
Mercy Watson to the Rescue (DiCamillo), 187
messaging, 7
Mexican White Boy (de la Peña), 136
Middle School Matters (Fagell), 134, 154
The Midnight Children (Gemeinhart), 52, 188
The Midnight Library (Haig), 189
Miller, D., 31
Miller, L., 172
Miller, P. Z., 179, 182
Mister Tiger Goes Wild (Brown), 182
The Mitten (Brett), 185
Mohamed, O., 45–46, 188
Moke, J. E., 34
Monday's Not Coming (Jackson), 33
Montgomery, H. L., 182
Moore, J., 187
Mora, O., 91, 181
Morales, Y., 182
More Than a Peach (Woodard), 182
Morgenstern, S., 179
The Mortal Coil (Suvada), 189
The Moth Presents All These Wonders (Burns), 160
Mrs. Tony Is Full of Baloney (Gutman), 184
Muhammad, I., 91, 137, 181, 183
multiliteracies, 29
music department, 174
My Footprints (Phi), 181
My Heart (Luyken), 179, 183
My Life as a Potato (Costner), 34
My Life collection (Tashjian), 188
My Papi Has a Motorcycle/Mi Papi Tiene una Moto (Quintero), 91, 137, 181
Myers, J., 113

N

The Name Jar (Choi), 181
The Napping House (Wood), 187
Narwhal and Jelly #1 (Clanton), 46
National Center for Families Learning, 173
National Council of Teachers of English, 173
National Geographic Kids, 187
National Geographic Readers (National Geographic Kids), 187
New Kid (Craft), 45, 47
new literacies, 29, 81–82
newsletters
    classroom connection, 42
    creating, 40–41
    designing, 27, 39
    sharing, 42
    soliciting recommendations, 40–41
new-teacher mentor program, 3
Nosrat, S., 35
Not a Box (Portis), 183
Numeroff, L., 184

O

O'Connor, J., 185
O'Neill, A., 21
Oddbird (Desierto), 183
Ogle, R., 52
Oh, E., 160
The Oldest Student (Hubbard), 184
One Book, Many Stories, 171–172
One of Us Is Lying (McManus), 52, 188
ongoing reflection, 161–162
online text discussions, 90
Ordinary People Change the World collection (Meltzer), 187
originality, 6
Orozco, J.-L., 34
Osborne, M. P., 188
Oshiro, M., 33
Oswald, P., 137, 182–183
Other Words for Home (Warga), 185
Our Table (Reynolds), 182
Out of My Mind (Draper), 188
outdoor spaces, 21
Outliers (Gladwell), 189
Owl Diaries series (Elliot), 187

P

Padlet, 42–43
Palacio, R. J., 136
Parachutes (Yang), 136
parent teacher associations
    hosting book events, 3
    promoting learning academy for caregivers, 152
    sharing information about the campaign, 16
parents. *See* families and caregivers
partnering with librarians, 23, 168
Pashmina (Chanani), 188
Passionate Readers (Ripp), 85
Patchwork (de la Peña), 181
patience, 179
Patron Saints of Nothing (Ribay), 52, 61, 189
Paul, M., 182
Paul, P., 145, 154–155, 157
Pauw, I., 28
Pea, Bee, & Jay #1 (Smith), 46
Peanut Butter and Jelly (Clanton), 187
Peebles, A., 9
Penfold, A., 137, 182–183, 185
Perfect (Amato), 185
Perkins, M., 182
perseverance and determination, 6, 105, 124
    recommended books, 184
personalizing culture, 62
Pete the Cat and His Four Groovy Buttons (Litwin), 187
Pham, LU., 35
Phi, B., 181
physical education and play, 174
PicCollage app, 92–93
picture books to share community values, 90–93
The Pigeon Will Ride the Roller Coaster! (Willems), 187
Pilkey, D., 46, 185, 187
Pizza Day (Iwai), 184
Pizzoli, G., 46
planning a book swap, 27–32–39
planning and launching your campaign, 9, 13, 15–17
play-based learning, 97
The Playbook (Alexander), 52
Players in Pigtails (Cory), 184
The Poet X (Acevedo), 136
Poisoned (Donnolly), 52, 188
The Popcorn Book (dePaola), 184
Portis, A., 183
Presley, E., 123
Prett, M., 183
Prislin, R., 144
problem solving, 6
Probst, R. E., 166
professional learning
    incorporating an author's visit, 135–136
    time for, 2
The Proudest Blue (Muhammad & Ali), 91, 137, 181
purchasing books, 110

Q

Questioners collections (Beaty), 184
Quiet (Cain), 189
Quintero, I., 91, 137, 181

R

Raising an Entrepreneur (Bisnow), 154
rallying students to prepare for an author visit, 123, 127–129
    generating questions, 129–130
    preparing fan materials, 130
    reading the author's work, 129
Read Across America Week, 139
Read Around the World experience, 91–93
Read the Rainbow displays, 32–33
read-alouds
    chapter books, 88–89
    online, 88–93
    picture books, 90–93
    scheduling, 94–95
    to reinforce math concepts, 175
    to support new content work, 168–169
Reader, Come Home (Wolf), 154
readers and leaders
    choosing reading events, 116
    deciding when, 115
    defining how it can work, 115
    group, 130, 135–138
    making it a complement to other programs, 115
    program, 103, 114–116
reading ambassador teams, 168, 172
reading calendars, 111
reading culture, 1
    making visible and participatory, 4–5
    supports content-area work, 5
reading culture–building, 4
    is a commitment, 6–7
    principles, 1
    requires risk taking, 6
    social/cultural experiences influence, 28–30
reading directories, 87
reading is important, 1, 13
Reading Magic (Fox), 154
reading schedule for a book, 66
The Reading Strategies Book (Serravallo), 36
Rebound (Alexander), 33
The Recess Queen (O'Neill), 21
recruiting musicians, 99
recruiting the art department, 99
recruiting the technology department, 99
Red (Shurtliff), 188
reflection questions
    author visits, 139
    continuing to prioritize reading, 176
    developing role models, 63
    engaging families and caregivers, 163
    helping students become literacy leaders, 116–117
    launching your campaign, 24–25
    sustaining the culture, 101
reflections from other teachers, 5
    author visits, 138
    continuing to prioritize reading, 172
    developing role models, 35, 38, 42–44, 47–48, 51, 53–54, 60, 60
    helping students become literacy leaders, 104, 112–113
    launching your campaign, 10, 22
Rekulak, J., 189
The Remarkable Farkle McBride (Lithgow), 185

The Remarkable Journey of Coyote Sunrise (Gemeinhart), 52
Remarkably Bright Creatures (Van Pelt), 189
representation and resources, 5
Restart (Korman), 188
Rey, H. A., 184
Rey, M., 184
Reynolds, J., 33, 52–53, 136, 188
Reynolds, P. H., 130, 137, 182–183
Rhuday–Perkovich, A., 160
Ribay, R., 52, 61, 189
Rideout, V., 9, 87
Riley, S., 182
Ripp, P., 85
risk taking, 6
Rita and Ralph's Rotten Day (Deedy), 34
Robb, M, B., 9
Rodriguez, J. L., 144
Romanelli, P., 35
roots of the work, 5
    author visits, 124
    continuing to prioritize reading, 165–167
    developing role models, 27–28
    developing role models, 27–31
    engaging families and caregivers, 143–145
    launching your campaign, 11–13
    learning from literacy leaders, 30–31
    sustaining the culture, 81–83
    why social/cultural experience literacy development, 28–30
routines, 3
A Rover's Story (Warga), 52, 188
Rowell, R., 52
Rubin, A., 184
Rubinstein, G., 183
Ruiz, D. M., 189
Russo, M., 145, 154–155, 157
Rylant, C., 179, 187

S

Sachar, L., 34
Salt in His Shoes (Jordan & Jordan), 184
Salt, Fat, Acid, Heat (Nosrat), 35
Same, Same but Different (Kostecki–Shaw), 181, 185
Santoro, L. E., 159
Saturday (Mora), 91, 181
Say Something! (Reynolds), 137, 182
Scheel, J., 60
Schinel, L., 184
Scholastic, 54, 98, 100
School libraries
    evaluating, 3
school resources tool kit, 107, 118–119
school values
    recommended books, 182
Schu, J., 182
The Secret Letters (Haddix), 88
Secret Pizza Party (Rubin), 184
self-efficacy, 103
self-perception, 105

Sénéchal, M., 143–144
Serravallo, J., 36
sharing reading through book covers, 85
She Persisted chapter books (Clinton & Boiger), 136
She Persisted collection (Clinton & Boiger), 136
Shouting at the Rain (Hunt), 52, 112
Shurtliff, L., 188
Shusterman, N., 189
Sichol, L. B., 188
Sing with Me/Canta Conmigo (Orozco), 34
Slater, D., 189
Slobodkina, E., 185
slogans, 9–10
    creating, 12–13
    samples, 14
SMART Boards, 92
The Smart Cookie (John & Oswald), 183
smartphones, 9
Smile (Telgemeier), 47
Smith, B., 46
Smith, K., 53, 183
Smith, M. W., 56
Snapchat, 12
Snicket, L., 34
social constructivism, 48
social engagements, 5
social media, 9
    can help enhance a reading campaign, 4
    connecting reading to, 12
    growing use, 12
    sites, 89
    using to launch your campaign, 16
    using, 126
social-professional relationships, 28–29
A Soft Place to Land (Marks), 52
soliciting book recommendations, 40
    sample email, 40
    suggested submission format, 41
Solo (Alexander & Hess), 136
Some Places More Than Others (Watson), 136, 185
Sotirovska, V., 105
Sotomayor, S., 172, 183
Soup Day (Iwai), 187
The Sour Grape (John & Oswald), 183
Space Case (Gibbs), 88
Spaceman (Massimino), 34
spotlight book of the month, 170
    choosing books for a focus, 170
    engaging students, 170–171
    preparing to evolve, 171
    sharing with community, 170
    storing your collections, 171
stakeholders, 3
    sharing the reading campaign with, 4
    soliciting feedback, 24, 179
Stamatogiannakis, A., 14
Stamped (Kendi & Reynolds), 53
Stantat, D., 188
Stargazing (Want), 188
Stead, R., 52

STEAM programs, 167
Steier, S., 51
Stein, D. E., 185
STEM programs, 165–167
Stepsister (Donnolly), 52
Street, B., 20
Strictly No Elephants (Mantchev), 183
student choice, 3
    book fairs, 100
student reading ambassadors, 103, 105
    coaching, 106–107
    introducing, 107
    opportunities, 106
    prepare resources, 107
student-led book talks in the classroom, 103, 114
    boosting reading morale, 114
    integrating book club units into the curriculum, 114
student-led schoolwide book talks, 118
    checklist to initiate the book–selection discussion, 108
    choosing a book, 108–110
    engaging participants, 111–112
    introducing, 110
    options for book access, 110
    planning the logistics, 111
    recruiting students, 107
students as literacy leaders, 5
Stuntboy, in the Meantime (Reynolds), 52, 136
Stuono, D., 51
summer book fairs, 3
Sunny (Reynolds), 33
Super Interesting Facts for Smart Kids (Moore), 187
Superman Smashes the Clan (Yang), 45–46
Supernova (Kibuishi), 33
The Superpower Sisterhood (Hager & Bush), 183
supporting a new focus, 165, 167–168
    book clubs, 169
    partnering with a librarian, 168
    read-alouds, 168–169
    reading ambassador teams, 168
surveying colleagues, 31
sustaining momentum, 17–20
    anticipate and prepare, 20
    making T-shirts, 18
    sharing the campaign with new teachers, 19
    using slides, 18
    using your logo, 18
sustaining the culture
    book fair, 81, 98–100
    declaring your own celebratory month, 81, 94–96
    hosting community events online, 81, 87–93
    importance of shared planning, 100
    kindergarten reading parade, 81, 96–98
    making reading culture visible, 81, 83–87
    reflection questions, 101
    roots of the work, 81–83
Suvada, E., 189

T

Table Topics Book Club website, 36
Tashjian, J., 188
Taylor, D., 20
team building, 6
technology, 9
    allows for connectivity and access, 82
    as a distraction, 12
    growing use, 5–6
    hosting reading events online, 87–93
Telgemeier, R., 33
Thank You, Omu! (Mora), 181
thank-yous, 38–39
thinking routine for selecting a schoolwide book talk book, 108, 121
This Is a School (Schu), 182
This Is How We Do It (Lamothe), 185
Thompkins–Bigelow, J., 181
Those Kids From Fawn Creek (Kelly), 188
Those Shoes (Boelts), 183
TikTok, 87
Today I Will Fly! (Willems), 187
Track series (Reynolds), 136
Travel Team (Lupica), 184
Tullet, H., 183
Twins #1 (Johnson), 47
Twitter, 12

U

Uncomfortable Conversations With a Black Boy (Acho), 53
The Undefeated (Alexander), 169, 184
Unsworth, L., 29

V

Van Allsburg, C., 185
Van Dusen, C., 171, 183
Van Pelt, S., 189
van Veen, K., 28
The Vanishing Half (Bennett), 189
Vaughn, M., 105
Verde, S., 137, 182
videoconferencing, 89
visibility of reading, 81–87
visuals, 5
Voege, L., 157
Voss, J. D., 183

W

Wang, A., 181
Wang, J., 188
Warga, J., 52, 185, 188
Watercress (Wang), 181
Watson, R., 136, 185
The Way Things Work (MacAulay), 189
Ways to Share Joy (Watson), 136
We Are Water Protectors (Lindstrom), 184
We Don't Eat Our Classmates (Higgins), 185
We're All Wonders (Palacio), 136
webinar style, 89
Westover, T., 189
What Do You Do With a Problem? (Yamada), 183
What Do You Do With an Idea? (Yamada), 183
What Should Danny Do? (Levy & Levy), 187
What to Do With a Box (Yolen), 167, 183
What to Do With a String (Yolen), 170, 183
What's In Your Pocket? (Montgomery), 182
The Whatifs (Kilgore), 137, 183
When Sadness Is at Your Door (Eland), 183
When Stars Are Scattered (Jamieson & Mohamed), 45–46, 188
When You Are Brave (Miller), 179, 182
Where Are You From? (Méndez), 181
Where the Mountain Meets the Moon (Lin), 136
White Bird (Palacio), 136
white elephant gift exchange, 36, 39
Who Was? series (various authors), 188
why social/cultural experiences influence literacy development, 28–30
Wilhelm, J. D., 56
Willems, M., 179, 187
Williams, A. D., 53
Williams, L., 185
The Winter Duke (Bartlett), 34
With the Fire on High (Acevedo), 33, 52
Wolf, M., 154
Wood, A., 187
Woodard, B., 182
Woodson, J., 136–137, 182–183
World Economic Forum, 165–166
World Read-Aloud Day, 139

Y

Yamada, K., 179, 183
Yang, G. L., 45–46, 52, 136, 188
Yang, H., 14
Yang, K., 136
The Year We Learned to Fly (Woodson), 137
Yes, We Will (Yang), 136
Yolen, J., 167, 170, 183
Young, L., 143–144
Your Name Is a Song (Thompkins-Bigelow), 181
Yousafzai, M., 182
youth programs
    partnering with, 21–22
YouTube Live, 89
YouTube, 12, 87

Z

Zirogiannis, B., 138
Zoom, 48, 89–90, 161

Read Alouds for All Learners
Molly Ness
In *Read Alouds for All Learners: A Comprehensive Plan for Every Subject, Every Day, Grades PreK–8*, Molly Ness provides a compelling case for the integration, or reintegration, of the read aloud in schools and a step-by-step resource for preK–8 educators in classrooms.
BKG116

The Literacy Triangle
LeAnn Nickelsen and Melissa Dickson
Accelerate learning with high-impact strategies. Beginning and veteran teachers alike will find insights and practices they can use immediately. No matter what content area you teach, this book will help you develop the strategic reader in every student.
BKF983

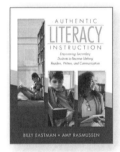

Authentic Literacy Instruction
Billy Eastman and Amy Rasmussen
Imagine a thriving English classroom. One that's active, experiential, collaborative, and rigorous. *Authentic Literacy Instruction* will help you not just imagine this classroom, but also create it. Use the book's doable action plan to reinvigorate your practices and tap into the passions and strengths of every student.
BKF948

Literacy Reframed
Robin J. Fogarty, Gene M. Kerns, Brian M. Pete
Discover a game-changing new way to think about—and teach—literacy at all levels. With *Literacy Reframed*, you will discover a dynamic path forward for creating classrooms that fully support students on their literacy journeys and prepare them to become lifelong lovers of reading.
BKF959

Remaking Literacy
Jacie Maslyk
Maker education—an instructional approach that emphasizes hands-on learning—empowers students to become passionate, creative thinkers and problem solvers. With *Remaking Literacy*, you will learn how to transform literacy teaching and learning by integrating maker education into K–5 classrooms.
BKF890

Solution Tree | Press

Visit SolutionTree.com or call 800.733.6786 to order.

Wait! Your professional development journey doesn't have to end with the last pages of this book.

We realize improving student learning doesn't happen overnight. And your school or district shouldn't be left to puzzle out all the details of this process alone.

No matter where you are on the journey, we're committed to helping you get to the next stage.

Take advantage of everything from **custom workshops** to **keynote presentations** and **interactive web and video conferencing**. We can even help you develop an action plan tailored to fit your specific needs.

Let's get the conversation started.

Call 888.763.9045 today.